THE TRAN

# DO SHIT, GET SHIT DONE

Your No BS Guide to Making Life Your Bitch

and Winning Every Day

Lee Bridges

*This book is dedicated to you for reading it, and my friends and family for either:*

a)      *Putting up with my crap*

b)      *Putting up with my shit*

c)      *Not mentioning my crap*

d)      *Not mentioning my shit.*

# CONTENTS

# Thanks

Mum and Dad. Thank you for being the most supportive and loving parents a boy could have. You have had my back since dot and if there is a thing that has more weight than 'eternally grateful' then that's where you're at! I love you both more than you will ever know and I hope you don't think I'm too much of an idiot! xXx

Hannah. Unlike my parents, you choose to put up with my shit. I have no idea what is wrong with you, but I am not gonna question it. You are the most amazing person I have ever known, and the fact you have no idea how amazing you are just adds to the wonder! I love you, and I swear on my eternal soul I will always do whatever I can to give you the life that you deserve. You are my perfect angel cherub sunshine (I just got slated hard for that, so hopefully that shows you how much I care). Mine! xXx

Cal. My boy! My guy! My little legend! I effin' love you bro! You're better than a kid, you're a best friend! I have got your back forever and I couldn't be more proud of you! You, my son, are going to have a phenomenal life, and it's all down to you! Keep doing you, little buddy! xXx

My friends that go way further than friends need to (in no order whatsoever): Ryan A, Ryan H, Rich Cruden, Jake Skinner, Steph Maciuk, Tessa Wilson, Roy Gifford, Jack Herbert, Matt Brown, Simon Faiers (I still can't spell your surname), Ben Melmoth, Rachel Palmer, Bang & Jo, Wiggy Kipper, Mr Lek, Adam Woolard, Vater Sticks, Remo heads, Liberty Drums, The 100 Club, Abiola GiwHa Otusanya, Herbie

Cuffe, Scott Gentry, Steve Beak, Kia Larbay, and everyone I've missed. I really can't believe I'm lucky enough to know humans as amazing as you, thank you! xXx

A special thank you to Maddie Karlsson and Ryan A for putting up with an unreal amount of shit throughout the making of this book, and also for believing and putting their money where their mouths are. Thank you! You have put yourself out time and time again to make this project happen and you've always seen the bigger picture! We got this... xXx

# Introductions

Suuuup! My name is Lee Bridges. How's it going?! I am the author of this book and I'm here to serve you! Before I do anything else I want to let you know I fought tooth and nail and still lost the battle to fill this book with emojis.

The most important thing I wanna get across immediately is that I'm not a self-help guru or whatever other wanky things those folks label themselves. I'm not telling you what to do, nor am I suggesting I am any better than anyone else or have all the answers. The following pages are the way I am doing life and it is working great for me. If you can take anything beneficial from it that makes your life better then I'll be happier than Charlie Sheen at an all-you-can-eat bro... er, let's not start that kinda shit yet!

At no point in this book will I tell you that if you do X it will guarantee Y, and I definitely suggest you make your own choices. I also recommend you add your own spins to the life hacks I am offering to turbocharge them and make them your own, and then I suggest you pass them on to others, maybe in your own manuscript. And I also guarantee you that there are grammatical errors and dumb sentences throughout, read 'til the end to find out what I learned... Also the last few chapters are about 20 times better than the rest of the book so...

This book was written as a self-help bible for... well... me. I'm super pumped to share it with you. The life hacks and exercises in this book got me my dream job, got me my dream partner, got me my dream family, got me in the best shape of my life, gave me the capacity to turn negative into positive at the click of my fingers, got my kid brain working again, got me pushing harder and faster than I previously thought possible, and amongst countless other game-changing positives these life hacks and exercises got me clean after a horrible battle with addiction, after suffering countless relapses and attempts to quit.

Ultimately they are continuing to push me towards my full potential, happiness and success. I have used all the hacks and exercises in this book not only on myself, but with countless clients, students, friends, and family, and they work. No bullshit! They are easy to implement but with massive results.

Thank you so much for giving me a chance and thank you for making the first commitment to absolutely dialling your life. You will not regret this, pinky swear 5,000!

You can hit me on my social @_lee_bridges or @drum_hacker or swing by my site www.leebridges.co.uk where you will find loads of new and regular content. There are a few little bits of info you need to know before we get started, so without further ado...

## Ethics

I am going to be showing and explaining to you some extremely powerful methods and life hacks that can be used for both good and evil. I want you to make a vow to only use these techniques for the former. This is very important for your happiness and also for my conscience. So no evilness, swearsies?! Cool!

The other thing I want you to know before starting this programme is that I will never tell you to do something I haven't done and I will not lie to you about where I am in my own life and transition. I am not yet financially free, but I am on my way. I am not yet a best-selling author, but I am on my way, and I am not yet a household name, but I am on my way. Think these are big statements, statements that you could never feel confident enough to make, let alone make a reality? You are gonna be pleasantly surprised. If you are not ready to smash your life sideways then maybe return this book and pick up something more comfortable, or Netflix and chill...

## My oath to you

I need to make you an oath because I need you to believe me to be able to get the most out of this, and the last thing I want to do is put any of you at risk or push you to do things that won't help you. So, I solemnly promise I will never lead you astray, or tell you lies, or make stuff up. I promise that I know the exercises and advice in this programme totally work and that all you need is commitment. I promise that I will do everything within my power to make sure you not only love this programme but in turn, you absolutely live by it and it makes your life exponentially better with every day that you continue your transition. And lastly, I promise that I got your back and I want you to be happy, successful, and owning your life.

# Introduction 1.1

Welcome to *The Transition: Do Shit, Get Shit Done.* Your one-stop shop to change your life for the better. I want to explain why this book is integral to you. In this programme, I will show how you can be the person you always wanted to be and in turn give your children, peers, friends and family the same opportunities. More often than not, the opportunities you never thought you had. I can make you better, faster, stronger, funnier, happier, and ultimately super successful.

Compared to the average Joe, and the world is full of them, this book will be the hand that you've been reaching for your whole life! You just gotta take hold of it and not look back! I am gonna explain every step and it's gonna be so easy that the only thing you will hate about the transformation is that you didn't do it sooner. Prepare to actually feel alive for the first time since you were a kid. Your perspective is gonna shift and your world is gonna start glowing! This book will teach you how to be successful! I don't mean just monetary! I mean in all walks of your life!

To be completely successful you need to find your true love; learn anything you want; get the body you want; close deals and make money; start a business; be part of an amazing relationship or ask the person of your dreams to marry you; raise a happy and confident child; smash your A-levels, college education or uni degree; invent cool shit, and pretty much anything else you can think of.

There are a very absolute set of rules that when followed can be applied to any part of your life. I'm gonna explain all of these in super simple little baby steps that you can implement so easily that your transition will feel effortless. My name is Lee Bridges, and I'm ya boy. I've got ya back and I'm here to help. So let me ask you this...

Are you completely done?! Like proper done?! Fed up, tired, shot to bits? Constantly working your ass off with nothing to show? Shit relationships, bad health and run down?! Lost, numb, depressed? Worried, anxious and with no confidence? Broke, sad and useless?!

I know how you feel! It sucks. Every time you take a few steps forward you have to run a marathon backwards? Same blah routine each day, week, month, year? Unhappy with your body? Unhappy with your mind? I got ya! I've been there, for years and years and years! I've had my 'enough is enough' day and I want to get you to yours as soon as possible!

A great man once said, "They tried to bury us, they didn't realise we were seeds." Sounds hippy AF, I know, but roll with the premise. Problem with seeds is they need specific things to grow, and if they don't get them, they don't even make it out of the ground! Your brain is like a seed, amongst other things that we'll come to later, and I'm gonna show you how to get it bursting outta the soil and grow it big and strong, positive and powerful! I am gonna show you how to feel pumped, gassed, and positive 24/7, 365. You need change. A fresh start. So no more excuses and self-deception. No more playing the victim and pointing the finger. You, my friend, can be fucking awesome!!! Let me tell you a bit about myself...

## Why should you trust me?

So, why should you trust me? There's a bunch of other motivational, self-help douchebags out there, and they are better known than I currently am! So what's different about what I am teaching?!

I always found I was that guy that people would come to when they needed advice. In my time so far I have been a teacher, lecturer, business owner, musician, step-dad, husband, poet, lover... Seriously though, I have always wanted to help people. My level of empathy for others is off the charts. Problem was, for the longest time I couldn't sort myself out!

I bent over backwards for years coaching students in college to get their lives on track but the whole time I was lying to myself! I managed to keep it under the radar but there was a huge amount of time where I was barely holding it together, and nobody noticed. I was drained, hooked on drugs, drinking way too much, talking loads of breeze, and fixing everyone else when I couldn't fix myself.

I was unhealthy, unfit, lost, and watching my life just float away. I tried everything I could. I have read, listened to, and attended more self-help books, audio programmes and seminars than you could imagine and although they got me started, I found that I could never keep them up, or I'd get confused because one person was telling me all my problems would be solved by doing X while someone else was preaching Z.

I was soooo confused!!! And that just propelled my self-destruction and lameness! One day, after having a serious self-inflicted medical problem, after already having a plethora of slightly less serious self-inflicted medical problems, I hit my rock bottom. Finally! If you've ever hit rock bottom, you know what I'm talking about. If you haven't then let's keep it that way!

Everyone was telling me to delve into my past and figure out what the issue was, then I could fix it. I heard this from countless professionals and in plenty of books. But whenever I thought about the past it just made me sad or angry or depleted of energy and I'd just end up doing nothing. I decided to start taking the advice I had been dishing out, and fuck me, it started to work. Immediately.

I kicked my addiction myself and sorted my life right out and I swear I have never been happier! I did this using the techniques I'm gonna teach you in this programme. I am not a recovering user, I am Lee and I am killing it at the moment and will continue to kill it! And I can show you how!

As well as successfully quitting one of the most addictive substances in the world by using these hacks, I changed my diet, I got fit, I started a successful business, I made better relationships and I got the best family I could ask for! I literally beam constantly these days, and on the odd occasion that I do feel rubbish, I can snap myself out of it within seconds, every time!

So why should you trust me? Because I absolutely want what is best for you and I care about you and I've spent the last 17 years studying the behaviour of humans incessantly and to the utmost degree! And I do care about you, all of you! Might sound soppy but it's completely from my heart and I mean every word! I want everyone to feel like I do now and I know how you can get there!

I believe the only way to get where you want to go is to take action and get shit done. You will find no quick fix here, no diets, no money-making schemes or similar. Instead, you will find the most sincere and obvious life hacks that can get you wherever you choose to go, and for the most part with a massive smile on your face.

Why should you trust me? Because I have successfully changed the lives of so many people when they had nowhere else to go and no idea how to start. I've got so many success stories from ex-users, self-harmers, procrastinators, worriers, cynics, losers, non-believers and wasters that had no belief in themselves or what is possible.

Why should you trust me? Because I quit my full-time safety-net job to write this book and I have never worked so hard at anything and I feel AMAAAAZING!!!! Why should you trust me? Because you've tried listening to self-help gurus, family, friends, teachers, the news, and whatever else and you're still not where you wanna be! I could go on! I got you, and I know that these techniques work. This programme is for you and nobody else, and I trust you to do the right thing and commit to it. So let's stop fannying about and begin to dial your life...

# Introduction 1.2:

# What you need

Before starting this programme you need to have the right kit. I highly suggest you invest in these and don't try to find them around your house or borrow them from someone. This is really important and I will explain why later.

**You will need:**

1. A small journal; I suggest leatherbound and pocket-sized with DsGsD embossed on the front.

2. A pen; make it one you feel comfortable writing with, no crappy Bics allowed. Maybe get one of those ones from the 90s where when you turn it upside down the person's clothes come off and after hardly any time at all the clothes get stuck on and you become frustrated.

3. The ability to set alarms; you can use your phone for this.

We are about to go to war. War on the life you aren't content with, war on the job you hate, war on the body you are sick of seeing in the mirror, war on your penis-butt boss, war on the lack of business you got coming in, war on your confidence issues, war on your anxiety. WARRRR!!! And in the same way, you wouldn't wanna go into battle with a pair of bongos and a personalised number plate that reads 5ex p3st; you are gonna need to be battle-ready, so fix yourself up a journal and a pen and prepare your ass to fight...

# Introduction 1.3:

# Good Lee, Bad Lee

Don't freak, it's cool, there's no Intro 1.4!! This is the last part of orientation before we get stuck in. You are gonna notice immediate results from this book and Chapter 1 is only a few moments away. In the meantime, I wanted to give you an insight as to how I see the world. But first I need to explain the shit I've been through/put myself through so you can get a feel of where I'm coming from. I am a recovered drug addict. I am a recovered sex addict. I am a recovered fatty. I have had every confidence issue under the sun. I was anxious, lost, useless and troubled.

I realised a long time ago that I was being bombarded constantly by my surroundings. The absolute garbage that is drilled into us daily and the regurgitations of this utter crap from friends, family, lovers and peers had moulded my world. It was such a habitual part of life that I spent many years not even questioning it, I thought it's just how it is. But it's not how it has to be!

The news, radio and TV, my friends, family, and peers all played a part in my belief system, and in turn, my actions, thoughts, and feelings. I always felt stuck bang in the middle! Not enough energy, self-belief, confidence, or self-esteem to get out. Scared to leave the middle. But if you are honest with yourself then you know as well as I do that nothing ever happens in the middle!

You're born, you school, you college, you uni, you job, you family, you die. Owning your dream house, running an awesome business, being a world-class dancer, musician, actor or artist, being a phenomenal parent, changing the world for the better, running charities, inventing stuff, creating solutions, being totally proud of yourself, being a role model, leaving a legacy. None of these things happen in the middle.

The middle is not scary, or uncomfortable, or demanding, well at least it isn't until you step out of it and see how scary, uncomfortable and demanding it really is. A lot of you will start this journey in denial! You will think things like "my life's fine as it is", or "I just want an easy life". If that's the case then I don't know what to tell you. Maybe you aren't anywhere near your 'enough is enough' day yet? But I absolutely guarantee you that if you have picked this book up then your life is not fine where it is and your life is nowhere near as easy as it can be, and it is definitely not anywhere near as rewarding as it can be.

I am going to teach you how to be so fucking awesome that your kids, family, friends, peers and acquaintances will follow! Everything in this book works and is tried and tested and is so easy to use that, for the most part, you will end up thinking: "Holy catfish! How the Jeff did I not think of that before?/Holy catfish! How the Jeff did I live for as long as I did?"

So, as I mentioned, I need you to understand how I now see the world for this all to make sense. So let's talk about spectrums...

I believe we are all on a spectrum. By definition, a spectrum is used to classify something between two extreme points. Your personality, body, and mind have these two extreme points. Think of it like duality: yin and yang, hot and cold, up and down. Your personality can be happy or sad, your body can be fat or thin, and your mind can be open or closed. Most of us land somewhere in the middle of the spectrum. Various parts of you will hang out more towards the positive end and some more towards the negative end, and sometimes the positive and negative ends swap and change.

I Have 'Good Lee' and 'Bad Lee'. They are at opposing ends of my behaviour spectrum. Remember, I believe there is a spectrum for absolutely everything. For instance, we all have behaviour spectrums, health spectrums, work ethic spectrums and whatever other things you can think of, there's a spectrum for it. Anyway, let's talk about my behaviour spectrum! At the positive end is 'Good Lee'! And towards the negative end is 'Bad Lee'. My good Lee is effin' awesome! I just wanna warn you, I am about to talk about myself in the 3rd person, and for that, I am very sorry...

Good Lee will make you laugh, he's got your back, he's fit and healthy, he's aware, he's courageous, he's badass, and he inspires. He's awesome in bed, he is thoughtful, he treats people with respect and remembers to call his nan just to check-in. He is an amazing parent and role model and amongst other things, he is happy and confident. He does shit, and gets shit done!

Bad Lee! Oh God, this guy!! Eurgh, man, I hate this version of me! He's moany, he watches too much porn, he is selfish, he does drugs, he is lazy, he forgets about others, he lies and cheats and doesn't think. I could go on. Bad Lee is a grade-A dick head! Not evil, definitely not evil, just a complete dick!!! And not all the time. In fact, the problem is that up until my mid-20s I was never completely good or bad, and I was both!

Sometimes one would hang around longer than the other but more often than not they would fight each other and I would run from one end of the spectrum to the other multiple times in a day, and sometimes simultaneously. 'Bad Lee' is exhausting, and only creates negative energy. 'Good Lee' is full of beans and lights up a room. 'Bad Lee' worries and stresses. 'Good Lee' makes life his bitch and kicks ass. 'Bad Lee' is an anxious mess. 'Good Lee' is a legend! I know you have the same good and bad versions of yourself.

Living at the bad end of the spectrum leaves you disabled, drained and weak, a complete mess running on fumes and navigating on autopilot. It propels you into your very own private prison. The bad you is so conniving that the majority of us never even notice it! Living at the good end of the spectrum leaves you rejuvenated, powerful and unstoppable.

I am speaking from the heart here. When you learn how to live in a good place you will never look back, and in the worst-case scenario that you do look back, you will realise and get back to the awesome version of you quicksmart so it doesn't wreck your life and take you too far off track! You will learn to be aware.

We all have the option to live our lives through our bad self (which definitely isn't as cool as it sounds) and whether your bad version prevents you from leaving the job you hate, dating the right person, starting a new business or something effin' awesome like that, or even worse hinders you from being your true you, the real you, the happy one, then it is time to squash it and start living your best life!

Not in control? Got an addiction? Can't start the gym or eat healthily? Tell lies to others or yourself? Can't kick your bad habits? Can't get confident or believe in yourself or your future? Go to bed worrying? Wake up anxious? Whatever negative bullshit wanky thing it is that's ruining you, don't worry, I'm here to help, I got you!

Let's be real, it's time to sort your shit out!

This programme uses a mixture of super-easy mind and life hacks that you can start using immediately with instant results. They are things I have learned, worked out, and implemented in my own life and the lives of others with staggering effects. In a week you will feel recharged, fresh, and good to go! In a month you will have started to forget the old you, and in a year, who knows! The bar you set for yourself is limitless...!

This programme is focused on absolutely everyone no matter where you are in your life. Whether you are starting out with a new business venture; you're a high school, college, or university student;

you're raising a child; turning a thought into a hobby; turning a hobby into a career, or anything else you can think of, this programme is for you! And the only thing you need to do is make a very small commitment. You CAN do this! Just trust me and I promise you won't look back! Welcome to *The Transition: Do Shit, Get Shit Done...*

At the end of each chapter, you will find a summary to remind you of the important points and life hacks so you don't miss anything or forget to do something.

We are gonna' start as we mean to go on, with immediate action....

# Chapter 1

# Commit

This is a nice short chapter, more a bit of reconnaissance for me to see where you're currently at. I need you to answer the following questions – you NEED to write these down because we are gonna track our progress, later on, to prove everything is working! Grab your journal and pen, or phone if your journal hasn't been delivered yet...

Answer all of the following questions honestly.

If you are doing something where you can't currently write then make a mental note of each of your answers but make sure you write them down later. If you do do this though (hehe, do do), then make it the only time as we need to start getting used to doing stuff as opposed to just thinking about doing stuff!

---

**Current you** (% between 1-100)

1. Happiness
2. Productivity
3. Confidence
4. Fear

5. Anxiety
6. Self-esteem
7. Doubt
8. Belief in future
9. Friendship group
10. Diet
11. Fitness level
12. Self-control
13. Overall

## Future you (% between 1-100)

1. How confident are you in your current abilities to smash your future?
2. How committed are you to your future?
3. How fearful of your future are you?
4. Are you ready to make a change?
5. Do you want to take control of your life?
6. Do you want to be healthier?
7. Do you want to be fitter?
8. Can you picture your life being much better than it currently is?

## A little bit about you (up to 3 for each)

1. What are your best traits?
2. What are your worst traits?
3. What are you amazing at?
4. What are you terrible at?
5. What are your favourite activities currently?
6. What are your least favourite activities currently?
7. What things do you want to change in your current life?
8. What things do you want to try (small)?
9. What things do you want to try (big)?
10. Who is your biggest inspiration?

We will come back to these later and you won't believe how different your answers are...

Now though, I need to talk to you about commitment! Commitment is the only thing that you need to complete this programme with flying colours and to the utmost avail. Commitment is the most important skill you need to fully-fledged dial your life!

We will go into all of this in detail later, but in the same way, I don't want you wasting my time (because it is precious like a Chow-Chow puppy in a wicker basket). I don't wanna waste yours either.

Commitment is the only thing I need you to commit to! So, what is a commitment? Well, the dictionary definition is 'the state or quality of being dedicated to a cause, activity, etc.'. Let's just take that as it is: what is the 'cause'? The 'cause' is your life! And you have the capability and opportunity to make it effin' amazing beyond your wildest dreams! Facts about your life:

1.  It is yours! And as far as I'm aware, or as far as anyone else seems to be able to prove, it's the only one you got! Better make it count, eh?!

2.  It is totally changeable and reprogrammable – which I am gonna explain to you later!

I want to leave you with one more thing before we get right into it... And remember this! As in, write it down, set it as your screensaver/home screen/lock screen, set it as a reminder on your phone, write it on Post-its and stick them places you will see them and whatever else you can think of to get it in your head – it will save your life countless times...

"You can never fail if you never quit."

*Let's begin....*

# Chapter 2

# Do Shit,

# Get Shit Done

**DsGsD ma' fuckers!**

For this programme to be completely effective we need to start immediately and with no hesitation. We need to break through the wall, not work around it or climb over it, just straight fucking through! I will only ask you to do this once, but it is integral you do it and without question: take your clothes off and kiss the first person you see! Do it, get it done!! And make it a big sexy French kiss. Joking! Seriously though, keep this mantra in your mind: Do shit, get shit done. You are about to begin the most amazing transformation and we need to start correctly.

The main reason we never finish anything is that we don't start it properly and I'm sure you can think of a bunch of things you haven't finished recently... We know what we want but we can't see the light at the end of the tunnel, and in a lot of cases, we don't even know where the tunnel is, or that a tunnel even exists in the first place!

Ever said or thought something like this before? "I'm so ready to get healthy, I'll join the gym tomorrow, and because I am gonna start being healthy tomorrow, I'll have one big blow-out meal tonight, my last meal!" Or, "I'm gonna quit smoking, I'm gonna do it, I'll have this one last cigarette, and then I'm free."

The 'last' bad meal or 'final' cigarette is the reason you are not going to do either of those things. "I'll ask that person on a date, I will, but my hair doesn't look right and I haven't showered... I'll do it tomorrow when my hair is right and I'm clean," or, "I'll take you to the park later little buddy," or, "I'll do that (insert whatever it is you are about to wuss out on) later, I'm busy at the moment!" Yeah you are busy, busy making excuses.

So, seriously this time... I will only ask you to do this once then you are going to have to make the conscious effort to change and maintain the change. However, this first one, the one you are about to do, that's the hardest one. Well, it seems like the hardest until you've done it... So...

Stop what you are doing right now! Don't be a smartass, I don't mean stop reading! But I do mean prepare to stop what you are doing after reading the following instructions. Unless it is life-threatening to stop what you are doing: I guess some of you may be juggling venomous snakes right now but for those who aren't, stop what you are doing right NOW.

Do not pause here and tell yourself you will do this later, you must stop now. You just paid for this programme so you might as well give this a try. I'll give you 30 seconds to stop what you are doing and grab your journal, do it now while I sing you some countdown music. Dududuudaa dadd adadadadadda daddaaa...

This exercise is going to take less than a minute. It doesn't matter if you are late for work or running behind, it will take a minute, and if you picked this programme up you are probably often a minute or two late anyway! This minute is soooo important! It's a minute that will change your life for the better, forever. If you don't have a minute to put into yourself now then stop reading and close the book and come back when you're ready, if you're ever ready... For those of you that are ready to go, then let's do this...

---

## Exercise 1.0

Now, open your journal (and for those of you that have already slacked off and don't have it with you: firstly, bad form, secondly, use your phone or whatever you can that allows you to scribe). DO NOT FORGET YOUR JOURNAL AGAIN! It is paramount to your progress and success.

K, write down one thing that you have been meaning to start. It could be join the gym; send someone you love a nice letter, email, or text; book a table to take your partner out on a date, or get a date; learn how to cook; learn how to play an instrument or sing; write a book; finish your coursework etc., etc.

I can't stress enough how important this step is.

Now I want you to write 3 mini-steps involved in securing this thing, whatever it is. For example, if the end goal was to join the gym, 3 mini-steps could be:

1. Find a gym near me
2. Get phone number for the gym
3. Make a call to book an induction.

If your end goal is to write mum a letter (cuz you have never done that before and she would literally shit her pants with happiness if you do), then your mini-goals could be:

1. Get some paper, pen, envelope and stamp
2. Write a letter
3. Post the letter

Or paradoxically:

1. Open laptop
2. Close porn pop-ups
3. Send email

FYI she will prefer the written letter tenfold...

Now, you have 1 hour to accomplish your first mini goal.

---

Something magical will happen upon completion of the first mini-goal... Now I know a lot of you will be having your standard naggy brain-loops: "But I'm on my way to work, where am I gonna' get an envelope, paper and stamp!" Or even worse and my biggest pet hate: "I don't have time!" Or the almost equally lame, "This won't work," without putting any effort into trying it. These neg-loops will not help you, they have never helped you, and will never help you.

We are going to start replacing these meh loser traits with legendary baller traits. "Ah sweet, there is actually that post office I drive past every day en route to where I am going and I can grab an envelope there, and get a stamp and some paper too!" Winning! "I can actually write the letter to my mum on my lunch break instead of doing what I normally do." (Probably talking about last night's reality TV show or gossip or some other random bollocks to a colleague or peer – no judgement.)

Do what you've always done, you will get what you've always got.

By now you will have a plan and a hard copy of your main goal and 3 mini-goals. Use your phone to set a stopwatch or reminder to get the 3 minis done within the next hour. DO NOT DOUCHE OUT ON THIS!!!

The clock is on. You can imagine you're on a gameshow if it helps. I often find playing the opening credit music to Pirates of the Caribbean or Jurassic Park helps get you amped too!

The minute you just spent writing done did save your life.

So, haters, I imagine you are saying, "How the Jeff did that stupid little exercise help save my life?" Two reasons, hater:

1. Baby steps. I said these were gonna be easy little life hacks – you can think of them like the tiny little snowflake that bonds with other tiny little snowflakes until there are enough of the little fuckers to cause an avalanche, and avalanches are powerful AF, they are just out of control! We will speak about this later: I'll show you how to control your avalanche.

2. You did something new and outside your comfort zone that had an immediate effect and was so easy to do that you now have no excuse for not just getting on with stuff in the future. You need to start super small and build it up – we will get to the huge stuff in due course.

I would love to hear what you came up with as your first goal and what the repercussions were. Lemme know on my social or email.

Remember I said I actually wrote this book as a self-help book for myself? It started as a bunch of notes I had made over the last few years while I was trying to kick a vicious addiction that nearly killed me twice and absolutely took control of my life. The tiny hack I just mentioned was the first one I wrote down in my journal.

Before implementing my own life hacks I had tried everything else I could think of. From meetings to counselling, to seeing my GP, to ODing... I started taking heed of my notes and then I realised they worked and I was beginning to live my life by them, and it very soon it became immeasurably better. I want the same for you (not the drug addiction). You must remember that there is no limit to success, there is no quota! If 100 people are successful it doesn't mean 100 others have to wait or fail. Never wait, never fail: you can have it all...

## Do Shit, Get Shit Done 1.1

When I first decided to commit to reaching my full potential and effin' owning my life I realised I needed a slogan. Something to live by, something to change my world with. A mantra for my life. Nike has 'just do it', Phillip Sydney had 'either I will find a way or I will make one', Grant Cardone's uncle has 'if you can, you must', McDonald's have 'I'm lovin' it' (this one is soooo lame cuz it's McDonald's, but it totally works) and S Club have 'don't stop, never give up'.

I wanted something snappy, something I wouldn't forget, something I could bark at people whenever they need it, and something that I could bark at myself whenever I needed it, which in the early days of my life hacking journey was pretty much all the time! I came up with a bunch of non-starters... like, 'oi, Lee, mate, do some stuff', and 'stop wanking', but none of them stuck! One day I came up with 'Do Shit, Get Shit Done'! It kinda rolls off the tongue, eh!? It fits the description: simple, easy to remember, abbreviate, ya know?!

Point is, DsGsD is not just one of my mantras, it's actually a way of life for me now! It works! Do you have a mantra? Something you can utter to yourself to override your negative thoughts? You may have a bunch! I've got loads now! You can change your mantra whenever you want, and add as many as you want, kinda like Pokémon. I actually often have DsGsD etched on my hand in ink, or on a Post-it note hanging off my rear-view mirror, or as a reminder on my phone. FYI auto-suggestion is a boss and making your subconscious do the work, pre-realising you need to do the work is badman! We'll come to brain reprogramming later...

You may have reeled in disgust when I said the word 'mantra'. It kinda conjures depictions of hippies doing yoga next to a waterfall saying 'Namaste' at every opportunity. Don't be a hater. Mantras come from Hinduism and Buddhism and are sounds that are repeated to aid concentration while meditating. Whether you meditate or not, having a strapline that helps you concentrate is entirely important. If you think about it you more than likely have a bunch of these already.

Chances are though, they aren't necessarily positive or any good for you! And they may not necessarily help you concentrate. Think of it like your own private coach or personal trainer. The difference being, you are the coach or personal trainer. It's a reality check, and once honed, will be the beginning of your new life. Having a sick mantra will allow you to make better decisions and do the right thing. This isn't a hack, this is just the truth. The more you can surround yourself with motivational and positive shit, the easier it is to navigate your life like a winner.

So let's get you a new mantra. One that works better than the ones you may already have. You have to make it yours, make it work for you, make it personal, and in the beginning, write it down at every opportunity. Travis Barker, the tattoo-laden drummer of Blink 182 fame, got his tattoos so he wouldn't have to get a 'normal' job, and it totally worked. I'm not saying you need to go get tattoos all over your body to win at life but I am saying that if you had 'just do it,' or 'never give up', or the like tattooed on your hand where you can constantly see it, it would save your life a bunch of times.

I drilled my particular mantra so deep into my mind that I don't even have to think about it now. Whenever I start to slack off (and I do, just like everyone else) my mind reality checks me by default. Imagine if every time you began thinking negative, or being lazy, or needed a push in the right direction, or felt anxious or scared or worried, someone came and tapped you on the shoulder and said, "I got you, my dude, don't worry, let's get back to work and make your life better." You would be much less likely to F your S up.

Imagine if everyone treated you like this! Always perking you up and helping you get through the negative crap. The brain will actually do exactly what you program it to, just like a phone, or a computer, or a car, or a toaster, but it tends to overthink shit and get in the way, and this slows us down and makes us question our validity and purpose, which often results in giving up or settling.

One of the reasons your brain tries to override you is because you are surrounded by bad media and people that listen to the media as gospel. People that lead their life how they are told (even if it goes against their heart) because their predecessors led their lives how they were told and so on. They say you are what you eat and you are who you hang around with. The former isn't 100% true as I am not currently a papaya or a spoonful of Meridian peanut butter but you know what I mean.

However, I completely agree with the latter. Even though you physically aren't who you hang around with, your mind starts to think like theirs, and theirs like yours. Think of it like this: you hang around at the bar, you're bound to drink. You live in a crack den, even with the best will in the world, there will be a point when you will consider honking up a fat pipe. It may take a year, but there will be a point. Hang around with negative people, and guess what?! Yup!

Aristotle said: "We are what we repeatedly do. Excellence, then, is not an act, but a habit."

Habits can be broken or created. They don't have to be bad! Think about it, and be honest, if I tell you to choose positive or negative when I say a word, and the word is habit, most of you would answer 'negative'. Why?!?! Cuz' that's how you've been programmed! Spectrums people! What about the habits at the positive end of the spectrum? We need to start fucking up these invisible chains that have been shackled all over our darling little brains and seeing them for the prisons that they are! Anyways, enough of that for the moment! We will come to that later on so let's get back to the task at hand...

How often do you take advice from people that are in the same position as you?

Broke, overweight, unhealthy, living hand to mouth, bags under their eyes, drinking and smoking too much...? If you think about it, and I mean actually think about it without disrupting the thought cuz your phone just pinged a notification or your brain started worrying about something that definitely doesn't deserve your time...

If you REALLY think about it, I bet your general set of values and accomplishments, and things you are proud of, are someone else's ideas and beliefs. We grow up trying to be what we are told is nice and normal, not to strive too hard or be too obsessed so we don't have to deal with the crippling failure and anxiety that goes along with it. WTFF!!!!

Who told us this?!?! Being the average Joe is failing! In fact, it has always failed, and you only know this for sure when you get the fuck outta Dodge! Living hand to mouth doesn't work! Being tired all the time doesn't work!!! Being anxious, having low self-esteem, not doing something because of what might happen all don't work! You know this! Is it working for you?

If it is, then why the hell did you pick up this book? Who are these people that make us content with living a life of normalcy?!?! Well, not me! I got ya! I'm gonna make sure that by the time you have finished this programme you have an awakening! I am going to tell you now. It is okay to ignore everyone else and do your own thing and run YOUR game!!!

It took me a long time to realise this but everything is down to you! If you're happy – you! Sad – you! Ashamed – you! Lonely – you! Wealthy – you! Popular – you! In control – you! Out of control – you!

Point is, you have the power to do anything, and the reason most of you still have that doubt, that nausey little D-bag of a voice in your head that doesn't believe in what I am saying, is because everyone you know feels like you do! If you were surrounded by only people that are saying what I'm saying (and there are shed loads of us, you just don't know us yet) your belief system would be different! If you grow up in Thailand you are way more likely to practice Buddhism than if you grow up in Jamaica! You are what you eat and most of us have been lapping up every last morsel of this absurd BS since we could hear! It's everywhere! But it's wrong!

You don't have to believe it anymore. The fact you have reached out to change your life is the beginning of freeing yourself from, well, you, 'bad you' I mean! You did this, you listened to the bullshit! You and nearly everyone else on this planet. And there is absolutely nothing to feel bad about from listening as we really don't have much choice. However, you should feel terrible if once you know and are aware of it you don't do Jack to fix up!

Now let me tell you about some people that didn't listen to the bollocks...

Martin Luther King
Gandhi
Steve Jobs

Socrates
Thomas Jefferson
Nelson Mandela
Abe Lincoln
Bob Dylan
Jay-Z
Rosa Parks
George Orwell
Princess Diana
Etc., etc.

You think for one minute that these badass mofos listened when they got told, "That won't work," or, "You can't do that," or, "That's impossible!" Hell to the mother flipping NO!!! They did shit, they got shit done!

Benjamin Franklin – did shit, got shit done.
Alexander Graham Bell – did shit, got shit done.
Nikola Tesla – did shit, got shit done.
Leonardo da Vinci – did shit, got shit done.
That guy from that TV show you watch – did shit, got shit done!
Bob Marley – did shit, got shit done!
Plato – did shit, got shit done.
Jim Carey – did shit, got shit done.
Usain Bolt – did shit, got shit done.

That person at your gym that is in better shape than you – did shit, got shit done.

That absolute don driving the car you want or living in the house you want – did shit, got shit done.

Whoever is making moves at the time you are reading this – DOING SHIT AND GETTING SHIT DONE!

The TV you watch, the magazines or newspapers you read, the 'news' you listen to, all affect you! And even if you don't listen to or watch the aforementioned puke, your nearest and dearest will relay it to you anyway. It's all absolutely bonkers! It holds us back and it prevents us from thinking straight. It distracts us from being the real us. We exert so much energy worrying about what might happen that we end up doing sweet FA to take control of our future so it doesn't happen.

I want you to come up with a mantra for yourself. If you already have one I want you to come up with a new one. Take immediate action and write it somewhere you are gonna see it every day! Even if it's just a Post-it note on the bathroom mirror, or a phone reminder or tablet screensaver. I wanna know what you came up with. HMU. If you are really struggling you can steal someone else's for now, but make sure you get your own real soon and make sure it's life-affirming and works for you! Think big!

It's time to stop! I'm giving you permission to break away. You no longer need to follow the herd. And I absolutely guarantee it will be the best move you ever make!

## Daily Goal Practice

Let's go back to our journal. We need to start something right now! A new commitment, a commitment to getting out, and ultimately a commitment to ourselves to be happy, to be strong, to be better and faster!

One of the most phenomenal changes I noticed in my transition was something I originally scoffed at. When I first heard people mention this I used my cumulative knowledge (which was everyone else's knowledge, not my own gut) to come to the conclusion that writing stuff down was dumb. I mean not dumb, but dumb for me. How could writing get me a better job, a better partner, better friends, a better life, a bigger bank account, a better body, a better mind?! I mean, it's writing! And nobody writes... apart from authors, and writers, and er... well, you know, I wasn't a writer then.

Now before you start freaking out I'm not gonna get you to write a book (although it is a very beneficial process). We are doing baby steps, remember, so we will start small. We are going to start a daily goal practice. This, without a shadow of a doubt, is one of the most powerful exercises you can begin. You don't need to do much research at all to hear super successful people talking about writing down their goals daily. Check for yourself on the interwizzle!

So, grab your phone and set a reminder saying something like "DO YOUR GOALS MOTHERFUCKER!" that goes off every day at the same time to tell you to write down your daily goals! Make it a time that you won't ignore. I started by doing mine just before bed and first thing when I wake up. These are both great times as your last actions before bed (as long as they are positive) really set you up for the following day and your immediate actions upon waking set you up for the day ahead. But you can set the alarm for whenever you want. You do you, baby.

When the alarm goes off though, make sure you follow its instruction! Get into the practice of trusting yourself – you set the alarm for a reason, don't ignore it when it goes off cuz you feel different to how you did when you initially set it! Trust that you set it for a good reason and don't let lame you or autopilot screw up your progress. Remember, it has to be daily as if something is worth doing, it's worth doing EVERY day!

As before, this will only work if you start it right now. After doing a few of these exercises you will see why the most important part is that you do things immediately. Change your life immediately, don't wait.

I want you to write down 10 things that you want. There are only two rules to this, and we will come to the second rule after we have written our initial 10 down. The first rule is that they have to be unrealistic. This is so important. Most of you will struggle with writing down anything unrealistic, and when I begin to tell you the sort of things I write you will initially think I am high as shit or I have completely lost the plot. Don't question it; do shit, get shit done, init. Start to become obsessed with your future and understand you need to be able to believe it to be possible to stand a chance of attaining it.

These 10 things need to be things you actually want and they also need to be about you! You can't write things like: "I want my family to be happy," or, "I hope my partner gets the job they are going for." These are both very sweet and totally understandable things you would want to happen, but in reality, they are wants and hopes, and wanting and hoping won't get you shit! They are also about other people and this exercise is solely about you! Your goals have to reflect that. You cannot make anyone's life better until you can sort out your own. If you can't love yourself, ain't nobody else gonna love ya!

Try and put yourself into kid mode, when you thought everything was possible and you didn't care if people thought you were stupid for dreaming big. Remember, this is YOUR journal and unless you want to, you don't have to show it to anyone so write as huge and crazy as you can imagine.

Write em' down now!

Rightio, all done?! Coolsies. For some of you, this would have been super hard and a lot of you wouldn't have even got to 10. That's cool, no problem. Soon you will find it hard to stop at 10 but we'll hit that in a bit. So what kinda stuff did you write down? Maybe some of you had "I wanna be rich", "I wanna be famous", "I want a better car", "I want to have a rockin' body", "I want the perfect partner", "I want to be a world famous singer, dancer, or movie star", "I want to be the best parent in the world"... If so, good job, but we need to talk about the second rule!

The second rule, and here's where the magic is and I'll explain exactly how this works later... for now just roll with it. Rewrite the same goals as you have done them. "I am famous", "I own my dream car", "I have a rockin' body", "I am in a relationship with my dream partner", "I am a world famous singer, dancer or movie star", "I am the world's best parent".

It's gonna feel double weird the first few times and you will feel like a bit of a dick, but I promise if you go with it you will start to feel the magic immediately, even if that magic is a little smile or titter to yourself. Yes, I did say titter. Yes, it does have the word 'tit' in it. Heh. Also, while I got you, chardonnay has the word 'hardon' in it. Double heh.

You will start to feel a change in your thought process and this is a huge factor in reprogramming your brain to be fucking awesome and essential to your success. The next thing I need to point out is that most of you will have written your initial goals way too small. This is fine but we need to get to the extreme end of the spectrum of what is possible.

You have to understand that when we think small, we get small and when we think big, we get big. It has to be possible in your own mind and if it isn't it stands no chance of working. And worst-case scenario, coming up short on a HUGE goal will still be better than coming up short on a small one!

Steve Jobs never would have dented the world as he did by thinking, "I want to build average computers." Imagine the advertising slogan for Apple being "Alright computers that may make your life easier". Why do you think Snoop Dogg says his own name multiple times in every song he's ever recorded?! I mean maybe cuz he's high AF but... Do you think that NASA ever believed anything other than "we going to space, motherfuckers!" They are dominating. Let's have a look at some of the top advertising slogans and taglines ever to get this point across...

1. A DIAMOND IS FOREVER – DeBeers.

   Imagine if this was: "Our diamonds might last you a year or two."

2. FINGER LICKIN' GOOD – KFC.

   Imagine if KFC's tagline was: *"It tastes alright when you're drunk."*

3. IT'S THE REAL THING – Coca-Cola.

   Would never have worked if their slogan was: *"It could be the real thing, but we're not entirely sure."*

4. WHEN YOU CARE ENOUGH TO SEND THE VERY BEST – HALLMARK CARDS.

   What if this was: *"When you have to send someone a card cuz it's their birthday or some shit."*

5. I'M LOVIN' IT – McDonald's.

   *"I'll hump it but I don't want anything to do with it after."*

6. IT GIVES YOU WINGS – Red Bull.

   *"Don't even think about jumping off a building after necking a can."*

You see where I'm going with this... Fact is when we eat McDonald's, we aren't actually in love! We're not gonna take Ronald out for dinner and try and get him into a stand-up 69 afterwards. We don't wanna put our winky inside the burger bun or French kiss the patty, well, most of us anyway... When we drink a Red Bull, if we take the time to think about it, we know we aren't gonna fly off anywhere.

When we drink a cola we know it's the real thing, it's cola!! WTF does that even mean anyway?! These huge claims that mostly make no sense at all but completely work. They lull us into a false sense of trust. We begin to believe them. We trust these companies to deliver what they say they will. We need to take this approach with our own lives. Huge claims are still claims, they're just bigger. But turning these claims into reality, woooooah, gamechanger.

So how does this relate to our mission? Well, you need to start making bold claims and taking massive action. The only reason we know of McDonald's is that they made bold claims and took massive action. They did this over and over until everyone on Planet Earth recognised their logo and branding and slogans and know exactly what to expect when they visit the golden tits of America.

We have all got used to taking minimal action and getting minimal results. It never just falls on your lap, dude! Ever! To win the lottery you have to buy a ticket: you done did an action. To get your hair cut or styled you need to go to the barber or salon. To get good at something you have to put time and effort in, and usually money. All of these are actions, and every action has a repercussion. However, most of our actions are meagre and result in meagre repercussions. If you wanna be an Olympic champion, invent a top-grossing app, get the body you want or anything else that makes you feel alive, you have to take HUGE fuck off massive action.

We all take action every day, but I bet the majority of these actions are detrimental to your success and happiness. Things like the action to turn the TV on, or play on Candy Crush, or hit snooze 5 times before eventually rolling out of bed. They all take effort and energy and all hold you back! Later on, I am gonna show you how to easily replace these negative efforts with completely positive ones!

For now, let's go back to your goals list. The importance of writing your goals way huger than you can initially imagine starts to train your brain into thinking they are possible and not impossible. Remember, nothing is impossible, you just believe it is cuz someone else told you so. And writing your goals like you have already accomplished them also further solidifies the fact that they are completely attainable. Keep telling yourself you can't do something because you are scared, anxious, unconfident, or whatever, just means your brain starts to believe the bullshit. So, lemme tell you how I started my goal writing. My first few entries (and I do mine at least once a day, usually before bed and when I wake up) were completely lame, and I really struggled to get to 10!

1. I want to be fit
2. I want my family to be proud
3. I want my family to be happy
4. I want to have more money
5. I want to be clean of drugs
6. I want a bigger house
7. I want to be a well-known drummer
8. I want to go on holiday this year

None of these were of any help at all. Want is another way of saying haven't yet, or even worse: won't. Compare these to the goals I wrote this morning... And bear in mind I haven't accomplished the following, I am just writing like I have.

1. I am a best-selling author of 10 books which each sold over 5 million copies and have been translated into over 30 languages
2. I am a household name and regularly appear on TV, Popular YT channels, and radio
3. I hold shares in over 10 multi-billion £ companies
4. I have over £750m in assets, bonds, shares, stocks and liquid cash
5. I employ over 1000 people and pay them 10x the standard wage for their work

6. I am a trusted and caring philanthropist that uses 80%+ of my own wealth and time to incubate start-ups, help charities, disrupt industries, and change the way education and politics 'work' for the benefit of humans

7. I give opportunities to those less fortunate in the form of free mentorship, programmes, and institutes

8. I make 1000x more money each day than I spend

9. I have offices in 5 different countries including the UK, France, Switzerland, the US, Japan and Thailand

10. I have proved everybody wrong and pushed the envelope of what is humanly possible

I know what some of you are thinking... But the only reason you are thinking about what you are thinking is that you have never thought big. You think I'm unrealistic, or just a wanker. That's hater territory, my dude, and where the F has that got you up until now?! I bet some of you are so stuck in your ways that you know your dreams and you can't even say them out loud because you don't believe they are even slightly possible! If you feel like this then remember that you were brought up with these limiting beliefs and passed on this useless info from everybody else. Well, fuck everyone else, you don't want to be like everyone else! Right?!

I have been writing my goals down for a long, long time now, daily. It takes about 3 minutes and it affects the rest of your life. After a while, you will notice some goals come up every day, and some come in and out. It doesn't matter, just write, don't think, don't spend too much time on it, go with what first comes to mind, your desires!

Don't fight them like everybody else, they are desires for a reason. It's your soul telling you what it needs. When a child desires food, you feed the little bubba. They would die otherwise! And that's exactly what's been happening to you, you're dying! Your brain, mind and body need purpose!!! Otherwise, what's the point!?!?!

You may be thinking, "You want £750m!? That's mental! And selfish!" BS, it's selfish, with that much money and power I will help the world in a way I currently can't. Think of it like this: I used to volunteer at soup kitchens and needle exchanges. I would spend an hour a day helping dish out soup and fresh needles. I remember feeling proud of myself every time I volunteered because I had put someone else's needs first. I would feel like I'd made a change, made a dent, done something to better the world.

Of course, it did help, but it only helped a handful of people. I am also not that interested in dishing up food and passing it to people. I am also not very good at it – I would spill, I would get the portion sizes wrong, I would mess up constantly. Why the hell would I waste my potential on something I'm not good at or passionate about?!

Well, at the time I figured that it was worth it cuz I was helping people, but I can't stress enough that I was helping very few people. Last time I counted, there were over 7.5 billion people in the world! And I was helping about 10-30 a day. That is less than a drop in the ocean. With FU money I can multiply the number of people I can help.

I can open more soup kitchens, with actual staff, with better food, and care and educational and support services. I can open more shelters, I can actually make a difference! When I say 'I am a household name', I don't wanna be a household name like Donald Trump, or Simon Cowell, or Jimmy Saville. I mean like Marie Curie or Florence motherfucking Nightingale. I know you're still laughing but you know what I mean. Stop thinking small! Someone's gotta do it!!! And the only reason you can't conceive of it being you is that you have always been told it wouldn't be.

So, the deal with the daily goals – you NEED to do this every day. Make that commitment. Some of you legends will have already set your alarm for twice a day, or even three times a day! Commit! I'm buzzing just knowing you have started thinking bigger. Hit me up with your first set of goals, I can't wait to hear what you came up with!

If you are still listening, you have already begun the process to transition, from Bad You to Good You. You have made the initial steps to creating the life you had forgotten was possible, or never knew was achievable. You're killing it! Let's move on...

---

## Summary

- Ex 1.0 Complete 3 mini-steps to attain the first goal
  - Make this small and attainable
  - Make sure you write the goal down in your journal
  - Make sure you tick off each mini step as you complete them
  - Make sure you tick off the first goal when you complete it
- Find yourself a new mantra
- Start daily goal practice (minimum once per day).

# Chapter 3

# The Scale

One of our biggest problems as modern-day humans is taking responsibility. We point the finger, act like victims, and ultimately put the majority of our effort and energy into doing things that are detrimental to our futures. These things actually more often than not take waaaaaay more effort and energy than just getting on with it.

I saw a documentary once. I wish I could remember what it was called, it was really good. The basic premise was that these two Canadian brothers had decided to live on the streets for X amount of time, I can't remember how long, a couple of weeks I think.

They decided to do this because they had come to the realisation that without experiencing something it is impossible, and ethically wrong, to have an opinion on it. The guys got to the point in the documentary where they realised that even though they were experiencing the initial hardship of living on the streets, they were missing one vital element – they had no reason to be on the streets other than to make the documentary. And this wasn't enough to actually experience how it feels to be homeless which in turn took away from the validity of their original goal.

After interviewing countless homeless people they ascertained that one of the main reasons for living on the street was hard drugs, namely crack cocaine, meth and heroin. One of the brothers decided that if they were to make the documentary true to the cause he would have to take one of the aforementioned narcotics to help better understand how their subjects were feeling. The other brother tried to talk him out of this but he would not relent.

The crux is that after he had lived on the street taking heroin for a few days he began to understand the absolute nightmare the majority of these people were going through. And that more often than not these people were ending up on drugs and in turn the streets after experiencing horrendous life events, events that a lot of us will fortunately never have to experience.

My point?! I realised a long time ago that everyone has an opinion about everything, right or wrong, and with or without experience and education on whatever the subject is. We are going to tackle this full force later on but for now, you just have to think a little bit to remember an experience where either you were talking passionately to someone about something you actually had no idea about, or the other way round.

This realisation turned into something entirely useful when I began hacking my own life. I realised that the majority of the time I was on autopilot and just going through the motions. However, on the odd occasion that I actually thought about what I was doing, it was so much easier to control myself and stop. For example, the number of times I would light up a cigarette, get halfway through it, and then realise I didn't even want it in the first place (I'd still finish it), or I'd turn on the TV to watch my favourite show, and then realise 4 hours later I was zombie-watching some shitty reality show that I had no interest in.

Most of you will have made the "I'm never drinking alcohol again" or the "I'll never date another asshole" pacts before. Fact is, in most cases, the realisation comes after the problem. If the realisation comes first then we can control ourselves enough to prevent it, however, without the actual problem how do we know we need the realisation? Chicken/egg! Time for a reality check! I want to get you started making positive changes right from the get-go and I want to get you used to taking action immediately and without pause for thought. Here is a hack I use that not only changed my life but it stopped me from dying, a few times to be exact.

---

## Exercise 1.0

The premise is simple, and all you need is a pen (which you should have on you at all times), and your hands. The idea is that you use your dominant hand for good and your non-dominant hand for bad. Let me explain.

The idea is totally up to your actions throughout the day: good actions are displayed by a single cross somewhere visible on your non-dominant hand. Bad actions are displayed in the same way on your dominant hand. The reason I chose to do it this way is, like most people, I can't write for shit with my non-dominant hand (in my case my left), and even holding a pen or pencil in my left hand feels alien and weird.

Every time I do something bad, something I feel ashamed of, or something of a detriment to my life, I grab the pen with my left hand (which feels alien and weird) and mark a cross on the base of my thumb on my right hand. When I do something good, something life-affirming, or wonderful, or something to be proud of, I do the same thing but using my right hand (the hand my pen feels natural in) to put a cross on the base of my left thumb. It feels awkward to use my left hand, and this helps the brain to remember that bad actions feel awkward and aren't right.

Now obviously you don't need to put a cross on your hand for every little thing you do: brushing your teeth, holding doors open for folk, and doing the washing up does not constitute a good action. Well, not good enough to cross your thumb. In the same respect, swearing when you stub your toe, shouting at your partner while you're on your period, or breaking the speed limit every now and again by a couple miles per hour doesn't constitute a bad cross.

Every single person bar none that I have taught this simple hack to has raved about it. Not only does it begin to prevent you from doing bad things but it actually encourages you to do more good things, and all for one simple reason: you are starting to become aware of your own actions. I don't believe that humans are bad but I do believe we can be utterly terrible when we are not being mindful or conscious.

I used this method to quit hard drugs after a loooong battle. I have had clients that have used this to quit drinking, cigarettes, drugs, and detrimental behaviour. And have also used this technique to learn new skills, start successful businesses, treat people better, and ultimately control themselves.

Your aim with this particular exercise is to get used to not even needing a pen and to not end up walking around with what looks like it could be the beginnings of leprosy on the base of your thumbs. I have found with most people, assuming they commit, that it only takes 2-5 days to not need the pen, and it is a skill that maintains itself and grows without extra effort.

The commitment, as with everything, is completely key though. This will not work unless you can at least manage the first few days. A good way to hack this hack (yeah man, multihacks) is to write a little B for 'bad' on your dominant hand and a G for 'good' on your non-dominant hand – make them visible so they remind you to be conscious of the exercise.

Imagine your life as a scale. You can even think about it like the classic pearly gates scenario where if you've done more good than bad you get to go to heaven. Or Santa's naughty and nice list... If you want them presents then you gotta have done did more good than bad to get your red Power Ranger or Barbie doll on Christmas morning.

The scale never lies, and the simplicity of only having two outcomes (win or lose), makes it really easy to understand and utilise, and also to make a game out of it, and we all love playing games, right?! The idea of this exercise is to give yourself one short-term primary goal – outweigh the bad with the good, and one long-term secondary goal – to eradicate the bad completely.

So, let's make a list of things that could fit on both sides, good and bad. The bad list could be things like lying (fair to big lies – answering your partner with a sweet and immediate, "Of course not, baby," to, "Do I look fat in this dress?" is okay from time to time), cheating, being unethical, being closed-minded, doing drugs, being immoral and a plethora of other discerning character traits. Oh, and the biggest one of all: lying to yourself, but we'll tackle this little fucker later...

Things that you would dot your thumb for good could be: being selfless, beating a personal best, making a hard decision, making someone's day, helping people, helping yourself, facing fear, and a myriad more. Basically, we always know if what we are doing is wrong or right but unless we think about it we more often than not make the wrong decision based on, well, pretty much nothing, and usually an impulse in our brain that I call the IGMF, or instant gratification mother fucker.

You know the guy, the one that gets you in trouble and brings out your Bad You. If you ever feel ashamed of one or more of the actions you have made, or repeatedly make, then this exercise is gonna change your life, and how simple is it, eh?! Told you guys, baby steps! The other absolute boss attribute of this exercise is that when you become aware that you are about to do a bad thing, the sheer thought of having to admit to yourself that it was a bad thing will stop it dead, and 99 times out of 100 you won't go through with it.

Now if you have proper demons, like a drug addiction, or you habitually lie or do things you shouldn't in secret, you may find that the first few times you try this, you will choose to override the thumb crossing, and in turn, lie to yourself, believing that there is no repercussion to your action. If this is the case, then just add crosses for smaller things to begin with, taking note of your progress each night, and build up to the big stuff. Remember, doing something shit is 100% better than doing nothing at all, and all progression is worthwhile no matter how small. Snowflakes, init.

To triple hack this exercise, make a note of your score each day in your journal before you do your daily goals Good – 10 Bad – 8 for instance. Keep check of your personal bests and try to beat them each day until you either just have crosses on your non-dominant 'good' hand, or you don't even need to cross yourself. This will work effective immediately.

Don't tell yourself that you'll start the day off tomorrow with this exercise. Start now! Begin to be aware of yourself, your actions and your thoughts. Think about how you could get a cross or two on your good hand right now.

This exercise will also start to make you aware of how often you think negatively. What is the first bad thought you have from now? You can even stick a timer on to see how often your brain is being infiltrated with negative shit – it's actually fully worrying! It's definitely less worrying when you notice and can remedy it though!

The most interesting part of this for me is the fact that as soon as you are aware of the scale, you can control it. The fact we rarely, if at all, are aware of the scale means there is no way we can choose to add weight to either side and we need to be sticking tons down on our good side. We want that motherfucker strong and unmovable. We want so much weight on it that our bad side has no chance of getting up into the air while our good side stays completely grounded.

Talking about staying grounded...

## Summary

- Ex 1.0: Play the Scale
  - Be aware which of your hands is dominant. You have a 'strong hand' or 'weak hand' – they both are awesome at different stuff. Your dominant hand is the one you write with, or throw and catch with.
  - Keep your pen on you at all times (I would highly suggest keeping the pen in your hand or getting one of those pens you can have on a chain around your neck that will make you look like a complete D-bag.
  - Every time you have to make a decision that could leave you in the shit if you pick the wrong route, use your pen to make a cross on the thumb of the corresponding hand. I.e. If I go to kick a baby in the face and realise it's a bad idea and don't do it, I give myself a cross on my 'GOOD HAND'. If I end up hoofing the poor little bubba in the chevy then I give myself a dot or cross on my 'BAD HAND'.
  - Repeat this process whenever you need it.
  - Count the crosses on each hand at the end of the day, or at different points in the day, and see which side of 'The Scale' you are on – good, or bad.
  - Set an alarm to go off throughout the day to remind you to be aware of the scale
- Awareness and mindfulness are key
- Autopilot ruins lives.

# Chapter 4

# Who's Puking On You?

I really hate the word 'puke'! It really does what it says on the tin! I was going to change the title of this chapter but I wanted to make sure you understand the absolute monumentalism of this. First, ask yourself the question: "How would I feel if someone puked on me?"

I guess you didn't actually have to waste any time answering that! There was no deliberation, right?! Nobody likes to get puked on. Well, maybe a very, very, very small percentage of the population, but most of them are getting paid for it! You do you, pukey-people!

I am not talking about the physical act of people puking on you, obviously, that would be weird in a self-improvement book. I am instead talking about the mental puking that's covering your brain daily. You're being puked on!!! Even worse, your brain is being puked on!!! And I'm almost certain nobody wants a pukey brain!

Lemme share some insight as to who is puking on you, and how you can stop them.

In no particular order: TV, friends, family, ads, radio, news, teachers, bosses, co-workers, your kids, movies, YouTube, etc., etc.

Basically, every facet of your life can be puked on by someone else. You currently have no shield to prevent it and 99% of the time it will be unwarranted. It is a useless, negative piece of BS that is passed on from person to person, usually extracted via the media, and regurgitated by autopilot us. It is a pandemic.

Every time you talk about something that you only know because someone else told you and they only know because someone else told them, you are spewing vile crap over whoever is unfortunate enough to be listening.

Remember, this is about beginning your journey positively and breaking your bad habits, replacing them with killer obsessions, and being super awesome! Think to yourself now, and be real: how often do you pass on information that you actually have no idea about?!

Every time there is an election on my social goes mental with everyone's opinions – they are obsessive and full of energy and passion but they only last the 2-3 weeks running up to the election before going dead and returning to their usual subject matter of food or dogs or bathroom selfies. No stress if you love making that kinda content, that's not what is important here. What is, however, is learning how to be obsessive and full of energy and passion...

If you have spent time perfecting a trade or skill you will relate to what I am about to say. Think about your answer when people that don't do what you do ask you what you do... If you are a teacher, you say, "I'm a teacher." You don't talk about syllabus or safeguarding, or school or college infrastructure, or EBS. If you're a basketball player, you say, "I'm a basketball player." You don't talk about drills, training regimes, diet, self-promotion and branding. If you're a mum, you say, "I'm a mum." You don't talk about the daily routine, food prep, the laundry cycle, or all the business start-up ideas you've had and talked yourself out of because you're 'just a mum'. Now think about the difference in conversation when you talk to someone that really understands your industry, job or lifestyle, someone that understands the nuances of your daily life, because they do it too!

The reason we don't go into detail with certain people is that we know they won't understand the jargon of our life and won't have the attention span or interest for us to explain to them what we actually do in full detail.

To put this into perspective, picture a 10-year-old asking you how you drive a car... Most of us would say something along the lines of, "Well, my dear, you go forward with this pedal, and brake with this pedal, and steer with this wheel." You wouldn't even imagine getting into a conversation about drive chains, combustion, timing belts etc. Why? Because you know the kid won't understand what the flip you're talking about!

We speak to people on the level we expect them to understand us. This is true of the media, and all your friends and family that regurgitate the absolute dross the media spouts at us 24/7, 365. How many times have you heard someone tell you like it's already a dead cert, with uber confidence and gusto: "it's gonna rain tonight", "you don't wanna fly to Asia, a plane went missing and now you'll probably die", "vote for this party", "don't listen to this radio show, they don't know what they're talking about", "don't shop there", "oooo you don't wanna do that" etc.

God forbid you have given people similar advice yourself, shame on you! :P Don't stress, we all do it. It's not our fault we are brought into this, but remember: it is entirely our fault if we know and don't do anything about it!

When you have an opinion without any education, back-up or research, it means absolutely nothing. It's kinda like when someone asks you for directions, and even though you have no idea how to get them to their destination, you really wanna act like you do, or when you don't go eat somewhere or watch a certain film cuz your friend told you they didn't like it without having been there or watched it themselves. Listening to this bollocks is a waste of your time and resources. So let's do an exercise to stress this point so we can get on with fixing it...

---

## Exercise 1.0

Grab your journal and pen... a line down the middle. On the left: people you know who do this incessant and ill-informed banter regularly enough that their names popped into your head when I just asked you to think about them. On the right: things that you can think of that you have lied about or pretended to know about when you definitely don't have a clue. Be real here!

If you are doing this correctly you will have stopped writing names on the left. It's nearly 100% of the people you know. And you will have started feeling ashamed and stupid about the things you've written down on the right! Or, you haven't admitted that you do do this, resulting in nothing being down on the right! I don't want you to feel bad, quite the opposite, so let's fix it... And yes, I did say 'do do'. Heh.

---

## Exercise 1.1

The following exercise is hard, like really hard. It took me a few weeks to get it correct just once, and then a further month to be able to do it 90+% of the time. I am still working on it daily 7 years later. I guarantee you that it makes your life immediately better! People start to notice your new positivity, and more so you will start to notice people who are a negative influence in your life allowing you to choose how much of your precious time you want to spend with them in the future. Remember: you are who you hang around with, but we'll come to that later...

The following sounds like a simple task, but it's waaaay harder than it seems. It works immediately and will allow you to start seeing how negative you are being without even knowing it. As soon as you are aware you will start to make changes with ease.

So, here's the task... You have to go 24 hours without saying anything negative or giving someone misinformation. The latter constitutes information based off of something you haven't spent time researching or experiencing, AKA telling people what's best for them when you don't actually know.

---

It is integral to your future happiness and success to be able to cut through everyone else's BS and make your own decisions. You need to be in control of your life and this starts with you being aware of your own BS, even if you currently believe otherwise.

The best way to begin with this exercise is to make a tally chart. Jot down a tally for every time you notice yourself saying something negative or something you have no actual knowledge of. For example, you're driving around looking for parking and you can't find any. Your blood starts to boil and you start muttering obscenities under your breath, you begin to get stressed... why? It's a parking space, you're going to find one, and you just wasted energy thinking about it.

A little problem, well, more of a mild inconvenience in the grand scheme of things, has now changed your mood and affected your decisions and thought process. It takes away from your now and we need to be using our processing power for monumental good and not for minor inconveniences. You will find when you first start doing this exercise that you may not even last one conversation or thought process without having to score a tally on your chart. It is so easy to be distracted and taken off topic THINK OF YOUR BEST FRIEND NAKED. See!

Once you've got used to not puking on yourself you will notice immediately when someone else is puking on you. I stopped watching the news 8 years ago and it was one of the best moves I could have made. No matter where I am I hear people puking on each other. Talking utter crap that they know nothing about. You have two options here: either don't say nothin', or research and experience for yourself to instil understanding and wisdom, and then have your say.

You can't just talk – actions are the only thing that matters! This is why keeping your journal is imperative. It's real! You are manifesting your thoughts into real shit! Thoughts only have worth when they are manifested and turned into something real. I'm not suggesting your thoughts aren't real but I'm suggesting nobody gives a hoot until you back them up with actions.

A good idea is only as good as the follow-through. When someone tells you they will meet you at a certain time and they don't show it is frustrating and annoying and a waste of your time, right!? What do you do when an employee doesn't turn up to work on time and the reason isn't valid, or they lie to you? Three strikes and you're out?! Nah man; go for the one strike!

We do this to ourselves all the time – "No problem, I'll do it properly next time." WTF?! That's an excuse! And we want results, not excuses!

Do what you say you will, in fact, do more than you say you will! Over-deliver your promises every time! Would you take the same approach with your kid or partner? If your kid gets caught skiving off school or doing drugs, or you catch your partner cheating, you wouldn't say, "Strike one – I'll do something about it when you do it twice more!"

Anyway, I digress. Point is we need to stop puking on people! I'm 33 years old now, and I can't remember a time the news didn't make people scared, or worried, or act a certain way. It hasn't changed since I've been around! But it's just some bollocks that some mush is spouting. Does it actually have any benefit to you or your life to listen to it, let alone act on it?

There was a 'petrol' crisis a few years back in the UK. At the time I lived right next to a petrol station and man, I couldn't believe the amount of passion and obsession people were putting into practice. People immediately stopped what they were doing and headed to the nearest fuel station and then fought tooth and nail to get the last drop of fuel. Why? For what? Media says, "Jump," you say, "How high?!" It doesn't help your cause. It just makes you act like a dick!

Were you one of those people schools worked for? I speak to so many people that struggled at school – you probably all had that one teacher, the one who you related to and got the best out of you. What was it about them that worked...? They related to you! They listened and worked with you, for you! They took on board what was important for you, for your life, and they worked on it with you – they had your back! If all of your teachers were like that, you would have loved school!

Fact is that one way doesn't work for everyone. All of us are different and have different needs and wants and when we are put in a position where we aren't allowed to flourish and grow we just turn off. Even worse, with time, we begin to act that way and get stuck like it – you've just gotta think about your cantankerous dad/uncle/boss to see it in the flesh.

The media is the same. It doesn't fit most of us and it's just utter wank. If the media was all about you being your best you and related to your life then it wouldn't be so bad. But it isn't. It just scares us and makes us back into a corner! The worst part is that it's so rife that we end up listening to it and believing it and basing our lives around it! But I believe deep down, we always know what is right, if we take the necessary steps to educate and work on ourselves. Think about it... you always know...

## Summary

- Ex 1.0: List your negatives
  - Draw a line down the middle of a page in your journal
  - On the left side make a list of all the negative people in your life
  - On the right side make a list of recent times you have lied or pretended to know something you didn't
  - Cringe
- Ex 1.1: Tally your negatives
  - Make a note of every time you say something negative or pretend you know something you don't
  - Make sure you question yourself constantly to test the validity of the statements you are making
  - Take note of how often you hear something negative that doesn't affect you but takes your mind from its previous task
- The media gives zero fucks about you
- The media has an agenda
- Your job is to be able to navigate your life through choices based on truth without getting caught in the crossfire of the media
- Always use talc before a long flight.

# Chapter 5

# You Always Know

I believe you always know. Like always! Problem is we don't often take time to acknowledge our thoughts, to really spend time on them, work out where they came from or if they are of benefit to us. I believe that I have always known: when I'm lying, to other people or myself; when I am slacking; when I'm working hard; when I'm right; when I'm wrong; when I'm unsure. I have always known, and so have you.

We get a feeling, some people call it heart or gut, call it what you want! It's there and you know it well. Whether you choose to trust it, that's an entirely different thing! It's like the car keys you can't find and after turning the whole house upside down looking for them you realise they were in your fucking pocket the whole time.

The knowledge and information is within us, we just don't spend any time with it. We get complacent and distracted and we don't learn from ourselves. You know that expression: "the world doesn't revolve around you"? It bloody does! Your world revolves completely around you, and mine around me, and hers around hers and his around his!

You are the only one that can affect it, and change it, and make it better or worse. Like I mentioned before, until we can become conscious of our own BS, we can't even begin to remedy the problem.

When you get ill, you go to the doctor, get a prescription, take the meds, get better.

How many times have you been to the doctor and not taken the meds?! And then while you're still feeling like shit had a family member, partner or friend say "...Well have you taken anything for it yet?" and your answer is, "No," or even worse, you say, "Yes," knowing you haven't just to get them off your back – God forbid they wanted to help you out!

Why?! You had an opportunity to fix your problem and you didn't. And how frustrating is it when the shoe's on the other foot? You knew you could have done something positive to remedy the problem, and you lied to yourself and didn't.

You know! You always know! You just didn't stop to actually think. If you had spent 10 seconds writing the problem and its solution in your journal, you would have taken the meds or gone to the doctor immediately, and in the long run, saved yourself loads of time and effort.

Instead, you had a headache for ages, affecting your mood and in turn your work, career, relationships or whatever else. I believe that a lot of the issue here is because we are taught not to take responsibility for our actions. We grow up watching politicians passing the buck, family and friends pointing the finger, and the rest of the world spinning stories.

Ever caught yourself pretending you don't know about something you did so you don't have to own up and it was totally your fault? Just cuz nobody realised it was you, you still know it was you!!! There was an expression one of my old bands had whenever we went on tour – "what goes on tour, stays on tour"! No, it doesn't, it follows you everywhere, in your pretty little brain box – you take that shit with you AND it affects you, whether you admit it or not. Even if nobody else knows, YOU do!!!

Ever overridden your gut because 'you know better'? Problem with your gut, or heart, or whatever you want to call it, is that it tells you what to do, but it doesn't tell you how. The 'how' scares us. "It must be hard work, I don't know what I'm doing, what happens if it doesn't work???"

Personally, I try and trust my gut whenever it gives me a signal, and then I figure out the 'how' after committing. Let's face it, nobody knows what they are doing, but only a few of us take the time to try and begin to figure it out. Fool me once shame on you, fool me twice shame on me.

Fool myself... repeatedly: quadruple shame on me!!!! I know you all know what I'm talking about! You all feel it, you know when your body is trying to tell you something, but how often do you ignore it?! It's screaming at you!!!! It's giving you a clue. You gotta learn to trust it. Pick up the clue, baby. The previous chapter's exercise will have allowed you to start noticing when you are lying to yourself and when other people are lying to themselves.

It is so important that you become aware of this. You can totally be in control, and in turn, you will improve the quality of your life and those around you. An awesome by-product of this is that people will start trusting you more and hold you in higher regard, and they will want to spend time with you because you are actually being real. That fart that you did, that absolutely stinks, that you know everyone else can smell... OWN IT!!!

Do you really think other people's shit don't stink?! It does. Everyone knows it was you anyway and will be more likely to remember you as the 'poopy-butt liar' if you don't come clean. When you own it, the moment passes as quickly as it came.

If your desk is messy – clean it. If your car is dirty – wash it (or pay someone else to wash it!) If you need a new pair of shoes – buy them. If you can't afford them then work out a way to be able to afford them! Stop window shopping on your own life and start living it.

Invest in yourself – it's the only thing that doesn't go down in value unless you let it. Whenever you tell yourself: "I'll do it tomorrow," you are denying your core instinct. Your body will tell you what it needs, so learn not to deny it.

When you need something and someone denies you, how do you feel?! How would you feel after going to the cinema and asking to buy a ticket to Toy Story 23 and the teller saying, "Er… no, unlucky dickhead, you can't have a ticket!"

You are waaaay better than that, we all are. Do you really believe you have been put on this earth to be average, riddled with problems, boring?!?! I believe not! I believe you were put here, amongst other things, to leave a legacy, to live on long after your body has dropped and to accomplish amazing things that make the world better.

Stop lying to yourself!!!! It is one of the worst things you can do, and when it has gone on too long you begin to believe your own crap! And then you teach that crap to your kids, family and friends and the struggle continues! Break the chain, like a powerful chain-breaking mother-bitch!

You know you have a purpose, you may not be sure of what it is yet but you know you have one, and if you don't think you do then put this book down and come back when you're ready. I'm telling you for a fact that you have a purpose!!! You may have to do some work to find it, but you definitely have one, or more likely a bunch.

Sick of waking up groggy and moaning about your day to come? Exhausted all the time?! Not buzzing on anything?! That's not life! That's a prison. That's not having free will or choices, that's a prison. If you live for the weekend then your life is around 5/7ths shit!! If you respond to, "How's it going?" with, "Not too bad," then what are you living for?!

I'm gonna get you to the point where Mondays are the best day of the week... along with Tuesdays, Wednesdays, Thursdays and Fridays, Saturdays and Sundays! This is your life!!!! Every single moment has the potential to be riveting, beautiful, inspiring and fucking awesome – but it all starts with you! And it begins with the commitment to being in control of your life and making every day awesome!!!

---

## Summary

- Stop lying to yourself
- Own your shit
- readthisifyou'reapoopyhead.

# Chapter 6

# COGTFO

Think of all the things you do every day, the important things: breathing, sleeping, eating, drinking, showering, brushing your teeth, getting dressed. You do them every day because they are integral. Other integral things are your happiness, your success, and your future.

You don't freak out when you put your underwear on in the morning, you just do it – you don't even acknowledge what would happen if you didn't. It is so inherent that you just do it. We all go through life, but only a few have life flowing through them.

For a long time, I was a course leader lecturing at a college, tutoring 16- to 20-year-olds. The majority of them in tutorials explained to me that they suffer from anxiety, depression, and low self-esteem.

They were nearly all on medication that their doctor prescribed because of their anxiety, depression and low confidence. I don't believe for one moment that any of them are any more anxious, depressed, scared or worried than I have been in the past, or any more anxious, depressed and scared than ANYONE can potentially be.

Taking a pill masks the issue and often dishes out more negative repercussions than the initial problem did! It actually takes a hella load more effort to submit to the fact that you are depressed and start taking medication for it than it does to work out what work needs to be done to kill the fucker dead in its tracks.

The reason I rarely take any medications myself is that I don't want to fool my brain into thinking there isn't a problem – if the meds mask the pain then the urgency to fix the problem dissipates. I FUCKING HATE toothache, but I am glad it exists. Without it, my teeth could start falling out without any prior warning, and I'm not the best looking guy already!

There is no time spent on self-help or progression in most people's lives. Instead, we often feel so done in that we resort to quick-fix remedies that are just IGMF. Ever got sucked in by a get rich quick scheme or fad diet?! Me too! Did it work?! Fuck no! Did it waste your time and money?! Fuck yuh-huh!

We all too often take the easy route, which when you know the real deal is actually the hardest route. I know a lot of you will be saying, "That's bullshit, I have a chemical imbalance," or something like that. I really don't want to offend any of you, I'm just going on my experience of being on both sides of the fence.

I am not for one moment saying that some of us don't NEED particular meds to help, but to rely solely on them with no extra effort to fix the problem is ridiculous and a coward's way out. Before you get mad at me though please understand that a lot of what you are thinking will have come from the puke we spoke about a couple of chapters ago and being told a pill will help is not your fault until you know otherwise.

Unfortunately, when we are so desperate to fix a problem we become frantic and will often take the path of least resistance which is more often than not the 'easy way', and the easy way is definitely an instant gratification mofo! One more time: I am absolutely not trying to upset or offend anyone, I just want to give you another option, and one that I know completely works.

Let's talk about diets. What is a diet? The concept of going on a diet is a short-term answer. You don't need a diet, you need a change and an absolute one at that. Think about how many times you've gone on a diet and not seen it through. Or in fact, anything that you have started and not seen through.

Think of that feeling you get from starting something new, you know the one – it's exciting, it gets you pumped, but it doesn't last. We are not talking about quick fixes here, we are talking about actual life changes. If you think about joining the gym and you get excited about it, excited enough to actually sign up and go for your first session... you rock up, do your first workout, and then don't go the next day or you give up after the first week.

You didn't make an actual commitment, you made a short-term decision. A short-term decision is not a commitment. If you go to the gym once you are gonna wake up a day or two later, muscles aching, with no gain whatsoever and a bad taste in your mouth.

When you commit to something, you actually have to commit. If you get married, that doesn't mean you're married 99% or the time but sometimes you stand-up 69 with someone else. That's not a commitment. A commitment is 100%. Nothing more, nothing less. A commitment is for life, not just for Christmas.

But this is how a large majority of people are. We start something, we do it for a bit, then we bail, and then get jaded and think it doesn't work. The reason it didn't work is that we didn't actually commit. You need to commit! Look how many fucking exclamation marks I put there! That's how serious this is!

The goal-writing exercise will not work unless it's something you are gonna maintain. In fact, everything is useless unless it's something you are going to maintain. How many hobbies have you started in your life and not seen through and then wondered why some people are living the life you want and you're not? They committed!

Starting is super important but it means nothing without finishing. They are the opposite ends of the spectrum. You have to run your game every damn day! Imagine if the internet only worked 9 days out of 10. Or if your best friend only didn't murder people 87% of the time. Or your parents only loved you 20 days out of the month. Or your left nut turned into an empty Lucozade bottle every Harvest Moon. Okay, so the last one not so much, but you get my drift!

You have to commit to your future, and your future happens every day, for the rest of your fucking life!!! USE IT!!! Later on, in the burst practice chapter, I am going to teach you how to learn any physical skill in under 5 minutes a day but for now, we are going to do another exercise.

Some of you will have been skipping the writing parts of the exercises = you guys can't commit yet. Commit Or Get The Fuck Out. Seriously, this is your life! Grab your journal. I want you to draw a line down the middle of the page and on the left side write all the things you do every day that are positive, and on the right side, all the things you do every day that are negative.

My list from a few years ago would have been harrowing, inclusive of lying, cheating, using, etc., etc.

Here's my list from 5 minutes ago.

## Positives:

Send someone a thoughtful message, exercise, write, play music, meet with potential clients, stay outside my comfort zone, tell my partner and son I love them, get up early, don't watch TV, don't smoke, don't do drugs, goal practice, eat healthy, practice getting better, scheme, create, make progress, mentor etc.

## Negatives:

NONE! Well some, but now they are pretty much just 'thought fires' that as long as I am mindful and not on autopilot, I can extinguish pretty quick!

I reeled this list off to a client yesterday in a session and she said: "God, that sounds boring!"

Thing is, old me would have been the first person to agree but I can tell you now for an absolute fact that I have never ever been so happy, confident, successful and at peace in my life.

I've been on both sides – partying like Charlie Sheen, no structure, no goals, chilling and eating what I want when I want, sessioning video games, picking up girls like it was going out of fashion, banging untold amounts of narcotics and all the other stuff I am saving for a future book entitled "stuff I didn't want my parents to read in my first book".

Parts of the old me were crazy fun, of course they were, but I swear on my eternal soul that my life now is infinitely better.

Point is, if you do heroin once a month you are still a user. If you cheat on your partner, if only once while you were really drunk, you're still a cheat. If you tell a lie, no matter how small, you are still a liar. What do you want people to think about you? Would you be hurt, upset, or ashamed if people thought you were a liar, a drug addict, or a cheater? I would! I was!

Imagine overhearing a conversation your friends are having about you, or even worse people you don't know, and they are saying things like, "He's a nice guy but he lies a lot," or, "I really like him most of the time, but I can't get over he cheated on his partner, what a dick," or, "She is great to work with, but she always stinks of cigarettes."

As far as we know, we get one shot! And in the grand scheme of things, we have very limited time to make a dent. No eulogy reads "really good cigarette smoker", or "established cheater". Ya dig?! Think about people you know who are dead but left a legacy. I'll reel off a bunch and I want you to think about why you know who they are...

Bob Marley
Princess Di
Mother Teresa
Albert Einstein
Bruce Lee
Walt Disney
Christopher Columbus
Mozart
Jesus Christ
Buddha

Come on, man, these people made a name through massive action, not for little amounts of effort spaced over the years. These guys and girls were in 100% 24/7, 365!!! You have the same 24 hours in a day that they had. What makes you think you have less potential power, wisdom, opportunity? Stop thinking small and COGTFO!

Commit to your life! It's yours!!! Your world completely revolves around you and you are the only one that can change it, make it better or worse, establish it or ruin it, create a legacy or let a potential legacy slip away. You can make history like these guys, even if it is just in your little town or for your little family.

Michael Jackson's Man in the Mirror – 'if you want to make the world a better place, take a look at yourself and make that change'. Never a truer sentence has been spoken! It's all you, baby! All of it. We create our own landscape and we grow our own crops. Stop growing shit crops!! Start growing your future. Yes, I was just a little sick in my mouth when I wrote that, but fuck it! Literally, fuck it!

Now let's talk about power hour! What in the hell is power hour, I hear you ask?! Well, power hour is (and I know you are gonna know exactly what I am talking about) the first hour of the day. For a lot of us, it isn't power hour but it completely has the potential to be. What do I mean? Well, the first hour you are awake counts for more than you probably know.

Ever had that thing when you get up and do something awesome first thing? Like you get up without hitting the snooze button, and then go straight to the gym, or start making calls, or practising drums or dance or whatever awesome thing you love. What happens after you manage to do that? The rest of the day is amazing! I used to kid myself that I did my best work at night, and then cuz I went to bed late, I'd wake up late, and then spend the first part of my day just flicking through Facebook or wanking or whatever, and then guess what?! The rest of my day was wank!

Power hour, mon frere! Your first hour will define your day! Lemme say that again: your first hour will define your day! It's similar to the idea that you are what you eat and you are who you hang around with. Your first hour is the one. Let's consider your average morning. What do you do in your potential power hour?!

Do you have a plan? Is it working for you? Are you in control of the first hour you are awake?

For myself I changed my diet, I got super healthy, I changed my bedtime, I drank way more water, I quit doing drugs. You name it, I changed it! Every aspect of my life became unmeasurably better after doing all this, apart from one thing! What was the one thing? Waking up, man, it STILL sucks!

I still have the same horrible initial-hit-snooze-nause that everyone else does. That first few moments that you are awake, that literal moment when your eyes first open and you have the option to get up or hit snooze is one of the main keys to the transition. I can't bear that decision every morning, I haven't jumped out of bed with a spring in my step since I was a kid. I want to press snooze nearly every day, even this morning I nearly pressed it.

But I know there is so much to lose by not pressing it – the reason? Self-control. When I want to get up and I hit snooze I am out of control. Then my power hour is just a shower hour! So, how can we hack this?! Let's tie in our daily goal practice with power hour.

Ever done that thing when you tell yourself what to dream and you dream it? Or you go to bed worrying about something and then all your dreams are about that thing? If you don't dream at all then get off the pot (heh). Anyway, in the same way, that your first hour defines your day, your last hour defines the following day's first hour – get me?!

Let's say that you want to get down the gym at 6:30am. The night before you get your gym clothes ready, trainers by the door, breakfast planned out, audiobook loaded on your phone and your headphones in a place where you know where they are. And then, to top it off, you write on your to-do list – "go to the gym for 6:30".

They say the last thought you have before bed is the first thought you think about in the morning. I don't know about that, but I do know to be in control of your morning the night before makes it 100 times easier to just wake up and stick to the plan.

Accountability.

Same goes no matter what you wanna do – start making business calls, start a project, eat healthily, practise, rehearse, whatever. Make your day count right from the start and plan it the night before. Later on, I am gonna show you exactly how to reprogram your brain and all of this will become a lot easier, but for now, you can put it to the test by planning tomorrow's first hour now, or tonight before bed.

As soon as that first hour is on point your day will follow. You know this. When your power hour is rubbish, your day will tend to be rubbish. You need that first hour to be a game-changer! Stop telling yourself that you work better at night, or you aren't good in the mornings – I did that and it cost me years! Not months, years! I was out of control. Power hour, motherfucker! Do shit, get shit done! If you are questioning this, please just give it a try. Even if it is far from your standard reality, you will be pleasantly surprised.

## Exercise 1.0

1. Plan tomorrow morning now. Make sure you encourage all movements to be positive.

2. Set an alarm to go off before your bedtime tonight to give yourself time to get everything ready you may need (i.e. gym clothes, ironed shirt, food prep etc.)

I know some of these initial exercises will seem pointless but you need to remember the snowflake analogy. Also, some of you will already be on top of this and have a regime, but for those of you that don't, it is important to make sure you are trying new avenues, no matter how tiny they may seem to begin with.

Remember in the last chapter I said you always know...? Well you do, which means deep down if you are questioning some of the things I am suggesting then it is because you know better, but if you stop to really think about it, you probably don't.

Trying different things (like planning your morning tomorrow), will not only keep everything fresh and new and shiny, but in turn, it will get you thinking and learning, and not just going through the motions (Netflix etc.).

Really, how do you know if you hate ballet, or cooking, or knitting, or bungee jumping if you have never experienced it?! For those of you saying, "I just know I wouldn't like it..." Grow up, dude! You might, and that's enough!

Every experience will lead to the possibility of learning something that will make your own journey so much better! I remember taking the piss out of all my yoga friends before one day being faced with the "stop being a dick and give it a try" sound byte. At the time I was a stubborn mofo so I couldn't resist calling their bluff. Immediately all of my previous misconceptions were shattered.

It didn't turn me into a tree-hugging hippy! I really enjoyed it! When I learned to play the guitar, it made my drumming better, it gave me a much deeper understanding of what to play from a guitarist's perspective, which in turn made my musicality better overall. Do new shit, get new shit done, make old shit better!

The main thing to take from this is that doing something outside of your comfort zone will keep you living, not just existing. Neale Donald Walsch says "life begins at the end of your comfort zone", and I couldn't agree more.

---

## Summary

- Ex 1.0
Power Hour
  - Plan tomorrow's first hour
  - Make sure all actions are positive
  - Do not add more activities than you can fit in (snowflakes)

- – Set an alarm to go off before your bedtime tonight to give you time to get everything you need ready so there are no delays when waking
- Commit and don't stop when shit gets hard or it doesn't seem like the end is in sight, cuz it is often only just a couple more chips away.

# Chapter 7

# Comfort Zone for

# Beginners

What is a comfort zone? In my mind, it's the walls we imprison ourselves in. It's easy. Well, it seems easy until you break free. It's familiar and it's, well, comfortable. These are the negative benefits. You have to understand that everything is changing, constantly, whether it be the cells in our bodies, the weather, or the relationships we have, it's all changing, all of the time.

Think about it like this, if you weren't meant to have new experiences there would be absolutely no point in anything, and there wouldn't be new experiences to be experienced. Think about how you felt when you tried something you had preconceptions about. It might be joining the gym, or starting a course, or asking someone on a date. Once you did them, they made you feel good, really good.

We spend a lot of energy trying to talk ourselves out of new ventures, new experiences, and the whole time we have no reason to other than we think we know better or we are worried or scared of the 'unknown', but no two days are the same so in theory, everything is unknown. The only reason you aren't good at stuff you don't do is that you don't do it! How mental is that?!

Being a drummer, I hear this all the time: "That's so impressive, I couldn't be a drummer because I have no rhythm." WTF! I didn't have rhythm either, I practised it. I put time into it and got good at it. Giving up is one thing but giving up before you've started is insane!! "I can't" is just a lame way of saying 'I haven't bothered!'

Steve Jobs couldn't build computers before he could build computers; Jay-Z couldn't produce music before he could produce music; Michael Jordan couldn't own a court before he could own a court. See where I'm going with this?! Skills and abilities take time, effort, and drive.

Whenever you hear of someone that had overnight success, it's only overnight because you didn't know about them until they were successful. I assure you it wasn't overnight for them! You never saw all the times they failed, cried, freaked out or wanted to quit. Difference between a winner and everyone else: winners keep getting up. Remember, you can't fail if you never quit! You get out what you put in, every time!

The first step is to work out where your boundaries are. Where does your comfort zone end? It's pretty easy to figure this...

Think of something awesome someone does that you wish you could do and then sit back and wait for your brain to tell you all the reasons why you can't do what they do. Try it now – pick your biggest hero and imagine yourself doing what they do and having what they have.

There is only one reason you can't do what they do... you haven't tried, and you haven't put in the required amount of effort to be able to. If your kettle only gets the water to 78 degrees then it ain't gon' boil! Soooo many of us don't realise the necessary commitment and effort it takes to complete something or become exceptional at it.

There is a picture I love. It is of a guy mining for diamonds. He has clearly been slogging his way through the dirt and stones for time to find the precious little fellas. From his perspective, all he can see is the same rocks in front of him, and the tunnel he has dug out behind him. He has no idea when he will find the loot he is looking for.

From the perspective of the viewer, he is only one more pickaxe chip away from hitting the jackpot, but the picture depicts him turning around and giving up. All the while the miner above him (that he can't see and isn't aware of) is hooning it full force towards the diamonds with no signs of stopping! If the giver-upper only knew there was only one more chip to make he surely would have persevered. But he gave up. No diamonds for you, dick 'ed.

Like I said before, the heart doesn't tell you why or how, it just tells you what! You can't give up. If you're anything like I was then you've been making excuses for years. So let's put a stop to it now! I was useless for years! I kept making excuses as to why I hadn't completed anything! It's exhausting. And soul-destroying!

I realised a long time ago that whenever I pushed myself to do something outside of my comfort zone I felt alive again, buzzy, excited. It works! I'd wanna talk about whatever it was to anyone that would listen. I bet you all have an immediate thought, or two, of things you really want to try that you keep putting off.

Might be travelling, starting a business, joining a fitness class, asking someone on a date, or asking someone to marry you. It's uncomfortable because you haven't done it before, but that's it. Why do you think the most comfortable shoes you own are the ones you've had the longest? It's because you know what you're gonna get with them.

Over time your foot has made a dent in the shoes and they fit in all the right places. Are they the most comfortable shoes you could ever have?! Are they the shoes that make you feel powerful, successful, in control? Probably not. They are just comfortable.

When you got them though, they weren't – they were stiff and new and a little awkward. You had to put the effort in to wear them through that stage to get them to the honourable title of 'most comfortable shoes'! You can apply this sufficient analogy to everything! Like, actually everything! We need to get you out of your comfort zone. Benefits are waiting for those brave enough to take the leap of faith.

How many of you run your own business and don't call clients, or knock on people's doors, or take clients to lunch? How many of you stay-at-home parents watch daytime TV, refraining from committing to anything else because you tell yourselves you don't have time because of the school run or some other excuse? How many of you sit there in awe at a concert and say, "I wish I could play the guitar," and never book yourself a lesson?

I can tell you this for an absolute fact that what you're doing feels like the easier option, but it is the hardest!!! For those of you living in a first world country, you are blessed with more opportunities than a large percentage of the rest of the world, and you are choosing prison. If you aren't making enough money from your business: pick up the phone and make some calls. If you're living within the confines of your child's life: start a business from home while they are at school. If you get excited watching people play music: learn a fucking instrument!

I know it feels horrible, but you have to understand that you have made an assumption with no backup – you cannot possibly have an opinion, well, a valid one at least, if you haven't even tried the thing you are opinionated about! I did this for years, I told myself I couldn't do something, or it was too hard, or that person's better and I'll never be as good as them. May as well get a drug problem and watch Netflix seasons back to back.

Let's do one of my favourite exercises. It's one of my favourites because it is the one that changed my life. It absolutely changed my life. It allowed me to practice being outside of my comfort zone pretty much constantly, and it gave me very obvious targets to hit and I knew immediately if I had hit them or not.

For a lot of you, this will be something you haven't done before, and it will feel immediately difficult and weird. Trust me, you can do it.

## Exercise 1.0

So here's the deal: it is a win, lose, or draw game. It is the only win, lose or draw game I am aware of where the draw is what you want; then the win; then the loss. Well, you don't want the L. Nobody wants the L!

The object of the game is to look into a stranger's eyes and maintain eye contact. Doesn't sound like much, but when you try it you will see how hard it is. The rules are simple: if you break eye contact first, you lose. If they break eye contact first, you win.

And if you both hold eye contact until the last possible moment when you smile at each other, you draw. Remember, the draw is what you want. The draw depends on the other 'contender' being at the same higher level of confidence that you will need to be at to win/draw this game.

I came across this idea when I completely lost the plot one day. I'd had a rough month. I had one of those months, one of those months you can't prepare for, that wipes you out. One of those months where you look at the sky and stupidly say out loud, "Surely it can't get any worse!" and it does! I lost a friend.

It was weird because it wasn't a best friend, and we didn't spend loads of time together, but it just got me – I was in total disbelief and complete denial. It was the first time someone that close had gone, and the way it happened was so sad. I had a flu-ey cold that week and felt horrendous too. I was on my way to rehearsal when I found out and I don't think it had properly hit me. I decided to do my 3-hour rehearsal feeling like death, believing it would help stop me from exploding into tears.

At this time my partner of 8 years and I were completely on the rocks – we shared a flat, but had both given up on the relationship 3 years prior. Neither of us had the bottle to end it even though we knew it was the right thing to do. I was sleeping on the couch and being at home was awkward AF. I finished rehearsal, got in my car, and started driving.

Five minutes into my journey the car starts smoking and the head gasket blew! I had no money to fix it. I called out the AA (for any Americans, this is not Alcoholics Anonymous), and they turned up hours later. It was winter, and I hate the cold. This day sucked. I've never been that emo, but when I eventually got home I did the most emo thing I have ever done. I sat at my computer and typed 'why is the world so shit' or something like that, I can't remember exactly what lame search I put into Google.

Now, I should point this out, up until this point my view on blogs was that of an uneducated idiot. I initially thought they were platforms for twats to preach their nausey lives to everyone else. God, I was wrong. I mean, some of them are, but some, well, some are game-changers!

The first thing that came up was a blog post. I was at my wits' end and did something I had never previously done! I clicked on a blog post and started reading... It was by a guy called Julian Smith, and it began the process to change my shitty month. The first blog post absolutely got me at the right time! You know when that happens, when the planets align and you get a sign. You know, that 'you couldn't write it' type shit!

Either way, this post started with something like: 'The world ain't shit, you are!' Fuck! I've finally decided to read a blog post and this motherfucker is calling me out. Introduce insecurity. For some reason, and I can't explain this as it wasn't a usual protocol for me, I kept reading. At the bottom of the blog, it had an option to be added to the mailing list.

Mailing list! God, this was out of character for me! In my desperate, confused state, I stuck my email address down and hit submit. I felt like absolute shit the rest of that week. I smoked more weed than Peter Tosh and drank a similar amount of booze to George Best. Forget, forget, forget. Numb, numb, numb! Ignore, ignore, ignore! About 2 weeks later I received my first newsletter. It was headed "thanks for joining, here is your homework for the week".

I was actually intrigued. Homework for the week? Screw you, blog guy! I read the email. It explained how everything is your own fault, and how you have to take action to change your life. The idea presented was (apart from my friend passing which we will come to in the next chapter) my fault. Feeling ill, being in the wrong relationship, my car bustin' etc. I realise now I was ill because I was unhealthy and malnourished.

I was in the wrong relationship cuz I was being a pussy, and I was done in about my car because it was my only car and I didn't have the money to fix it. I'll explain this in a minute. But first, lemme tell you about the exercise that changed my life.

The homework given in that first mail-out was the one I am telling you to do, it was explained a bit differently but the outcome was the same. I decided I was going to stop wallowing and give this a try, I mean, how hard could it be to look at someone? Then I tried... Daaaaayum!!! The initial anxieties that popped into my head were: "Well I can't stare at young girls, I'll look like a paedo; I can't stare at that guy that looks like he's just butchered someone with his bare hands, because he looks like someone that's just butchered someone with his bare hands; I can't stare at that overtly gay guy cuz he'll think I wanna suck him off, and I can't stare at that black guy cuz he might think I'm racist!" Jeez, I was an idiot back then! Thanks to the media and school.

A lot of you will be thinking, "Wtf is this guy chatting about? What an idiot!" Try it yourself, I dare you!!! It's not anywhere near as easy as it seems. So, because I'm a stubborn dick head, or used to be, I decided I was going to push myself to get this done. It sounded so stupid I figured I would boss it right off the bat. WRONG!

I failed daily for over 2 months. Seriously. I remember pretending the 'scary' prospects were not there and just started staring at people that I wasn't afraid of. COMFORT ZONE! I kept losing. As soon as I would connect eyes with someone I would hold the gaze for what felt like minutes, but was actually a tenth of a second, and feel like I was winning! It took weeks to get to the point where I could hold it for a second or two before the inevitable look at my feet.

I was, by this point, absolutely obsessed. It was the first time I had been obsessed with anything in ages. In fact, since I started playing the drums or wanking. But that's a different story (the drums, not the wanking). Every time I left my house I started playing the stare game, and then I played at every opportunity throughout the day. I was starting to get more daring; one day I even tried to keep eye contact with a gay black paedophile that looked like he'd recently killed someone.

Man, I was hooked. It seems like such a silly little exercise now, but at the time it was huge for me. It was totally outside of my comfort zone. It felt fresh. And then... one day, I won! For the first time. And when I say I won, I mean I drew. I had won a few times before this, actually a lot of times – turns out there are a lot of insecure people out there, less confident than me – crazy!

I was walking out of my house and I locked eyes with this girl; she was beautiful, but not in an "I wanna stick my thumb in her pooper" kinda way, more in a "this girl is a sister" kinda way. The little fucker held eye contact with me. I should stress we were on opposite sides of the road. I held it. It felt weird: not awkward, or bad, just different. We were walking opposite ways and we were seconds away from the critical point where we would pass each other, I maintained.

Our eyes were locked and my heart was racing. Not because I fancied her, or wanted to jump her bones, it just felt awesome, like I'd perfected something. It felt like slow-mo. We were milliseconds away from passing each other, on opposite sides of the road, never to see each other again, and then it happened...

She stopped. I stopped. We stared at each other from across the street. She started to cross the street. I started to cross the street. This was a compulsion and felt like I couldn't stop it. We met in the middle of the road – usually, I would have been aware of this, aware that there are other more deserving vehicles on the road, vehicles that pay tax and insurance, but this was effin' magical. If you are being a hater now, simmer down, I'll come to you in a bit! Embrace this awesome shit!

She held her hand out, I swear this is true, and grabbed my right hand. She said, "Man, I don't know what it is, but I really want you to be happy!" I returned the gesture, not because it was polite, I just felt it! Like completely felt it. For those of you that know, it was similar to coming up on a 90s ecstasy pill with a silly name like a Hot Carlos or Mitsubishi Turbo.

We took a moment, I said, "I want you to be happy too," we smiled, like a proper smile, a smile that meant something, and we went our separate ways! FYI if you are that girl, and you're reading this or listening to this, hit me up, I owe you a drink.

Look, the point is, something I thought was dumber than dumb manifested into something absolutely life-affirming for me. Try the game! It's amazing! A lot of you won't even tell the barber or hairdresser when you don't like the cut or do they've done, but you need to be able to. We all have to feel powerful in our own bodies, and breaking your comfort zone daily is one of the keys.

You can do this right now! You can work this in the same way as your scale practice, with your thumb dots: tally it up and get to the point where you start to feel more confident. Lemme know how you get on. I mentioned a minute ago about having different types of luck...

---

## Summary

- Ex 1.0
  Staring at strangers
  - Make eye contact with strangers
  - If you look away first it's an L
  - If they look away first it's a W
  - If you maintain eye contact and end up speaking or both smiling it's a D (which is a BIG WIN)

- Stay out of your comfort zone! When faced with a fork in the road, ask yourself, "Which route will I regret more if I don't take it?"

# Chapter 8

# The Two Lucks

I had always told myself there was only one kind of luck: luck you make for yourself. You can be the best artist in the world but if you never leave your house to network and sell your paintings, they will never sell because nobody knows about them or you. Luck = opportunities.

The more effort you put in and the more action you take, the more likely you are to have 'good luck'! Well, that's what I believed for a long time! Pushing hard does create a form of good luck, this is completely true, however, I hadn't taken into account the other form of luck.

The other form of luck is luck as most people know it, like finding 50 euros on the floor (good luck) and picking it up and realising that is a counterfeit with a marker pen phallus drawn on it and when you touch it you contract an STD (bad luck).

This luck is the luck that just happens and it's out of our hands! It's fortune, and it is gonna run its game no matter what. You can't do shit about it! If it's gonna rain on Christmas this year it's gonna rain on Christmas, and no amount of wishing, pleading, begging or palm reading is gonna stop it. The luck you make for yourself is not really luck, it's your life! There are only two things you can affect in your life – your thoughts, and your actions.

I'm not gonna talk about standard good luck as this is just a bonus, but we need to mention the standard bad luck. It is really important to understand that this is not the type of luck you make for yourself – it is straight-up luck as we know it, and in this case, it is at the bad end of the spectrum. Something as grandiose as a close friend dying, or something not so grandiose as spraining your ankle before a big game. These kinds of situations blow, and for very different reasons! There is nothing you can do about them!

They happen! They suck, but they happen. At some point in your life you may have to deal with losing your best friend, mum, dad, God forbid child!

A couple years ago, I had 'a year'. Within 6 months, I got fired from my job of 7 years due to government cuts; I broke my foot just before catching a 14-hour flight and ended up in a wheelchair for 3 months; I got assaulted in a bar while volunteering and ended up with a nearly fractured skull and severe concussion; I got sued for something I didn't do and it cost me $2k when I was broke as shit; I got arrested on NYE and was kept overnight in a cell even though they had nothing on me; and the worst one, the one that completely changed my life... I was in a brutal car crash.

I've been in wrecks before, but this one hurt. It crippled me if I'm honest, physically yes, but more mentally. To give you an understanding, I need to tell you a story, a true story... A good few years ago I met the love of my life. I had known this person for a long time prior – she was the sister of the singer in the band I was in at the time.

There was obviously always chemistry between us but we were both in other relationships, and you know how that is!? By the time we were both single, she had made a child. I have always been that guy: I didn't believe in marriage, and I definitely had never envisaged ending up with anything other than a huge bill at the brothel and a bachelor pad.

I never ever imagined I would have kids, let alone someone else's, but something felt right about this, in fact, it was magnetic AF and even when I tried to fight it, I was pulled back in! Before I knew it, I was driving 300 miles each week to go and visit her. I fell in love with the kid too! I couldn't help myself!

I taught him how to catch, how to ride a bike, how to swim. My now mother-in-law said, "I have never seen Hannah and Cal so happy!" I would have taken this as a compliment but it just felt easy for me. I loved them both! I wanted them to be happy and have opportunities. I still put my heart and soul into being the best person they could know!

Anyway, the car crash! As I mentioned, I've been in a few fender benders in my time, to be honest, I always saw them as opportunities to get some whiplash money or take some time off work, haha! Idiot! I know now that stealing or getting wins from something you haven't put effort into is completely unwarranted and does not leave you feeling proud or in a better position – it is just extra money you could have made tenfold if you just put the effort in. This is another book, but remember this: a thief can never steal more than they could have made from honest hard work.

Anyway...

The reason this car crash was different and affected me in a way I had never experienced before was solely because of Cal. I thought he was dead. By this point, I had been a step-dad for about 3 years. I thought he was dead. I pulled myself out of the wreckage and clambered to the back of the car. I thought he was dead!

There was petrol spewing out of both of the cars involved, and glass and debris everywhere. I pulled the back door open and undid Cal's belt. I picked him up and carried him to the nearest parked car. It was December, and December in the UK is cooooold! The crash happened at 4pm, but it was already pitch-black dark as it was so near to Christmas, and it was raining torrentially.

I was shaking with fear, cold and anxiety. I managed to find a car and a really amazing person who looked after my boy while I phoned the emergency services. The police were first at the scene.

They started singing Roxanne. Joking! Seriously though, they turned up, and I watched them stay in their car. WTF?! I was expecting them to jump out of their cars and run over. About 20 seconds passed and they hadn't moved, so I stumbled over to their car. I started screaming at them to help.

They replied, "Are you okay? Did you see the crash?!"

I explained I was in the crash, with my step-son, and the crushed square of metal they could see was once my car.

They said, "Jeeeeez, we stayed in our car cuz we called for backup, are you sure that's your car?!"

I said, "Yes!" and one of them said: "I've been a road traffic officer for 20 years and I've never seen a crash like this where anyone walked away!!!" We were more than lucky!! In fact, it was miraculous we both survived.

The crash did something to me. It wasn't about me. When I was in the ambulance on the way to the hospital my brain didn't allow for any thoughts other than the wellbeing of my Cal! I had never had this. Even in previous experiences, even when I would have wanted people to think otherwise, my thoughts were on myself, my own recovery and wellbeing. This was a game-changer. A new me! I began questioning everything!

Did I do the right thing for him, for his mum!? For his real dad??! I wasn't thinking about me!! At all! First time ever!!!! Now, there is nothing wrong with primarily thinking about yourself, in fact, it is integral, and I'll explain why later, but in this instance, I was spending all of my energy and resources on someone else.

This is the luck that you can't explain, affect, or choose. A drunk driver pulling out in front of you at 60mph is something that you can't pre-empt. It happens. It was so quick I didn't even have time to brake! Point is, I couldn't have done a goddamn thing about this happening – it just happened, out of the fucking blue.

So if some stuff just happens and is out of my control, why the Jeffin' Jeff would I let the things I can control in my life be anything other than monumental?! You have the power to affect at least 80% of your life, if not more, why would you just let it happen? You need to take control!!! Be in control of the things you can. You can't stop someone nearly killing you, that is them not taking control of their life, but you should take control of everything YOU can!

If your job is boring or shitty – your fault. If you are unhealthy – your fault. If you can't pay the bills – your fault. I was gonna leave this till later in the book, but start as you mean to continue, eh?! Do shit, get shit done. Take responsibility for your actions. If you can't take responsibility for yourself then you will have no ability over anything.

Remember, life is around 5% what happens to you and 95% how you react. You need to be in control!! What you gonna do?! Wait for someone to use their precious time on earth to take control of yours?!?! It won't happen!!! You are in control, well, you can be in control. If you're not in control, you are out of control. Spectrums, init. The car crash changed my life. It reminded me of all the things I should be doing, could be doing, wasn't doing!

Imagine going to the doctor because you have a pain in your chest, and the quack drops the bomb. "I'm sorry to tell you this, but we have found a cancerous lump." What would you change about your life after hearing this?! My dad got cancer and it was the best thing that ever happened to him!

Bear with me on this! My old man WAS that guy: went to school, went to college, worked, got a wife, had an amazing and wonderful child, paid off mortgage etc. I love my dad – he is the most caring, worried-about-my-happiness, hard-working motherfucker you could find! They were really poor at points in my childhood.

I remember Dad getting made redundant and having 5 crappy jobs he hated just to put bread on the table. Legend!!! I can't even put into words how grateful, thankful, and in awe of him I am! My dad worked his ass into knots just to keep me and my mum with food and warmth! He never spent a penny! The heating was always off – "Put more on clothes, boy!" – but he always paid for my school trips, or helped me buy a drum kit when I first wanted to take it up.

He always got presents for me and mum, and it wasn't until recently I realised what he went through to do this. I LOVE this guy!!!! More than he will ever know! I LOVE my mum too, so much, but I'll praise her later. For a long time, we had the same couch, the same kettle, the same broken ladle, the same 4 TV channels, the same tiny kitchen, the same cheap caravan holidays!

Dad was diagnosed with prostate cancer and something changed. We got a new couch. He took me and my bestie to Jamaica on holiday. He bought new clothes. He started taking regular getaways. He changed. Fight or flight, init! I am so angry and disappointed my dad hadn't had this realisation without having to get cancer first.

You can probably think of someone that has had a similar experience – they got cancer, or some evil illness or ailment, and it kicked them into actually living their life. The irony. I can think of countless stories of people that started raising money for charities after getting the illness that particular charity helps, or started eating healthier and looking after their body or some other super awesome thing. I know people who used to laugh at meditation and now meditate every day because they had a similar life shock, or ate fast food religiously and now only eat greens and fresh veg!

As far as we know, we get one shot at this – some people say live for the day, but I am saying just live, and live for the rest of your life, every day!! See what's possible, stay outside your comfort zone and embrace the fear the unknown brings. Everything was unknown to you at one point! You had to experience it, and then choose to learn from it, or act on it to better or worsen your life!

The keyword here is YOU! The luck that just happens, just happens. The luck we make, that's ours for the taking! I don't want you to get cancer or have a near-death experience to have this realisation, but I know from experience that sometimes you need something that big and profound to be the kickstart.

So let's figure a way to kickstart you without having to go through any trauma. Think of it like this – imagine you are a car. If it helps you can imagine you are your favourite car. In fact, that will help a lot. So, you're a car, a gorgeous car, but you haven't been used in a while, and when you were used you just mooched about on little journeys around your local town or to commute to work. Is that your full potential as a car?

I mean, you could drive from London to Turkey or South Africa. Point is, the longer you leave your car stationary, without use, the harder it is to get the fucker to start – and in most cases, if you leave it for long enough, it won't start at all. It will need a surge of power, in the form of a new battery, or bump start to get you going again. So how do we bump start a human? Well, we could grab the defibrillator, but I can assure that won't end well. We could also grab an adrenaline shot, but when it runs out we will need more.

There must be a way we can bump start ourselves. Hey! *waves* This is the type of luck you are in control of, the type of luck that allows us to do shit and get shit done! There are a plethora of bump-starts we can use on ourselves, and they all tie into daily planning and goal practice. Before you poo-poo this idea, yes I said poo-poo, recall a time where you were so excited and gassed on something and remember how it felt.

Take the next few moments to really remember how it felt when you created your own luck and began to win from it! It felt powerful right, like pure energy coursing through your whole body. So exciting that you felt like you were vibrating to the point you were about to burst! There's your bump start. It's just you didn't realise at the time that you were starting something, and in turn, the power-fuelled battery explosion more than likely went away as quick as it came. Why?

Because you didn't drive the car anywhere important – you drove it to run errands, or to the job you hate, or whatever. You shoulda driven somewhere fucking monumental and amazing. And furthermore, you should have used that surge of energy and confidence and sureness to pave the way for the next surge.

It's like a stone being dropped into a pond but without the stone having a purpose, it just hits the water, creates some ripples, and drops to the bottom of the pond. I don't wanna drive my car in circles, and I don't wanna live at the bottom of a pond. Nor should you! We will talk about 'the past' later, but I'll tell you now, one of the only things the past is good for is to learn from.

In this case, use your now to really remember that awesome thing you once did that made you feel like the most awesome version of yourself. It helps if you put your favourite song on while you do this, especially if it is a song that you listened to around the time this awesome thing happened!

Try and remember the smells, tastes, feelings, sounds and visuals from whatever it was you are remembering. We are gonna go DEEP on this later, I'm barely warming you up at the moment...

## Summary

- There are two types of luck: the luck that is out of our control, and the luck that is within our control
- Your reactions to what life throws at you are WAY more important than what life throws at you
- #YOLO.

# Chapter 9

## 24

I'm gonna say some names and I want you to think about what they have in common... Justin Bieber, Gandhi, Princess Diana, Bob Marley, Bob Dylan, Bobby D, Salman Rushdie, your nan/mum/best friend, Trey Parker, Usain Bolt, Michael Jackson, all of the dragons from Dragons Den, etc., etc.

Amongst a bunch of other things, they all had or have the same 24 hours as you each day to affect the world, their life, and the people around them. It's hard to believe that these people all have the same amount of time as me and you and started off with the same clean slate as me and you. It's crazy when you think about it! How the shit did Albert Einstein manage to get relativity while some people struggle to get a better job?! How did Bob Dylan manage to write hundreds of songs while some people struggle to write hundreds of words for a blog?! How did Julius Caesar run a country while some people struggle to run a mile?!?!

Same 24/7, dude! There's no movement on this! When I started thinking about this stuff I really struggled to get my head around it. It's like when you start thinking about why we're here on Planet Earth and you get to that critical point where your brain feels like it's gonna explode and then you give up and go back to your game of Fortnite.

You're not taught this shit at school. We are always told to think big when we're little, then told to be realistic when we get older. Being realistic is an illness! What are you being realistic about? The future? Soon as you're realistic and give in to the low bar that has been set for you, you will only ever be realistic. None of the people I just mentioned were realistic.

You can't be if you're inventing the telephone or internet or running a country, or running a successful business. Realistic is average and average is one of the biggest diseases on the planet. It's infectious. It's like negativity and stress! Soon as someone starts moaning or stressing about something, we relate and join in. Same with being realistic – just try telling anyone your mental huge goals and see what happens...

Remember, you are what you eat and you are who you hang around with. How often do you see the super successful hanging with Gary from the local BP garage? You think Jay-Z surrounds himself with musicians that practice once a month for fun?! Hell to the no-no. You need inspiration. Try saying out loud, "I have changed the world," or, "I have cured cancer," or, "I have put an end to poverty." I bet you can't say it! Like really say it, with belief and conviction. If you can, fair play, you're already on your way to being fucking awesome! For most of us, we have been so indoctrinated into normalcy that we cannot believe we even stand a chance at making such claims a reality.

## Exercise 1.0

Grab your journal... I want you to write down ALL of your accomplishments today, or if you're listening to this first thing in the morning, write down ALL of yesterday's accomplishments. Are they huge? Are they life-affirming? Game-changing?

The avalanche can't exist without the snowflake, the snowflake can totally exist without the avalanche. These guys were snowflakes, so are you and I, but they could see the avalanche! You have to be able to visualise the outcome.

You have to be able to see anything as possible. It is if you make it so. Your daily goals, because I know you've been keeping them up, should be starting to transform. They should be getting bigger, better, crazier! Think big! Then think bigger, then times it by 10, or 100, or 1000!

Remember, failing on a fuck-off-bonkers goal is waaaay better than failing on an average goal! Your 24 hours are precious. In fact, they are the only 24 hours you got. Granted you get to start them again as each day passes but you only get each one once! Then it's the next one! Did you take massive action today, yesterday, last week? Are you going to take massive action tomorrow?! You need to! It's imperative to your well-being, success and future.

Stop kidding yourself – just cuz your mum, dad, bestie, teacher, newsreader, local politician or whoever else told you, doesn't for one minute mean it's true, correct or helpful to YOUR success. And when I'm talking about success I don't just mean monetary, which is super important, but I'm talking about everything. Do you want your kids to live the life you've led?

Would you be happy knowing they were going to have a similar life to you so far? I wanna be proud when my boy asks me about my day:

"How was your day, Pop?"

"It was okay."

BULLSHIT!!! It was okay?! WTFF!!! Your answer needs to be sincere and nothing short of, "It was awesome, little dude, because of XYZ, and I'm so excited for tomorrow!"

Be the change you want to see!

If you're not excited, ain't nobody around you gonna be excited. If you're not courageous, ain't nobody around you gonna be courageous! If you're not happy, laughing, positive, well you know the rest! C'mon, it's time to put an end to feeling like this.

No more pointing the finger, no more feeling sorry for yourself, DO SHIT, GET SHIT DONE!!! I gave a lecture recently where I asked: "Hands up who likes Justin Bieber..." (Bear in mind it was a music college.) No hands!

Class: "He's a twat, he's talentless, his songs are shit." The barrage went on.

"You guys know the difference between you and JB?" I questioned. Silence. "He works harder than you, he has disposable income to allow him to do amazing things, and he doesn't have time to be talking about you, but you have time to be talking about him!"

Don't get me wrong, his writing team has made my ears bleed multiple times, and I definitely don't enjoy his music, and as a musician myself I hate mass-produced-equation-hit-factory-pop, but there's a high chance he does too!

He saw an opportunity and took it to make his life better. Don't you want to be able to know for a fact that you can always look after your family: they'll be safe, warm, fed, and you have time to enjoy them?! No child wants to hear their parents worrying. They want inspiration.

Think about what your kid says in class when the teacher, or more likely their friends, asks: "What does your mum or pop do?" Wouldn't you want them to answer something awesome?

"Errr, well my mum worries loads and I don't see Dad as much as I'd like cuz he's working like a dog just to make rent or buy me the Christmas present I want."

DO SHIT, GET SHIT DONE

Imagine your kid saying, "My pop invented Microsoft," or, "My mum is in the Olympics." Same 24 hours between an Olympian and a domestic cleaner that hates their boss; same 24 hours between a world-class singer and a daytime TV binger; same 24 hours between the mush that invented the telephone and Gary who you have small talk with every time you fill up your car (which is probably not your dream car).

You know what I mean?! You gotta work your 24! It won't work for you! It will just pass when you don't use it. It owes you nothing! But when you start to use it, to control it and make it your bitch, amazing things begin to happen. Take control and make each day work for you!

Ever had that thing where you forget to eat cuz you are so into what you are doing? Or you can't sleep because you are double excited about tomorrow? If you haven't skipped a meal because you are excited then you haven't yet experienced what I'm talking about!

You've given up and more than likely without even realising! Like I mentioned before, it's not your fault you were dealt the hand you were, but it's damn straight your fault if upon realising you don't do Jack about it! God forbid you play the lottery! How many times have you said the sentence: "If I had a million pounds I would..."

So you've got the ideas for when it happens, but you're missing the main part – doing the hard graft it takes to get it in the first place! We need to stop fooling ourselves just cuz someone else told us so. You can make this world better or worse, your call.

Think about it, even Hitler had a better work ethic than most of us. I couldn't be more sickened about his MO, and it baffles me to think people can be so evil, but the motherfucker worked!!! Now imagine if his message came from a place of good, not evil. All the opinions you got, all of those comments you have, they mean shit without backup or action! DsGsD!

93

Commit to yourself! Same 24 hours, brooo! You can keep lying to yourself (the worst person you can lie to) or you can start right now and get your shit sorted! If you had the opportunity to stop Hitler, wouldn't you have?!

The fact is, huge opportunities present themselves daily, you just miss them cuz you're worried and anxious:

"Shit, rent's due tomorrow."

"What if he/she doesn't like me back?!"

"Well I'll never be as good as (insert excuse), so I may as well not bother trying!"

"It said so on the news so it must be true!"

"I don't think I'll risk flying this year as there might be a terrorist attack!"

And just FYI, that D-bag reading you the news has the same 24 hours too! Have you ever had that thing where you wake up earlier than usual, and you get more shit done in the first 2 hours of being up than you usually get done all day?! It's not a fluke! You can do that every day, you just gotta control your 24! Here's a banging hack that will really open your eyes.

## Exercise 1.1

Create a weekly planner of cells to find out how much spare time you have. Just like this one:

| | Sun | Mon | Tue | Wed | Thu | Fri | Sat |
|---|---|---|---|---|---|---|---|
| 7:00 | | | | | | | |
| 8:00 | | | | | | | |
| 9:00 | | | | | | | |
| 10:00 | | | | | | | |
| 11:00 | | | | | | | |
| 12:00 | | | | | | | |
| 13:00 | | | | | | | |
| 14:00 | | | | | | | |
| 15:00 | | | | | | | |
| 16:00 | | | | | | | |
| 17:00 | | | | | | | |
| 18:00 | | | | | | | |
| 19:00 | | | | | | | |
| 20:00 | | | | | | | |
| 21:00 | | | | | | | |

I came up with this very basic week planner specifically to help you understand how much time you do actually have, and also to get you to the point where you don't use your 'lack of time' as an excuse. Remember, saying, "I don't have time," is an excuse, and ironically a waste of time! The successful make time, they don't surrender to it.

I first came up with this for two reasons:

1) I was sick of hearing people using their lack of time as an excuse.

2) Seeing your week in a super-easy-to-understand visual makes it 100 times easier to understand.

Our mind can often be a complete dick with what's real and what's not so sometimes it makes loads more sense to make it as obvious as possible!!

I have used this method with sooooo many people, of all ages, and in a bunch of different situations. I am gonna explain the results that I found when doing this with adults who are parents with full-time jobs, as this seems to be the 'worst case' scenario for having 'spare time'. As a side note: when I do this with young adults between the ages of 14-21 who study but do not have a 9-5, the results are mental.

Lemme explain. There are 105 empty cells on the planner. Fifteen for each day Sunday to Saturday inclusive. The day starts at 7am and finishes at 10pm. Obviously, you all get up at different times, but from my research, 7am-10pm is a good average, and also any later than 7am is detrimental in regards to smashing your life (I get up at 5am most days, and sometimes earlier).

The other thing to note is that I have left the cells as whole hours, but the better you get at this and the more serious you are about absolutely killing it, the more intricate you can make the plan – mine currently goes down to blocks of 10 minutes, but let's stick with hours to begin with.

The object is to fill up the planner with positive, life-affirming things that replace any dead time, or negative wasteman things you may already have stealing time in your day today!

Before you ask, the reason I have stopped the day at 10pm is that, and hear me out before you kick off: nothing beneficial happens after 10pm. That's not to say you can't have amazing experiences after

10pm, and sometimes you have no option, but I can't stress enough, for those of you saying, "I do my best work after midnight," or, "I'm a night owl." Quit it.

You only think that because you haven't committed to being in control yet. I have never met someone super successful that doesn't more often than not get up early and go to sleep at a reasonable time. Anyway, we'll come to that later.

Firstly, I want you to put an X in every single cell that you already have a complete commitment to that is beneficial to your life. For most of you that are working full-time with kids, you will be putting X's in your work hours, and the specific times you NEED to be with your child or have commitments with your child.

Really think about this before you start putting X's everywhere all willy-nilly like. Remember I said the X's have to go where you are already committed to something beneficial to your life. This means you can't put an X in a cell because that's the time you watch EastEnders or smoke a bowl or go to the pub.

When you have completed this I want you to count the remaining number of white cells across the week. I have purposely given you 9 hours outside of the plan, from 10pm until 7am – this gives you your recommended 8 hours of sleep, and a spare hour to do whatever you want.

As a further side note (sorry, I like side notes), you can, assuming your diet and health are up to scratch, live on 6-7 hours' sleep a night very comfortably, so you can shave yourself a further 1 or 2 hours if you take this approach.

Upon completion of X'ing your cells, what you will find is one of two things, and for most people, this is an absolute penny-drop moment. You will have either just realised you have WAAAY more time each week than you keep telling yourself, and everybody else. Or, you have filled up every single blank cell. Let's take these one at a time...

# 1. You have loads more time than you previously realised

This is the case for most people – when I have done this with students between the age of 14-21 the average amount of free cells was 80!!! Per week!!!! 80 hours per week!!!! These are the same kids that didn't get coursework in on time or commit to regular practice because they "didn't have enough time"! Haha! With full-time working adults, the average is about 10 hours over the whole week period.

Do remember that I have already given you enough sleep time, and an hour each day to do whatever you want! So, let's be conservative and say the average was 7 hours per week, not 10. Well, if you started a new hobby, in fact, 7 new hobbies, and spent an hour a week on each of them, within 6 months you would have spent 24 hours, or a whole day, on each new hobby.

This is without using my miracle burst practice, and all the other legendary hacks we are gonna dial later on in this programme. Anyways, let's say that you didn't do 7 different hobbies, let's say you did just 1, well, over a year that's 336 hours!! And that is enough time to get very good at something! It is also a much better way of spending your time. The time you didn't previously have...

This hit me like a ton of bricks the first time I sat down and planned my week into hour chunks. It also made me realise how much time I was wasting by doing micro activities. Micro activities are what I call an action that is executed outside of the allotted time when you were doing something else. A good example of this is checking your phone as soon as a notification pops up.

Unless you are waiting on a specific notification (an email that is urgent and needs immediate action, or phone call or similar) then this practice is entirely stupid. The reason being is loads of micro things make one life-losing major thing (just like snowflakes and avalanches). All those 10-second replies to texts or WhatsApp messages or liking peoples pictures when the tag notification pops up on your phone are taking up huge amounts of time over the space of a month.

The fact we never tally up this time up means we are unaware of it, and when we are unaware we make big mistakes! Well, that's what I'm here for. I tallied up the amount of time it took me just to reply to text messages across a day and I was stunned. Note that I didn't even take into account my other notification platforms – and to put a point on it, just like I imagine most of you, I have multiple email accounts – 8 to be precise, WhatsApp, Messenger, FB, and 4 Instagram accounts. This is without random calls and similar.

My findings were that each day my average time responding to just messages was about 10-20 seconds per message. On average at that time I was receiving about 30-50 texts a day. Let's work that out, an average of 15 seconds per text, an average of 40 texts = 600 seconds, or 10 minutes per day. Now let's work that out over a month... 10 x 30 = 300 minutes, or 5 hours!!! And just to twist the knife a little more – over a year would be... errr... 5 x 12 = 60 hours!!!

And remember this is just an average guy replying to an average amount of messages! Now, even though this is quite a scary thought, and it really did blow my mind the first time I worked it out, it isn't the actual problem. The real problem is the extra amount of time and focus that practising this immediate response takes away from what we were initially doing. It stops you getting anything done with full focus, which is absolutely crucial when you want to be a boss!

We will go through this in detail later. I just wanna plant the seed early on. So how do we fix this? Well, the best way to be in control is to dominate. You have to be able to choose when you check your phone, or go on Facebook or upload to Instagram, or nip to the shops or brush your teeth or whatever.

This isn't just phones, this is an instant reaction to something that wasn't the initial plan – it might be washing the dishes 3 times a day as opposed to smashing them out in one go or walking past the laundry on your way to sit down and write your first book and thinking, "Oh, I might as well put the washing out now while I think about it," or something like that.

Here's the thing, this is out of control! There is no plan or structure, and as much as my old hippy pot-smoking self would be turning in his grave to hear me say this, you can't do shit without control. You need control in every facet of your life.

As a rough idea, and this will change for each person and set of responsibilities, you could reply to all texts at midday for 5 minutes. If it's urgent they will call! You could check your social media and reply to emails, or upload to Instagram, or like and comment on other people's feeds or profiles between say 6pm and 6:20pm.

It takes a little self-control but as soon as you get used to it you will be making time as opposed to wasting it. When you focus on one job at a time and do it to fruition, you will do it better and faster in the long run.

When I started writing this book up from my notes, I spent the first chapter correcting my grammar and spelling as I went along – I type fast and every time I would look up from the keyboard to the screen I would see Google had waved its massive dick all over my work and underlined all my mistakes in red.

Each sentence I would spend a few extra seconds right-clicking to alter the mistake from illiterate to slightly less illiterate. Not only was this frustrating and took extra time, but it kept throwing me off my flow and then my mind would wander and it would be hard to pick up where I left off. As soon as I noticed this I started to ignore the red, as hard as it initially was, and soon got to the point where every other word was underlined in red, thousands and thousands of grammatical errors and spelling mistakes.

At the end of the book I will spell and grammar check in one session. I don't need to think about it now as it is not good for me to work like that – it's not good for anyone! It's counterproductive even though it feels like you are doing things as you go. So many people will tell you that this is the best way to do it. It's not.

The reason it feels right is that we haven't yet reprogrammed our brains to be able to focus and control our thoughts. The reason the errors were bothering me as I was writing were due to the fact I had no control – I saw a red line and I wanted to fix it, and it's the same with your phone, or computer: a notification pops up and we can't control ourselves to ignore it. Just like an impulse.

Just so you know: billions of £ are spent each year on working out ways to keep us 'busy'. You need to make life your bitch. You need to be in control, and when you do, man, does life get much, much, much easier, and in turn more prosperous, much more prosperous. What about those of you on the other side of the fence...

# 2. You have no time!

You filled up every single blank cell and there is no way you can fit anything else into your busy schedule. This is as detrimental as having more time than you realised. And I absolutely guarantee you that you are not living with every single cell full up with absolutely amazing and life-affirming activities. If you are, then kudos! You may not need this programme, but do listen on just in case I can help with anything else (there's a picture of me posing in a leopard print thong hidden somewhere towards the end...!)

However, I would imagine if you picked this book up in the first place that you are not in that position – if your week is water-tight: full of super awesome amazing things without any time wasted, then you may still have a slight issue as far as moving forward. One massive problem people come up against is thinking that they can add something to a busy schedule without amending their current schedule or replacing something to make room for something new.

This is more often than not why people don't stick to the gym, or keep up a new hobby or skill, or have enough time to commit, or start a business or whatever. Look at it like this – you're slammed sideways and one day you realise you want to be fitter, so you fix up and join the gym. You're gassed about it when you make the decision so you commit to going – you're initially obsessed with the idea, but then the next day, the next week, the next month, you realise you don't have time to maintain going and it's a bind to fit it into your already manic schedule. Then you quit.

You can't take, take, take without making sacrifices, and this also falls into the self-control category. This is why cheating never works: you can't have a partner then spend your time with another person without there being some sacrifice. This is where the long game comes in. For those of you that managed to absolutely fill in every single blank space, I want you to go back through the planner and really think about whether every single cell is valid and making your life better. If it is, then is there anything that would be better suited?

And when you figure out what those things are, how and what can you change about your current week plan to accommodate your new venture? The other way to look at this is to think of it as a vehicle. A car is a car is a car, right?! But some cars are slow AF and others are super whips! The faster the car, the more streamlined it has to be, and this is something that is always being perfected.

Your life can and should be the same. If you have a full schedule, I bet you I can make you some time. I bet you I can find you an hour or two that you didn't realise you had through streamlining your current protocol. By the end of this programme, you are gonna be like an Italian supercar.

And if you are already one of those, then you might wanna think about growing wings and being a fighter jet. You can always progress, you can always learn more, get faster, better, stronger. If you are telling yourself you can't then you are being stubborn and a bit of a winky butt. And not even your mumma likes a winky butt! Apart from your mumma, Cliff, she really does love a winky butt.

---

## Summary

- Ex 1.0
  Time Planner 5000
    - Use the planner to fill in each hour-long cell with an X if you are currently using it for something important, positive, and progressive to your life
    - Be honest with yourself when doing this
    - Count up the remaining amount of blank cells and begin filling them with new ventures
- Your 24 hours are the same as everybody else's
- Stop bitching about your lack of time. While you're bitching, people like me are getting shit done!
- Stay hydrated.

# Chapter 10

# Know Thyself

In the last few chapters, possibly without you clocking it, I have been getting you to think about yourself. I remember explaining to my kid once that golf balls were full of elastic bands to make them bounce – his mind was blown! You gotta understand yourself, and be true to yourself to stand a chance of growing into something better.

When elastic bands aren't the best thing to go inside a golf ball to make it bounce and someone finds a better solution, they will be replaced. If we don't know who we are, then how can we evolve and transition positively?! Here's a thing... How well do you know yourself? Like, really know yourself? I would argue that you actually know yourself really well, better than anyone else.

Well, at least you have the opportunity to know yourself better than everybody else. Fact is, most of us ignore all the pointers our body and mind are giving us, or we acknowledge them and then choose to override them anyway, usually because we are on autopilot or distracted, or brought up to believe X when the real answer could be 7@£$. Cheers, the media and the education system!

Imagine you are lost in the middle of a jungle and you come across a river. You follow it right?! It must lead somewhere! And at the very least you're near a water supply or a boat will hopefully pass and spot you at some point. The little pointers our body and mind give us are the river, they show us the way to go. If you've been in the jungle for a few days, bitten to shit, without food, running out of water, the last thing you would do is turn away from the river and walk aimlessly back into the jungle, right?!

You gotta trust your body, man! How many times have you lied to yourself about the real you?! You told your brain and body the same rubbish so many times that now it's your life! Where's your river at?! Some of us are so lost in the jungle that we haven't seen a river in ages. You need to trust your river to stand a chance.

I wanna talk to you about boxes.

Not the cardboard kind, but the metaphorical kind that people use to pigeonhole. I hate boxes!!! I mean, I understand why they exist. Imagine if everyone was called Barry! You wanna get the attention of your mate down the street and you holla him and everyone turns around at the same time. Funny once or twice but then entirely frustrating and a waste of time, and a nightmare for delivery drivers!!

Same thing with any other box, whether it be being gay, vegetarian, a maid, a wife or husband, a parent, a businessman, a doctor, a dancer or anything else that has a title. The title can be super helpful – if I wanna start dance lessons and every business was called Barry's Barry's Barry's, I might book into a mechanic or florist by mistake. It would be mental!!! Again, entirely funny for a bit, but it would soon drive you crazy.

However, these same boxes allow for a completely sinister outcome when used incorrectly. Racism, sexism, religion etc. They all have a specific rep dependant on what you've heard. Would you trust an ex-convict to look after your 5-year-old? Would you let an 18-year-old fresh out of college do your accounts? Would you forgive a paedophile?! I imagine the last one was an outright no for most of you. We need to dig a little deeper...

What if you found out that same paedophile was locked in a cupboard for the first 10 years of their life, beaten and raped daily, and then recommitted the same crime when they grew up, but they did it once and turned themselves into the police, and admitted everything, and were clearly manic and distraught, served 45 years in prison, started a charity that benefits children from abusive backgrounds, and were completely rehabilitated.

You probably still wouldn't trust them because of something that happened a long time ago based off of them being a product of their society. I agree that some things are unforgivable, but there is still a spectrum to at least consider.

## Exercise 1.0

I am going to say some words and upon reading them you will have an immediate mental image pop into your mind. You won't be able to help it. The images and thoughts that your brain conjures up will be based on a mixture of experience, media, and nonsense, and not necessarily in that order.

Let's go:

Homosexual
Vegan
Salesman
Cleaner
Ferrari driver
Fake tanner
Alcoholic
Musician
Homeless
(haha, the last 3 are one and the same! JOKING!)

Flight attendant
Single mum
Stepparent
German
Israeli
Actress

You will have had exact pictures in your head for each of those. However, if you are a single mum, I guarantee you would have had a different thought process when I said 'single mum' than someone that isn't a single mum. Why? Because you know first-hand. The majority of things people think about you are not correct.

They are assumptions and regurgitation. And the regurgitation comes from someone else who has puked a bunch of trash on you, and then you puked on someone else. Sorry, I still hate the word 'puke', I think this is the last time I use the word 'puke' in this book!

Let's take Germany for example, and be honest, how many of you immediately thought of Hitler?! Or the war? Some of you may have thought of BMW, or bratwurst or Oktoberfest. Now think about why you thought these things. Have you ever been to Germany before?!

Unless you meet and talk to, and experience every single German that has ever lived, you surely have no idea of what is actually true! If you think about it, you know that every German person isn't an engineer for BMW or a supporter of the Nazis.

What about flight attendants? How many of you pictured an uber gay overly fake-tanned guy?! Or a girl with a TIGHT bun hairdo, who is also fake tanned? It's impossible to prevent these bullshit impulse thoughts from entering our heads, but it is up to us to get the correct information before making our own decisions.

Don't get me wrong, there is sometimes no smoke without fire, and stereotypes can most definitely exist without being hate-fuelled, but the point of that exercise is to get you thinking about what people think about you, and if it is correct.

If you don't know who you are, then ain't nobody else gonna know who you are. They won't know what you are good for or what to trust you with, or how helpful to their lives you could be. We've all been tarred with an illegitimate brush before, it sucks! Try and think back to a time you weren't given a chance for some bullshit reason because someone had the wrong information on you! I remember getting put forward for an audition for a popular UK TV show to be the drummer in the house band.

The feedback I received after the call was "great player, really amazing drumming and professional, too tall". WTF!!! I was ornery for a while, but this is the world we live in, and we can learn to take advantage of the small-mindedness of people, embrace the situation and ride the wave. Sometimes you're gay or veggie! Spectrums, people! You know those kinda guys (see, I'm putting people in a box!) that are overly homophobic, or racist, or any of the other super-lame boxes. Narrow-minded, non-thinking idiots, right?!

Let's take homosexual people: I have heard so many proper laddy rugby sorts (more box) that happily take the piss out of gay people, then they get drunk after the match and all start running around the bar with their dicks out touching each other's nut-sacks.

I've met loads of people who are racist and xenophobic as sin: "they come into OUR country, and take OUR jobs" and then go order a kebab at 4am after smashing loads of Russian vodka – you didn't have a problem when they were frying your food or fixing you a cocktail!

And to put a point on it, my actual view on all of this is that I am a Lee – there is nobody else like me and I can go wherever I please and hang out with whoever I want. Hate and judgement are for idiots!

WTF is wrong with people? Don't be one of these small-minded idiots, pointing the blame and never taking responsibility. Imagine you are a racist, God forbid, and you uber-hate black people, and then one day you are in a car crash, God forbid, and the ambulance driver is black – what do you do?! Like, literally what do you do?!?!

Or you hate lesbians and you break down at the side of the road, and the first person to stop and offer help is homosexual! What do you do?! Or you're a homophobic racist with short man syndrome, and you're blind, and a gay Asian 6'7" basketball player holds a door open for you!? C'mon!

What do you want people to think about you? Do you want people to give you a chance? When you're starting a business, and you cold call people, how many times have you known full well your product was perfect for the person you called but they overlooked it because of XYZ. Or you made an impression that wasn't what you wanted by mistake and you lost out just because the other person didn't see your best you? Or you try and ask someone on a date and say the wrong thing cuz you're nervous and screw it up, and now they think you're a cockmuncher.

Stop worrying about everyone else and fix yourself first! You need to be aware and understanding of the fact that sometimes you're gay and sometimes you're veggie. For all you meat eaters out there, if you eat porridge or fruit, or crumpets, or toast with peanut butter for breakfast: that's a veggie meal, so sometimes you're veggie.

For all you straight, not-gay-at-all motherfuckers out there, I bet you watch porn where you can see a dick and get excited by it sometimes, or at one time in your life have had a naughty thought about someone of the same sex. Or you've open-mouth kissed your best mate on a stag do.

Or you had a 3some with someone of the same sex. You're a tiny bit gay sometimes, mon frere! And if you're not, that's cool too, but don't hate on anyone else for being them. Let them do them and you do you. Learn to be yourself in a world where everybody else is trying to make you something else.

Don't fight it. If you fight it you are just fighting yourself. Know thyself. Admit that you are you and then start using it to your advantage. So many people are fighting against themselves. Man, there's enough people in the world you will come across that will wanna fight you, for fuck's sake don't fight yourself!

In this world, the only thing that sells, whether it be in business, relationships, success, or whatever else, is being real. You have to be real. And that starts with you! The reason your daily goal practice is so important is that for those 3 minutes you're writing YOUR goals down. You are giving yourself time to think about...

YOU – what you want, what you want to be known for, what your dreams and desires are. Don't fight them! They are you: allow them. You don't need to lie about them anymore! You have to work at the transition. You have to be ready to admit yourself to yourself. It feels hard initially, but the more you do it, and the better you know yourself, the better you can sell yourself, and you NEED to sell yourself to get anywhere in this world. The whole fake thing is a farce, people always find out, they always know, and even worse, YOU always know!

You can smell fake a mile off. When I mentioned 'Ferrari driver', I bet most of you pictured some swanky D-bag with more money than sense. You know nothing about this particular person! You made an assumption. They very well may have started charities that have saved thousands or millions of lives, and if they have, they deserve a fast fucking car.

Either that or they have rich parents and a small appendage, haha! FYI check out the statistics for millionaires that came from an inheritance, it's not what you will expect!

When you thought of a homeless person, you probably imagined some bearded hobo who is probably addicted to heroin. You ever lived on the street?! Stop judging. Ever taken the time to talk to a homeless person about their life and how they got where they did?

If I was sleeping in a bus stop in the cold months after my wife cheated on me with my best friend, won custody of my kids, got half my house and ignored me last time she saw me trying to sleep in a bus stop in town I'd probably do heroin too! So would you!! Stop wasting your time judging everyone else and start working on yourself.

So how do we begin this process of being our real self without all the anxiety that comes along worrying about what others may think (others that have the same anxieties!)? Well, the great news here is that you've already begun the process. The previous chapters have started to get you thinking about you, what you want, what you really want and what is a waste of time, what you need and what you don't need, what your aspirations and goals are and what is killing you slowly. You have already begun the process.

I told you baby steps were the way! I bet most of the time you didn't even realise you were doing it! Let's see how you're getting on.

---

## Exercise 1.1

I want you to go back to your first page of daily goal writing. I want you to take a picture of it on your phone, or rip the page out so you can see it next to the next open page in your journal.

Now I want you to write those same goals out again. You should feel like it's a waste of time. And you should feel like you don't actually want to write them out again, because they are too small, or not what you really want.

In fact, you should feel as awkward rewriting these as you did when I first asked you to write out your unrealistic goals! Interesting, huh?! You've changed! You are better than you were and we haven't got into the good stuff yet! So it's almost time to see how we begin to reprogram our brain, but first, we have to understand how the brain works...

---

## Summary

- Ex 1.0

Word association
  - For a more complete version of this game just Google 'job roles' or similar and note the first thoughts that come to your mind when you see each one on the list
  - You can play this game with your family and friends by writing down a list of your own words and asking them to do the same thing

- Ex 1.1

Goals revisited
  - Go back to the first set of goals you wrote down at the start of the book
  - Rewrite them and note what has changed
- Commit and don't stop when shit gets hard or it doesn't seem like the end is in sight, cuz it often is just a couple more XYZs away
- Let them do them while you do you
- Don't prevent real you coming through.

# Chapter 11

# Your Brain Is

# Your Phone

So, here's where the magic begins. I'm about to drop some bombs, the good kind. Get excited, that's an order! I figured out the following a few years back, and it is one of the key realisations that gave me the power to take my life back, for me, and in turn help loads of others.

I want to remind you that success is not a limited resource, it's available for everyone – I get the biggest kick out of helping people, and I'd love you to take the information in this book to pass on to your network. Take it for yourself if you want, but after it has helped you, make sure you pass it on.

Let's talk about the brain. Your brain is not in control of you, well, at the moment it probably is, but it doesn't have to be! The answers are always already around us but we often miss them. We can be looking right at them, but if we don't understand them, then it's just like trying to read a book in a foreign language: confusing as fuck!

Using really basic shit everyone understands to explain unbelievably intricate stuff is so handy to get the ball rolling. I have always had a knack for using analogies, and this is one of my favourites as everyone gets it!

Enjoy...

Think of your brain just like your phone. There are four main obvious similarities between the two.

1. Your phone is full of applications, as is your brain.

2. Your brain, just like your phone, runs out of juice sometimes and needs rest, so we have to charge it.

3. Every now and then (if you're reppin' Apple then way too regularly) your phone updates, just like your brain.

4. Your phone only has a certain amount of processing power and storage, just like your brain.

So, let's talk about apps. An application is a program or piece of software designed to fulfil a particular purpose. In educated terms, it's some cool shit that has the potential to do cool shit.

## Exercise 1.0

Grab your journal. Think of all the applications you have on your phone, and put them into one of the following three categories – effin' awesome, meh, or embarrassed to own (ETO). I'll explain each, and remember to keep spectrums in mind and that anything can be anywhere on the spectrum, good or bad or anywhere in between...

1. Effin' awesome apps: Effing awesome apps are the ones that benefit you, and others. Your phone book holds numbers of those you care about most and drug dealers. Your camera and camera roll means you can capture the most amazing things and save them to look at later: friends, family, drug dealers. Fitness apps, brain training apps, poster makers, podcasts, music, calendar etc. can all make your life better, sweeter, easier, funnier, more full of love. Obviously, if you fill up your contacts with absolute mugs (like drug dealers), fill up your calendar with 'play Xbox and wank' or catch up on TOWIE, and listen to only racist podcasts, your life will definitely take a turn for the worse – we'll come to positives and negatives in a bit...

2. Meh apps: Your meh pile are all those apps that you kinda use but don't necessarily need, and as much as they don't make your life worse, they don't really make it better either – and if something isn't making your life better then it's not worth your time. Things like that 'learn Vietnamese' app you got but never opened a second time but won't uninstall just in case one day you go to Vietnam. Most apps can fit into this category.

3. Embarrassed to own apps (ETO): You know! Candy Crush, The Sims, any game where you have to build stuff but they don't give you enough coins without having to wait for ages, you know the ones.

---

Let's talk about #1 first. It's the only one you wanna spend time with! And after I've explained the following you will begin to understand why you should start shaking your phone up and switching up your apps. Your brain, just like your phone, has a limited amount of space, and more so, a limited amount of time. Your brain apps take up space, and time, so it is super important which ones you install, and how much time you spend on them.

They also take up different amounts of processing power and work better at certain times of the day. For example, making a call or listening to free-form jazz in the middle of the night while your household is sleeping (and you should be too) doesn't go down so well, whereas using your alarm to get you up at a decent time is paramount. In turn, having all your apps open at once slows your phone down, and drains the battery outta the little mush.

Something else to note is that all the most amazing apps are nearly always preloaded and have been there since day one – they get built on and updated, but they also need space to grow and if you fill your phone up with mehs and ETOs then there isn't always the space or time to update.

The meh pile is a bit of a weird one as it can go both ways and can be super beneficial if you use it, but can be entirely detrimental if you don't. Think of Instagram or similar. You can use Instagram to put up pictures of you pouting in front of the mirror, or your food, or your dog, or your dog food. I love a good Chow Chow puppy picture as much as the next man, in fact, it melts my heart every time and then makes me want one and then I get sad and then I eat chocolate and play Mario Kart to ease the pain.

You can also use Instagram or similar to your advantage – you can grow an audience, create new opportunities, and use it as FREE advertising and promotion etc. (I could go on for ages here!) There are loads of meh apps, and most of them can end up either effin' awesome or ETO.

Remember this rule – it is super important when we begin to reboot our 'phone'.

The meh pile also tends to take up the most space/time.

Now, for the completely soul-destroying, but unbelievably addictive ETO pile. Here's why you shouldn't own ANY of these types of apps. I'll say it twice so it sticks with you... first time: they steal your life.

Second time: THEY STEAL YOUR LIFE!!! If you think for one minute you are gonna remember level 243 of Candy Crush, or that time you upgraded your throw-rug in your gorgeous Sims house when you are on your deathbed, then I would argue you are a complete derp!

I don't even want to begin working out the hours, days, and probably months of my life wasted literally trying to blow up candy, or refreshing Facebook feeds to just scroll through a bunch of shit I don't actually care about!

You know what I'm talking about. They are battery drainers. In the same way, everything needs power, whether it be sunlight for plants or your car battery, your brain needs to be running, not ticking over. Your car goes nowhere when it's ticking over. And it doesn't even start if the battery is dead.

Something absolutely amazing about phones, though, is that you can factory reset. You can wipe and move and reorder anything on your phone. Take a few minutes to have a look at every single app you own and put them into the three categories I have mentioned – effin' awesome, meh, and ETO.

Upon doing this you have probably discovered that you have a bunch of meh apps that you had almost forgotten about, and a bunch of meh apps that you are not using to your benefit.

Now I want you to spend a few minutes flicking through your photo reel. When you come across a picture that really means something to you, I want you to think about why it means something to you. What was it that made your heart pour when you saw it or made you laugh, or gave you a knot in your throat, or made you proud? Whatever it is, we need more of that! It meant something!!

## Exercise 1.1

Now in true DsGsD fashion, I want you to take action right now: delete 1 app, right now!. However, the app I want you to delete has to have some of your time tied up in it. Candy Crush or the like is a great example cuz you are probably on level 672 and 'really don't wanna' lose your 'progress'.

---

Newsflash: THIS IS NOT PROGRESS!!! Every level is pretty much the same, and if you actually think about it, no matter how far through the saga of levels (it's called Candy Crush Saga for a reason!) you get, there are still levels you really enjoy (well, think you enjoy) and levels you don't. Using this methodology, it doesn't matter which level you are on. DELETE IT – NOW! Do shit, get shit done.

You may be wondering why I am getting you to get rid of, for good, some of your life's work (cuz that's what it is if you did it in your life, it counts as some of your life's work) because we need to replace it with something beneficial, that makes your life better. No motherfucker will ever have a Candy Crush legacy or a tombstone that reads: 'Mother, wife, upgraded curtains on Sims multiple times'!

The reason I call them ETO apps is not because you are necessarily embarrassed if anyone knows you have them installed, but more so because you would be embarrassed to mention them on your deathbed. We will talk about this in the next chapter... Anyway, now we need to talk about 'charging'...

Charging: you need to charge your phone (that's 'going to sleep' for the brain and body). If you charge your phone randomly, and for little amounts of time, after a while, the battery is not optimised and can even break or lose charge quicker than it should. To get the optimum battery life, you need to charge from near zero to full, then unplug and start using. If you leave your phone plugged in to charge after it's already full it screws your battery too – this is like oversleeping, staying in bed till 2pm, having over 10 hours sleep and feeling more lethargic than when you went to bed. GET YOUR ASS UP!!!

Another fact is that your brain is constantly updating. It processes experiences and uses them to make your future better/easier. The trick they don't tell you is that you have to put this in to practice to make it work. When a phone has an update it fixes the bugs: it makes the phone faster, better, more equipped.

Here's the kicker though: after an update you can still use the phone, with its new superpowers, to play the same crappy ETO apps that you were before! It's mental!

Think very carefully about the following statement: your phone will do what you tell it: you wanna make a call, make a call, but you have to put the effort into pressing the buttons to get it doing what you want!

It's you! It's always you! When you have given up in life, it's because YOU have given up. It's got nothing to do with anyone else. If your phone has no battery and it can't update, then at some point it won't be able to keep up, let alone set the standard! If it's hyper fucked you can't even turn it on – it's like when you've spent all your wages from the job you hate at the weekend to forget the job you hate and then you feel like crap on Monday, and then you rinse repeat.

How much time are you spending on the apps that don't help you? To be in control of your life and make money, get the partner of your dreams, enjoy waking up and feeling like a don, or anything else that makes life worth living, you gotta cut ALL of your ETO apps. Imagine that you are given the opportunity to talk to your hero – might be JC, or MJ, or JT, or whoever, and they ask you what you do most evenings, and you have to say, "Er, well I cook dinner for my kids, then I am so tired I just play Candy Crush with Netflix on in the background and then I fall asleep."

How often are you not making love to your partner cuz you are too tired! C'mon. You used to hump like motherflippin' rabbits! What changed?! Your apps! You installed too many BS apps that don't help you.

Imagine if you'd have installed the *How to Keep Your Partner Happy* eBook instead of The Sims?! You gotta work at this stuff! Replace your crappy apps! Think about what you do when you get home from work... make dinner, clean up a little bit, put the kids to bed, sit on the couch and veg the F out.

You should never come home from work – work implies it's a separate entity to the rest of your life. What is a holiday or a vacation to you? I'm guessing if you are anything like I was then it's a time to get away from your life, to relax, to enjoy your time, to not clock in. Successful people, and I'll explain this in detail later, don't need to vacation because their life is one thing – their life!!! Why would you do something you don't like to save up to get away from the thing you don't like, to then go back to the thing you don't like to pay off the extra money you spent while you were vacating from the thing you don't like?! MENTAL! It doesn't make sense! You're tired because you aren't doing what excites you.

Those times where you forgot to eat cuz you were so excited about something... You didn't feel hungry, cuz if you did you would have remembered to eat! You're moody because you're not overriding your neg-brain with exciting shit. You argue with your partner, kids, or friends because you don't have a reason not to argue. You go to bed late cuz you've got nothing exciting to wake up for! That's you, my dude! All you!

And that was 100% me too, for soooo long! I got sick of it! Life without purpose is not life, it's prison. Are you in prison? The job you hate, living hand to mouth month in, month out?! Always telling yourself it's not fair. It may not be fair! But you have the power to make it fair! Take your life back! Do shit, get shit done! If you don't have goals then how in the Sam flip do you think you will accomplish anything?! Your brain is your phone: change the apps, make it faster, make it better, make it clever. Make it work for you so you're not working for it.

If you want a wake-up call, then for the next 24 hours act like you normally do and time how long you spend doing things that you know full well aren't benefiting you.

You can compare your brain to anything, think of it like a toaster... What do you do if your toaster stops working? You either figure out what the problem is – blown fuse, age, technical fault etc. – and then you fix it (if you can), or you buy a new one. The only difference here is, you can't buy a new brain – well I suppose you can buy a brain on the deep web, but it ain't yours! If the toaster was the only toaster you could ever have I would hope you would do whatever it took to fix it (or prevent it malfunctioning in the first place) – surely you would work out how to fix it if you could because there is no other option.

So YOUR brain, we need to fix it, make it work faster and make it work for you! The reason I have related your brain to a phone is because we are led to believe the brain is something that we can't completely understand. Its intricacies make it a subject matter that we often shy away from figuring out for just that reason.

Something I have found over all my years of lecturing and teaching is that if someone doesn't understand something, YOU need to relate it to something they do understand. When someone talks jargon to you, you just switch off, but the only reason you switch off is because it's jargon. You just don't understand it yet. Does not for one second mean it isn't completely imperative information for your journey!

A great teacher will always work out why you don't understand and figure a way to relate to you. This phone analogy is the best way I have got results with regards to people understanding how to begin hacking their own brains, with incredible effects. You can relate your brain to most things, but a smartphone is something we pretty much all understand.

Let's do one more exercise before we move on, and I just wanna reiterate this point: you have to totally understand something and feel confident with your understanding of it to achieve the best results. We have all experienced beginner's luck, but again, this is us not being in control. Anyone can have beginner's luck, we want to be certain of the outcome every time! You think for one moment that any professional is guessing the outcome? Of course, other factors come into it, but for the most part, Michael Jordan knows it's going in the basket, Lady Gaga knows she's gonna hit the note, and Gordon Ramsey knows a fillet steak takes X amount of time to cook!

---

## Exercise 1.2

I want you to now install a new app. Your new app has to be a completely amazing effin' awesome app! One that you can start using immediately that will replace one of your ETO apps.

This will work better if you replace an ETO app instead of just installing a new effin' awesome app. Out with the old and in with the new! If you are stuck for ideas, try something educational, or life-planners or health and fitness applications. A great app for being on top of your diet and losing weight is MyFitnessPal, so this may be a good one for you if you can't think of one yourself. I'd love to hear what app you picked and why – hit my social and lemme know!

---

Awesome work so far, guys!

Let's talk about one of my boys...

---

## Summary

- Ex 1.0

Categorise your phone apps

– Organise your current phone apps into the following piles: Effin' awesome, meh, or ETO

- Ex 1.1

Delete one of your ETO apps

– This works best if it's the one with the most 'progress' on

– Stick a cross on your good hand when you have completed this task

- Commit and don't stop when shit gets hard or it doesn't seem like the end is in sight, cuz it often is just a couple more XYZs away

- Let them do them while you do you

- Don't prevent real you coming through.

# Chapter 12

# DWYAD GWYAG

We are gonna get right into some full-on brain hacks later but I needed to water the seed from the last chapter so it can start growing in your head for a bit before we go super deep. In the meantime lemme tell you about Ryan... I have a dear friend, his name is Ryan. He has been one of the key reasons I started to take control of my life. I need to tell you a bit about Ryan.

I used to live with him and two other guys a couple of years after I'd finished uni while I was bumbling about. I had recently split up with a long-term girlfriend and I needed a place to stay.

Ryan suggested I stay on their couch till I got my shit sorted. I lived with them for 2 years! My room transformed twice a day between bedroom for me and living room for them.

I found it really hard to relax at night cuz if I was tired I had to stay up until they had all gone to bed, it was their living room after all. Ryan hardly ever hung out with us. At the time I thought he was missing out. We seshed Mario Kart and smoked peng ganja weed and ate crap. We laughed a bunch while it was happening but I always woke up feeling like shit. No plans, no goals, no nothing. I wish I knew then what I know now!

The reason Ryan wasn't hanging in the living room was that he was always in his room. At the time we had no idea what he was doing. It turns out he was running his game! I just thought he was wasting his 20s while we were all having fun.

He missed out on filling up condoms with aerosol and exploding them; he missed out on cooking a 'sweet lasagna' made from 8 different types of chocolate; he missed out on making a profile on a swingers' website for one of our other mates... Here's the clincher though, he has time to do all that shit now if he wants cuz he spent his time wisely making contacts and getting boss at his craft.

He got so good at what he does that he now works high up for one of the fastest-growing companies in the UK. He did shit, he got shit done! Ryan realised early on that you get out what you put in, and the motherfucker put in! I don't know for sure if Ryan came up with this quote, but he sure as hell says it all the time – "do what you've always done, get what you've always got!!"

On a basic level, this sentiment means to eat chocolate every day – stay fat. Or smoke every day – get lung cancer. Or hang with the same people – stay with the same people. Nobody wants to be fat, nobody wants cancer, and even if you tell yourself otherwise, nobody wants to be stuck with the same people day in, day out, especially if they are moaners or down-and-outs or nause-bags.

The other understanding of this sentiment is much more vast, much more powerful, and much more real than the initial ideal. If you wanna be an astronaut and you spend your time working at KFC, ain't gon' happen. You wanna change the world for the better but you don't change your bad habits, ain't gon' happen.

You wanna be a professional or master at something but you spend your days doing sweet FA to get there, guess what: IT AIN'T GON' HAPPEN! You gotta make a change and believe in yourself enough to take the risks nobody else will!

You only got stuck in the rut you're in cuz you didn't move from the rut. Ya dig?! You always wear ill-fitting clothes cuz you always wear ill-fitting clothes. You always watch crappy Netflix shows cuz you always watch crappy Netflix shows. You always smoke cuz you always smoke.

I want you to think of the first thing that comes to mind when I ask you the following question, and I guarantee you that the thing you think about will be something completely out of your usual comfort zone. Something different. Something that means enough that you use it as an answer when presented with the following question.

So here's the question – what was the best day of your life?

Most of you will have a couple to choose from: might be marrying your true love, or going travelling, or getting your first big commission, or quitting drugs, or blah, blah, blah! Notice it?! The best day of your life was different from all the others! But YOU did it! YOU made that day happen because of your actions and persistence. Even something as minuscule as booking a holiday: you gotta check different charters, take time off work, get a dog sitter, save money to spend while you're out there etc. – but you did it! Go you! Imagine what else you can do!

That time that you pulled it all together, that time you threw all your eggs in one basket, that was you! You can do that every day! A few years ago if you'd asked me the same question I would have given a similar answer! Now, I have so many monumentally awesome days I just love the years! I can't pick out one thing!

There's too many! Even today, as I'm scribing this, today has been fucking awesome! So was yesterday and the same for tomorrow, because I chose it to be.

It's all me! When my days are shit – me! When I moan – me! When my relationships are rubbish – ME!!!

Anyways, back to the point: do what you've always done, get what you've always got! If it didn't work in the past, it probably ain't gonna work in the future. If you eat burgers every day then you gon' get fat. If you run a business without calling potential customers, you ain't got no pipeline. If you go to the gym once a week, you're gonna get once-a-week worth of results!

You smoke 'only' 2 a day – well you smoke 2 a day! It's a reality!!! If you aren't willing to stop acting like a victim, you ain't gonna get ANYWHERE worth going – you'll do what I did and get what I got, and go round in circles blaming everyone else, and everything else... and guess what?! You'll end up in exactly the same place you were before, but you'll be older!

It's all about the transition. Your body is changing daily, moment to moment, and you have the opportunity to make that change positive or negative. Those are your options! Not changing at all, that's actually negative. Having a negative change and learning from it, that's positive. But once again, it's all you!!! You should have already started making this change and if you're this far into the book then you must have! But now you have new problems. Let's talk about problems...

Your partner might be holding you back now, or you have had the realisation you need to quit your job to pursue your true calling but you've got kids and you're scared about the lack of a safety net from going self-employed, or you can't work out how to make the time to start your new venture.

Fact is: problems are awesome! You've just been told different your whole life! Even thinking of the word 'problem' probably makes you feel anxious or worried, right?! Just me saying the word 'problem' may have got your annoying ass-face subconscious to start worrying about some of the 'problems' you currently have.

You have to remember duality: up needs down as a reference, hot needs cold as a reference, pretty needs ugly as a reference. What does a problem have as a reference? A solution, of course, you silly goose! And a solution is employable. A solution is a game-changer, a solution is your chance to get out!

Think about it: your car breaks down, you need a solution! Your baby gets ill, you want them to stay ill or you want a solution? Your job sucks, you wanna stay working and hating it or you want a way out? A solution! All the amazing people in the world understand that a solution is an opportunity. Without the problem, you ain't got nothing to solve! If you ain't got nothing to solve then what's the point!?

We all have those times when we need help with something we know nothing about. Let's say you've locked yourself out of your house, or your car breaks down, or your house is on fire. Unless you are a locksmith, a mechanic, or a firefighter, you are gonna struggle to solve this particular problem. How much would you pay for that service?

Your house is burning down with all your personal stuff in it: photos, memories, your favourite bed sheets, your tax returns, hahaha. If someone could come along and wave a wand and it all went back to normal, how much would you pay?

Imagine you are the one that invents a time machine, and it works – you think how much people would pay for that!!! However, imagine someone else invented the same thing at the same time as you, but as well as being able to send you back and forward in time for a nominal fee, they also send you a congratulatory bottle of your favourite drink when you make your first purchase, and give you a loyalty card: 5 time-travels and your 6th one is free! Which one would you go for? What if the second one is an extra £100 – is the extra service worth it?

What about if the deals are the same but the first one is run by a Mother Theresa sort who has started loads of charities and gives 50% of their profits to said charities, and the second deal is run by

Hitler incarnate? Now, which one?! What if it's the same deal but the first one is now £500 more than the latter??? You have to remember this: do what you've always done, get what you've always got! You gotta change shit up, topsy-turvy that motherfucker!

We'll talk about how to sell later, but for now, we gotta get a grip on this! The following is an inescapable but entirely hard to swallow truth: you have to admit that if your life is shit then it's all your fault. I know it's hard. I know you are probably cussing me now, but I am not willing to lie to you! Your parents should have told you this, and their parents should have told them this...

Everything is you! And if you're living the same life, or you answer the question "how's it going?" with something like "same shit, different day", or "not bad, thanks" then you are nowhere near your full potential. I spent a long time taking the piss out of those people that seem overly confident, or overly happy, or overly positive. I used to think they were faking it! I was wrong! If you can't be happy for other people's success it's because you have no idea what they went through to get to where they are!

Did you know (the last time I checked) over 60% of the billionaires in the world are self-made!? That means they weren't born into it. Instead, they were born with shit-all, just like you and me! I was blown away the first time I heard about this! I just figured all rich people were born from rich parents and the money got passed down! WRONG! More than half of them just worked their asses off and made it happen. And this is just billionaires! A colossal 90% of millionaires are self-made!

Fucking AWESOME! If they had done what they'd always done, they'd have got what their parents got!

They had to make a change! They had to make a commitment to themselves, to take massive action and fuck shit up! Like I mentioned before, you CANNOT do any of the things I have been talking about, and definitely not do the things in the next few chapters, if you aren't ready to admit to yourself that you have to make some big changes.

If you're not there yet, then come back when you are, but trust me on this, cuz I lived it first hand: if you do walk away, you WILL get fed up again at some point, and you will have wasted that extra time not doing anything about your situation – do this now, make this commitment and make it to yourself. Tomorrow won't wait, bitch.

If you are ready, then tell people! It feels embarrassing talking about this shit, and a lot of people won't have any interest or understanding of what you are talking about! But those are the same people that have settled: standard life, average job, mediocre relationship. You know that saying: 'go big or go home'? I say, 'go fucking massive or go fucking passive!'

But what if people laugh?! I can't stress this enough: there are shed loads of us that won't laugh (you just don't know us yet!), and we are doing way better than those people laughing at you for finally starting to break free and live life.

Can you remember a time when someone you know told you something they were doing or going to do that was huge: like quitting their job and going rogue, or starting a new hobby, or taking on the world? Did you laugh, or did you feel jealous!?

If you are like I was then probably a bit of both. Be honest, a lot of the time you didn't want them to succeed because it makes your life seem double shit – bet you didn't even think about the amount of courage and bollocks/vagina it took for them to tell you about their crazy idea.

The actual crazy thing here is not living life and just existing, spending your energy cussing people that have worked so hard to be successful! You know that question: "if you could have dinner with anyone dead or alive, who would you choose?" Ain't nobody ever said, "Mandy from Tesco that has worked as a shelf stacker for their whole life," or, "Kenny from the KFC on North Street."

You wanna have dinner with someone that owned their life, right?! Someone who went all out and created a legacy! I want to leave a legacy, I don't want to be forgotten, and you know why? Cuz people who leave a legacy did something with their lives, they smashed it out the park when everyone else told them they couldn't, they went against the norm and believed in themselves and didn't take 'no' for an answer!

You think for one minute that some badass motherfucker like Mike Tyson gave up after the first fist to the face? You think Michael Jordan gave up when he missed his first bucket? You think Mother fucking Theresa gave up because there were too many ill people!? Come the fuck on! I wanna leave a legacy after I'm gone, and I wanna run ting while I'm here and I know you do too!

Everyone does! Stop fighting it and let's do this! I'm about to tell you the most obvious pen-behind-the-ear-but-you-can't-find-a-pen hack that is so obvious that nobody seems to even think it will work! Lemme show you that it works...

---

## Summary

- "The definition of insanity is doing the same thing over and over again, but expecting different results." AE
- Do what you've always done, get what you've always got!
- Your actions are everything. Thoughts that are not manifested will cause absolutely nothing to happen.

# Chapter 13

# The Switch

Think of all the answers to your dreams being in one room. The room is split into each and every one of your dreams, with an easy and direct route to achieving each one. The room is also split into every problem you have, with an easy and direct route to remedying each one. The room is split into every relationship you have or want to have with an obvious pathway to make each one a reality.

The room is full of all the things you desire and a paint-by-numbers, easy AF route to help you attain each thing. The only problem is, the room is pitch black. Like, blacker than charcoal. You can't even find the light switch. If only you could, all of these solutions and answers would be laid out right in front of you.

The issue of finding the light switch is a problem that the vast majority of the world never, ever resolve. They spend their whole life looking for the light switch, and for the most part, they get to the point that they give up looking and give in to the fact that they will just get used to living in the dark.

Human beings are fucking awesome at adapting to whatever situation they are in, naturally and without too much obvious effort. Without awareness, you are living in the dark and you will never know because your body and mind will just get used to it and figure out a way to deal with it. Even if the outcome is negative, humans WILL find a way. Humans are AWESOME!

Ever heard the expression 'burying your head in the sand'? It's not just a physical thing, it's mental too. You can have all the lights on but have no idea what you're doing! It's so frustrating not being able to find something: say you've lost your keys and you need to get to work. The kids are doing their respective lids and you're already late. Where the hell are they?!

You can do what everybody else does and spend ages frantically looking for them only to realise they were somewhere obvious the whole time, or you can cut out the shit and prevent the problem occurring in the first place. What do I mean? Well, you could get one of those lost key finders! Even better, you could already know where your keys were.

How many times have you, your partner, friend or family member lost something – it's hella frustrating and a waste of time and effort to find whatever it is you've lost. Or even worse, you never find it and have to replace it, spending extra time and resources. You need to be a control freak, a maniac, and an absolute dominating force in all walks of your life.

Let's go back to the black room analogy. Fact is, all the answers are often right in front of us. You've probably heard this a million times before, but it's often the things we have heard a million times that we don't take any time to actually comprehend, like where the expression 'steal their thunder' or 'in a nutshell' come from! You've heard them a bunch of times but are you now gonna Google them to see their actual origins?! Just cuz you use it doesn't mean you understand it...

Anyway, I'm rabbiting... The pitch-black room. Darkness is not the problem, not being able to illuminate the room is! If you can find the light then all you gotta do is flip the switch and turn it on! This is exactly the same with your brain, the way you manage yourself, the actions you take, the relationships you have, the businesses or hobbies you start etc. They all need to have YOU on board, and aware.

Trust me, I've put this into practice countless times, and it works! You can literally just flip the switch, whatever the switch is for, and start taking immediate action. You wanna eat healthier, flip the switch right now and stop eating bad! You wanna start a business, flip the switch and start taking action. You wanna build the business you've got, flip the switch and start making some calls! You wanna ask that person out you've fancied for ages and haven't mustered up the courage to even say "hello"... Guess what... FLIP THE MOTHERFLIPPIN' SWITCH AND ASK THEM OUT!

I know what you're thinking: "It's not that easy, Lee Lee, I've been trying for years and I'm still stuck in this rut." That's cuz you didn't actually flip the switch, like proper flip it. You probably did what I did for years and either didn't even know there was a switch to flip, or you flipped it on but kept flipping it back off every time you left the room! It's like a diet! I hate the word 'diet'! It's a cop-out!

You don't need a diet – diet implies that it is only for a limited amount of time – you need a lifestyle change! If you quit smoking for 3 months a year every year, you are still a smoker! What's the point in only part committing?! Why would you go to the gym once a week just to see absolutely no change in your body, and end up aching for days after – you need to go every day! Why would you not drink alcohol all week then get blind drunk at the weekend and punish the shit out of your liver, spend your rent money and not remember anything?!

You'd do better to have a glass of wine or a bottle of beer each day and really enjoy it. Why would you start a business, or a relationship, put shitloads of effort into it, excite yourself thinking about it for the first few months, then slip out of the honeymoon period and bongle it?! See, this is what I mean! Why is it called a honeymoon period?! Why does it have to only last for a while!

When I married my partner it was for life! I don't wanna just have a bit of a life with her, I want it all! And so does she! And so should you (but not with my wife!). You don't wanna watch half a movie, or eat half a meal, or only wear one shoe at a time! You need it all! You need your business to flourish, consistently, for the rest of your life! Same with your relationships, same with your health, same with your spirituality, same with your smarts!

Get the picture?! It's all integral and needs to be a full commitment, for life!! The biggest problem most of us have is that we have been told it's okay to give up. For some reason it's encouraged to have massive unrealistic goals and dreams when you're a kid, then spend the next few years being told to be realistic and settle down! Well, I ain't settlin'. Nu-uh, no way! This is my life and I'm taking control of it. This is my life until I die. I want control, right up until my last breath! You gotta flip that switch! And for those of you thinking, "I just don't have the time/energy/confidence," then that's because you haven't changed those things yet.

Remember, if you can't swim, it's cuz you don't swim! We are gonna learn how to rewire our brains soon, but for now... you are wrong! I hate to say it cuz I know I just pissed you off, and actually, it is not a good idea to tell anyone they are wrong, but on this one occasion I'mma say it, and I wish someone had told me years ago, or I had listened when they did!

Your time is not the problem, and I guarantee you your effort level is not the problem. It's the things you are spending your time and effort on. Think of it like this: most of you will have a vice, or two, or maybe a few. Let's investigate a few things you might be able to relate to.

Smoking: How much time a day do you spend standing outside with a cigarette in your hand? Let's forget the fact it costs you money and is pretty detrimental to your health and just focus on the time. If you smoke only 3-5 a day, assuming each cigarette takes you 2 minutes to smoke, and I'm sure it is normally more like 3-5 minutes, then you are spending around 10 minutes a day just 'standing there'. Doesn't sound like much, I'm sure you just told yourself that you deserve that couple of minutes a few times a day cuz you work so hard. Keep telling yourself that...

A lot of you don't smoke, but I bet you fit into one of the following categories. If you do any of the following daily or at least 5 days out of the week then the time you are wasting will be relative... Some of you will even answer yes to all the following but don't worry, it's a good thing as long as you are aware of it – that way you can change it and ante up!

So, do you do any of these things daily?

Watch over an hour of TV, refresh ANY social media page without posting something on it, play video games, press snooze on your morning alarm, have no set bedtime, have small talk with anyone, worry, complain, watch adverts, chase small amounts of money (this counts as trying to get back £5 worth of phone calls from your tariff or fanny about trying to get off of a parking ticket for £35 when in the same day you will spend an equal amount in the pub or on makeup or whatever), sit in traffic, pay attention to haters, tell yourself your relationship is working when it isn't, tell yourself your business is working when it isn't, saying yes to something you don't want to do, then spending the time at said thing moaning because you don't wanna be there, gossiping, listening to the news, doing drugs for no reason, drinking to excess, making empty promises, being messy or not putting things back in their place (you'll just have to look for them later), I could go on...

But there is one thing that most of you will be doing daily that is making all of the lists I just reeled off possible. The following is the reason you aren't where you want to be, with who you want to be with, looking how you wanna look and doing what you wanna do!

And the prize for the absolute worst time-wasting thing you can do daily: making excuses and playing the victim. You waste sooooo much time making excuses, over-thinking, blaming, pointing the finger, negging yourself! C'mon! Own up to it and let's move on, finally! I don't wanna make you feel bad, and you gotta understand I was the wooooorst at this for so many years!

I used to session video games for about 3-6 hours a day, whilst getting high and eating like an elephant. When I wasn't kicking ass on GTA or COD I was drinking and watching TV, endless reruns and trash, and making excuses and getting angry about how I thought the world owed me something, what a dick! Bad Lee! Don't get me wrong, there are some awesome video games, movies and TV shows that deserve our time! I'm not saying don't enjoy the arts, quite the opposite. What I am saying is don't stay up in a weed coma wanking 'til 5am, every day with nothing to show for it!

Once every few months, look forward to it, enjoy it, go and get a bit tipsy or watch 10 episodes of South Park, one after the other, but you should only do this as a reward, and to watch 10 shows in a row you better have made bank last month in some way shape or form!

You need to grind, man! Making excuses and acting like a victim puts you into a negative brain loop. We are going to go into detail on this later when I show you how to hack your brain, but for now, I need to reiterate the importance of your time, and how you use it. The 'flip switch' method is as basic as it sounds: think of something negative or time-wasting you're doing, and then flip the switch on your brain to correct it.

Turn the darkness into light. I know a lot of you are saying, "Whaaaa, I don't believe this will work." Well stop, that is you playing the victim, you haven't tried yet so stop being a WLB. We are starting to get to the part of this programme where the real change begins and to make it count you're gonna have to commit and ride the wave. The switch exists in your brain for all the things you do, and you CAN flip it, you just haven't done it before. If I asked you to invent me a time machine, you would have a similar thought process... But someone is gonna do it one day! And then it will be old news and something else unimaginable to our current brain will be the thing to strive for!

So let's go back to our dark room, our pitch-black, impossible-to-navigate room. I remember one of my biggest struggles when I was putting all of these exercises and hacks into action is that often they were so easy I felt like I wasn't trying hard enough, which was enough to question the validity of the process and in turn give up.

Often we are so anxious and worried that we can't congratulate ourselves for anything, and no matter what we do we feel like we're at the bottom of the next mountain as opposed to the top of the previous one. Think about how you treat a kid: you navigate them, teaching them the difference between good and bad, and offering treats for good behaviour and sanctions for bad behaviour.

I'm sure you've never put yourself on the naughty step as an adult, but I bet you often deserved to spend some time there! I also bet you have regularly given yourself treats when they weren't deserved. But if the treats have no purpose behind them then they ain't treats. We fall into a rut, and the thing that used to be a treat, like watching your favourite show or movie, or meeting friends at the pub, or having a night on the yay just becomes the norm and is no longer a treat.

Every time you flip the switch, in whatever situation you need to flip it, give yourself a thumb cross for flipping it, and a further cross at the end of the day when you stuck to it. If you don't stick to it, leave the cross on your good side, but add a cross to your bad side and start the process again. Rome wasn't built in a day, and neither is your new life. It takes time and effort, and a bunch of fucking up. The fuck-ups are the things that put us off and make us feel like the effort isn't worth it, where in fact they are just stepping stones to winning big. You can even flip the switch on this – every time you fail and start to give up and that dick of a voice starts chirping up in the back of your head to just give up, flip it.

The easiest way to flip the switch is to literally tell yourself whatever you need to hear. I'm sure you can relate to feeling nervous or anxious in a situation, maybe a job interview or date or whatever, and that awesome bad boy voice gets involved in your head and says something like, "C'mon dude, you got this," or, "You're gonna be okay, just go for it," or something like that.

That's the switch. And unless you ran home without turning up to the interview or date or whatever, then the switch worked. You told your brain what to do, and it did it. You controlled yourself. There is a lot to be said about spending time managing yourself, even if it is micromanaging in between different scenarios! I use the switch in between different jobs or situations and it has saved my ass countless times.

I spent a long time perplexed at how I could one minute feel on top of the world and the next totally off my game. For instance, I would power hour the start of my day by going to the gym and was in the mode there, then I'd get back in my car and drive home, and immediately be in a different situation where I had to be Daddy and husband until I next left the house, then I'd be working for a bit, then meeting man, then musician or book writer, then pitcher, then lecturer, then couch, then back to Daddy and husband.

All the time I wouldn't be preparing myself for the next event. Kill it at the gym, then come home and screw it with the wife or the kid. I'd crush it in a sales pitch, then have writer's block when I sat down to scribe. Dial writing, like totally on fire smashing out page after page, then feel nervous when I had to put the pen down and go to a meeting. So, in true style, we're gonna hack and multi-hack our exercise. The switch works anytime, and as long as you are aware of it as an option, it will work. To make it even stronger, you can learn to flip before you realise you need it. Prevention is better than cure type shit! So here's how to transition.

# THE TRANSITION

Standard example: You are on your way home after work. You walk through the door after a hard day's graft and immediately step into the whirlwind that is your other half running around like a nutter trying to cook dinner or clean the house, or whatever. Immediately you are forced into panic mode too, which doesn't feel relaxed after the day you've had. They bark at you and you immediately respond in defence.

Kick in the switch. Flip that bad boy. "I am not going to be angry or rise to them, they are obviously manic and they are not actually taking it out on me, I am just here." So instead of barking back, I'll either give them time to chill, or I'll do something really sweet to let them know I love them and I've got their back, cuz to be this manic they must be having a bit of a 'mare.

This totally works, and it works with any example. But let's go superstar version.

Ninja example: Same situation. However, before you get home, you choose to be conscious of the switch, and you flip it then. Lemme explain, and this is what I call a switch setup. The switch setup allows you to predict the need of the switch. The genius is that if you needed it, then you needed it, if you didn't need it (everything is chill and lush when you walk in the door) then it will allow you to reach much, much higher levels of being awesome due to dwelling in hyper-aware mode.

Lemme explain more: Think of your day like an alphabet. Break all of the different elements of your day into letters. To keep it simple, let's say we just have A, B, C, D and E. A could be gym, B could be work, C could be a hobby, D could be family or friend time and E could be cooldown time before bed.

All of these elements are completely different and require completely different abilities and skills to navigate. For instance, being at the gym with your headphones on takes a different skill set to being at work or family time. But more often than not we just end up in the next situation without even thinking about how we need to feel in preparation for that situation.

Turning up to school without your PE kit doesn't mean you can't take part, but it's awks AF and not as easy as it should be. So to get the best out of the situation we need to plan ahead – this doesn't mean writing the night before: "must be happy when walking in the front door tomorrow at 18:45". In fact, the brilliance of this hack is that it works almost instantaneously and you can do it at any point in between tasks.

All you have to do is be aware – noticing a trend at all? ;) As long as you are aware there is a potential switch to be had, you can flip it before you need to, and in turn force your mood. There is so much research on this subject. But I want the quickest, fastest version, I want the 2.0 bug-fixed track-ready version.

People often say you need to be in a meditative state to affect your brain – not true.

And I have tried both, extensively. All you need to do is be aware, that's it! So, let's go through our day with the ABCDE examples. I'll add my stacked-up, hit it from all angles mini-hacks in too just for good measure. And remember, in the same way daily goal practice works, and you write it like you've done it, with this we are telling ourselves how we are going to feel, not waiting to see how we feel!

---

Previous night: Write goals for next day and fall asleep telling myself I'm gonna wake up pumped and good to go.

Arise: Wake up feeling groggy but with last night's mantra ticking over so it only takes a sec to snap out of my bed coma. First job to do is go to the gym, so in the shower, I tell myself something like, "I am going to flip the switch on the following so I know I am in control of myself and my mood: I am gonna crush it at the gym and feel like a boss when I first walk in, I'm gonna train for X amount of time and I'm gonna feel great the whole time I'm there – click!"

Gym complete. Feeling great!

Next main job of the day is to go to work (for me as I'm writing this, it is writing this, so I'll use that as the example). On the way to my office, I tell myself, "I am going to flip the switch on the following so I know I am in control of myself and my mood: I am gonna feel amazing when I open up my laptop and start writing. I am going to still be buzzing from the gym and I will carry this energy across to my book writing so that I can get the best writing out of myself – click!"

Book writing complete, feeling great!

Next main task of the day is to spend an hour learning something new (in my case as I'm writing this I am focusing my hobby time on researching hip-hop sampling for an acoustic drum kit, for an important session I have coming up, but this could be anything from learning a language to learning to cook to learning piano, to mechanics 101 or brushing up on your string theory chops!).

On my way from the office to the studio, I tell myself: "I am going to flip the switch on the following so I know I am in control of myself and my mood: I am going to absolutely slam this sideways, I will research like a master, smiling the whole time, and absolutely engrossed in what I am learning without getting distracted. I am still buzzing from my book writing and I will bring this to my research for the next hour so I can absolutely own this project – click."

Hobby time complete, feeling awesome!

My penultimate main task of the day is to come home to my family.

On my way from the studio to my home I tell myself: "I am going to flip the switch on the following so I know I am in control of myself and my mood: When I walk in the door I am going to hug and kiss my partner and kid and with a huge smile ask them how their day was and make them feel special, and no matter what mood they are in, I will maintain my mood of positivity and love, and I will carry this into the evening – click."

Family greeting time is complete and I'm feeling amazing!

My last main to-do is to go to sleep feeling accomplishment, happiness, and success, and to set myself up to repeat the cycle tomorrow. While brushing my teeth before bed I tell myself: "I am going to flip the switch on the following so I know I am in control of myself and my mood: I will go to sleep feeling blessed and happy with my actions today. I will carry this with me tomorrow and wake up feeling amazing and full of life – click."

Then the cycle continues. The uber-cool thing is that you can do this with any situation, big or small, you just need to be aware and remember to know it is an option. For all you haters out there: I dare you to try this! I double dare you, motherfucker! It totally works!

Try it right now – whatever you are doing, whatever the next thing you are going to do is, even if it's really small and not a seemingly big deal, tell yourself you are going to do it the best, with the most amazing attitude, because it makes you awesome! The more you repeat this, the better it works.

The next element is to ask yourself this question: what do you want people to think of you?! I remember this penny dropping monumentally at a bar once... I've always been super matish when it comes to buying a round or getting the bill for dinner or lending people money or time. I have done this forever, no matter how broke I've been. I love treating people. And I never buy a drink for someone to get one back.

If I buy you a drink I did it because I wanted to, and you don't owe me anything – it's an entirely English thing to feel indebted to someone if they buy you something or do something for you – but that takes away the gesture. That's a different story for another book. Either way, this one time I was in a bar in Brighton with a bunch of my friends.

They were all at the bar trying to order a drink, and when the drinks order had been taken, I put my card forward and paid for everyone. I need you to understand that this was not for any other reason than I wanted to and definitely not to show off or anything like that.

At the time I was broker than an old record, like, in the black broke. The round was about 10 drinks and it cost about £45? My friends reluctantly let me pay, but that's not the point. As they were walking off with their drinks, the barman said to me, "Jeez, you must be sorted to get a big round in, what do you do as a job? Next drink you order is on the house!"

This was so funny to me as I was brassic, and at the time was doing very little work-wise and had no direction. The key here is that until I explained to him I was broke and I just liked sorting my mates out, he genuinely believed I must have some high-flying, well-paid job. The double funny thing was, this wasn't even a fake it 'til you make it plea, I genuinely just wanted to show my appreciation to my friends.

This got me thinking, "Hold on, he thinks I'm rich and because of that he is offering me a free drink." His preconception and misjudgement allowed me to get something. The point I'm making here is that by acting a certain way, things happen, and if you act positively, positive things happen.

And even if they don't, you won't care anyway because you have forced yourself into a state of positivity and will begin to see things differently. The power of the brain and how you can compel it to do what you want is something I have spent the last 10 years mastering.

I have my off days, but these only happen when I am not being aware. And these happen less frequently the more I own it. You can try this immediately.

Force yourself to act a certain way with a stranger and see how they react. I do this all the time. The difference is now I am not using it as an experiment, it's my life. Later on, we will get into this on a much deeper level where I will show you how to reprogram your brain – sounds scary I know, but it ain't. Now though, we need to understand the reality of purpose...

## Summary

- Humans are exceptional at adapting, you can adapt to whatever situation you are in, choose to be in a good one
- You can always choose to flip the switch
- Forward-think to ensure you are always in the best and most helpful frame of mind. Be aware of what situations you are entering and act accordingly.

# Chapter 14

# Purpose

What is purpose? The dictionary says purpose is: the reason for which something is done or created or for which something exists.

Think about that for a minute, this definition is huge! Purpose is pretty much the meaning for everything. And you are a part of that everything. So you need purpose. And purpose needs you! Without purpose we just float through life, we get average jobs, have average relationships, bring up average kids, go on average holidays, have average sex, you get the gist! Average breeds average.

Think about it, you go on a diet because you were in a long-term relationship that didn't work, you let yourself go and now you wanna get back in the game but you need to change your 'long-term relationship' lifestyle to get back to the point where you feel confident in your own body so someone will go home with you, and if you're lucky, they may even let themselves go for you in the future and get all chubby and lazy... There is a purpose there: you know full well that if you don't lose the weight or change your attitude from your 'comfortable years', you will struggle to get a new partner. Purpose!

You NEED purpose!!! It is the one thing that makes you wake up in the morning. I don't mean hit snooze and wake up just before you need to leave, rushing a shower and scrambling for your underwear cuz you forgot to put a wash on the night before! I mean actually choosing to get out of bed, ready to go, excited and pumped!

Honestly, ask yourself this: when was the last time you literally couldn't sleep because you were so excited?! Am I talking to you!?

So let's delve deeper into this. I want you to answer the following questions as fast as possible:

1. What is the purpose of a toaster?
2. What is the purpose of a boat?
3. What is the purpose of a light bulb?
4. What is the purpose of a school?
5. What is the purpose of a meal?
6. What is the purpose of a book? And finally, and remember to answer quickly...
7. What is the purpose of you?

The first 6 answers you gave should have come super quick and easy – they are pretty obvious. Let's go through the really obvious ones. Purpose of a toaster is to toast bread. Purpose of a boat is to travel across water. Purpose of a light bulb is to illuminate. Purpose of a school is to teach people. Purpose of a meal is to fill your belly. Purpose of a book is to read.

You could have answered more off-piste like – the purpose of a toaster is to take to bits so you have spares for the new circuit board you are making. Purpose of a boat is to party on. Purpose of a school is to ruin kids' lives (heh). Purpose of a meal is to alleviate the munchies after a bong hit, and the purpose of a book is to hide your porno in, or whatever version fits you.

Whatever you chose to answer when I asked you these questions,

I'm certain you had a distinct answer flash straight into your mind. What about the final question? What is YOUR purpose? What is the purpose of you? Did you answer quickly? Did you answer at all? Do you have any idea what that answer is or what you want it to be? When doing this exercise with loads of other people, over 98% answered that integral question with, "Errrr, ummmm," or, "Woah dude, I don't know?!"

Isn't that interesting, don't you think?! Lemme ask you this: if we were unsure what a toaster was used for, would you have even ever heard of it? To prove this you can think of all the things you haven't heard of yet! See, the thing needs a purpose to deserve a name. You got a name, but what does it mean?! What purpose have you given to your name?

---

## Exercise 1.0

Journal time, lovelies! I want you to write down the top 5 things you want people to think of when they hear your name. To give you an idea I have listed my current ones below, and these change as I accomplish new goals and continue to transition:

1. The most positive person in the room
2. Sick musician
3. Killer entrepreneur
4. Role model
5. Best-selling author

---

I want these things to be my purpose at the moment. When I have these goals or any goals, it immediately gives me purpose. Ever been to a party and felt like you wouldn't be missed if you left? Ever been in a meeting or group conversation and felt left out? Like nobody even knew you were there?! Why do you think this is? Is it because you are not interesting, or funny, or whatever? Is it that the people you were with don't like you?! Nope...

It's because you done brung no purpose. Think how it feels when you do a task at work that you have to do because it is protocol, and you know full well it doesn't mean anything and is just a waste of your time but you do it anyway because it is protocol.

Are you happy when you wash the dishes or hang out the laundry? Does it feel life-affirming? Of course, there is a purpose for washing the dishes or drying your clothes after a wash, but is it YOUR purpose? Like your true purpose?!

We need to talk about dreaming big! We have touched on this previously with unrealistic goals and daily goal setting. You should be getting to the point where you have started setting yourself crazy goals. Any of you yet written down 'I want to be the world's best washer-upper', or 'I want to hang out laundry' in your daily goals?!

Of course not. Why?! Because it's not your purpose!!! You want bigger things, just like me, and just like everyone else! My partner used to be a cleaner – an absolutely noble profession, but let's face it, it sucks! Nobody was put on this earth to clean shit off of somebody else's toilet bowl as their main purpose, surely?!

However, there is also sub-purpose. If you are working a cleaning job, or whatever job that isn't your dream job, with the intention of saving up money to be able to afford something that you need to make your dreams come true or similar, then that's cool – now the job has a purpose. Get me?! For instance, you are a college student and you want to be able to save up so you can go travelling for a year. In that instance having a shitty job stacking shelves is now worthwhile.

# Exercise 1.1

So let's work out your purpose score. Create a fresh 24 planner (from Chapter 9). I want you to fill it in just like you did last time, but this time, inside each cell, I want you to put a mark 1-10: 1 being absolutely no purpose, and 10 being the most purposeful thing ever.

As you know, there are 15 cells per day. Now we can figure out how much purpose your current life has. To do this simply add up all of your scores for each cell i.e. the 7am-8am cell you might have been doing something full of purpose, like perfecting your skills in a certain area, so you gave yourself a 9 out of 10, and in your 8am-9am cell you may have just watched a rerun of Friends (for the 18th time), so you gave yourself a -2 out of 10 (heh). Once you've filled in every cell, add all of them up! The best score you can have is 1,050, where every single cell has a 10 in it.

We all have off days and lose concentration, and that's without the bad luck just happens sometimes... So let's take that into account. To be running at the level of world-class professionals in their field, you need to hit a score between 85-100% purpose in this exercise, which equates as anything equal to or above a score of 892.5.

That may sound like a lot for some of you and you may be asking questions like, "How the Jeff do I keep up the pace to have that much purpose?" Or, "I'm nowhere near that percentile." The latter will have reintroduced the horrible naggy voice in the back of your head that always tells you to quit or that you'll never be good enough. Ignore it.

Throughout the rest of this programme, I am gonna show you exactly how to get your scores to over 85% - we are gonna do this together and I'm gonna show you how much easier it is to get to 85+% than it seems. Just bear with me.

Before I explain how to do this, there are a few facts you need to know, and there is no movement on this...

1. Daily exercise increases energy levels tenfold
2. Eating healthy increases energy levels tenfold
3. Working towards specific goals and being aware of what you want from life increases energy levels tenfold
4. Surrounding yourself with positive and/or successful people increases energy levels tenfold
5. Being happy and laughing increases energy levels tenfold
6. Being overweight decreases energy levels tenfold
7. Eating shit decreases energy levels tenfold
8. Having no purpose decreases energy levels tenfold
9. Hanging out with idiots decreases energy levels tenfold
10. Being sad and depressed decreases energy levels tenfold

To show what's possible we need to check out some people that already did it...

---

## Summary

- Ex 1.0

What do you want people to think of you?

- Write down 5 things you want people to think about you when they hear your name
- Be honest with yourself here and don't be afraid to put your deepest desires down

- Ex 1.1

Work out your purpose score

- Create another day planner (from Chapter 9)
- Fill it in like before but this time instead of a cross, put a score mark 1-10: 1 being absolutely no purpose, and 10 being the most purposeful thing ever
- Add up your score

- Everything needs purpose, otherwise what's the point?
  - You need to create a life of purpose by levelling up your current commitments, or by replacing them with better ones.

# Chapter 15

# There Was A Time...

Let's take a moment to think back, like really think back. Remember being at school and your teacher drops that classic line: "What do you wanna be when you grow up?"

Your answer would have been one of the most organic and truthful answers you have ever given to any question. You answered with no ego, no pressure and no limits. You answered honestly. You believed everything was possible. You answered with no reference points or ideals.

You weren't jaded. You answered before having kids to take care of, or a job you hate, or a shit relationship, or a loan to repay. Before money meant anything and the sky was the limit, and in most cases, it wasn't the sky, cuz you believed in dragons or wizards or invisibility or some shit.

So what happened? Cuz we all know you don't think like this now. I do! And I'm gonna show you how I continue to think big, then bigger, then huge day in, day out!

Think about your life: you're born, you're told anything is possible, you're left with that thought for a couple years then you're told everything isn't possible and you need to get real, get a job, get a partner, have kids, pay into a pension scheme and hedge your bets on everything turning out alright! And if you think about it, alright is just another word for average, boring, plain, meh!

Imagine how happy you could be after spending your whole life working to make someone else rich and then finally being able to relax on your 'massive' pension! With aching bones. And the start of dementia. FUCK. THAT. I'm not waiting and neither should you!

We need to get the kid back. Little you, no-limit you! The facts remain the same, nothing has changed since you were a kid, only your own belief and the absolute bollocks that you have been told and now probably live by. I believe we can do anything! You gotta work your respective dick or vagina off to get there, but it IS possible. If someone had told you that voice activation of the lights in your house via a smartphone would be possible 20 years ago, what would you have thought?!

Would it have been positive or negative? Would you have been excited for the possibility that someone somewhere was rewriting what's possible?! Or would you have chalked it out?! I mean in the last few years alone some of the most amazing inventions have included metal 3D printing, artificial embryos, the introduction of smart cities, AI that is so far advanced from anything else we have ever seen before... I could go on!

And this will have changed massively by the time this book goes to print! Think about how different the list I just made would be if I had written this book 20 years ago, or 100 years ago!

To really begin to understand yourself and believe in yourself in a way that gives certified results, you have to be true to your own mission. It's imperative that you can commit to being you, I mean, you ARE you, right?! To get this process going you have to start being the change you want to make. It's not about fake it till you make it, it's about living it till you are it. Doesn't roll off the tongue as well, I know, but it's the truth!

To be successful, in all senses of the word, you will have to make an oath to yourself to take the necessary steps. One of these steps is being able to have a reality check. So what do I mean by that?! Well, as I've said before, you are what you eat, and you are who you hang around with. So you need to start eating better and hanging around with legends!

Let's play a little brain game...

## Exercise 1.0

You are put in prison, but it's worse than normal prison, it's solitary confinement. In your tiny cell, which you have to stay in for 24 hours a day, you have a lamp and you are allowed to choose one book. You have been sentenced to life so the book you choose is ultimately the only book you will ever read again and will be your only source of entertainment/education/porn or whatever. What would you choose? Moreso, why would you choose it?

If you choose to spend your remaining years sessioning the Christian bible, you are either gonna end up a hardcore Christian, or a hardcore hater of Christianity. If you choose a memoir, you will end up thinking like the person that wrote it, or their beliefs and ideals will drive you madder than a bag of dicks!

Now, consider this, you haven't got a life sentence, you've got 25 years and you know you will get out at the end of it. You still have to choose one book. Does that change the book you would ask for? I would see this as an opportunity to read my chosen book over and over and over, for 25 fucking years, until it was indoctrinated! I know full well I wouldn't ask for a newspaper, or a celebrity magazine, or anything other than an amazing and inspiring piece of work.

If you knew you could, surely you would! Well, this is your life. You can! And if you are choosing to read any of the aforementioned BS then you might as well be in prison – I know I feel like I've picked up the soap every time I'm in earshot of the news.

I constantly reality check myself, I have to! It's easy to fall into bad habits! Your friends and family, your work colleagues and peers, your government and leaders will all allow it. They won't remind you to keep your brain in race-ready pristine order cuz it doesn't help their cause and they are more than likely living a scripted lifestyle. Don't allow it! You're better than that! You don't need leaders, you need to lead your own life!

Every day I need to reality check myself constantly – why?! Just think about what we're up against...

Advertising: literally billions are spent each year on keeping you the same, well within the machine, spending all your hard-earned paper! The same small, scared, anxious, worried version of you. You're told what to eat, how to eat it, and when to eat it. You're told it's standard to work 9-5 and then get blasted on the weekend. You're told it's okay to retire or work for a boss you hate just to pay the rent. You're told to take a pill if you're sleepy and a pill if you're over-excited!

You can prove this to yourself by just watching one set of adverts in between an episode of something. Take note of how these adverts make you feel. Remember, these ads are the ones that aren't even directed at you! Your searches on the internet allow for direct ads to be forced upon you constantly!

It's like having a fucking fishing rod attached to your head with your favourite thing hanging from it, just out of reach, unless you buy it! Without thinking we can succumb to them, and even if we don't buy the thing they are selling, they keep us believing we can't do any better and distract the shit out of us.

So, one of my favourite reality checks is the following...

There was a time when someone said... Keep this in your mind. This sentence changed my life! Lemme explain.

You gotta think about the accolades and accomplishments other people have aced: people with the same 24/7/365 as you! Alexander Graham Bell, the mush that invented the telephone – imagine the conversation. "So... er... Mum, I've got this idea, I've come up with an invention that allows you to talk to someone on the other side of the world!"

What do you think his mum said, or the bank said, or his friends and peers said?! "Lay off the shrooms, Al!"

To make that analogy more current and relevant, it's like me saying right now: "Guys, I've invented time travel and it totally works! I just need £1.5b to get the project off the ground?" What would you say? Would you believe me? Even if you did, would you believe me enough to shout me the dollar? You wouldn't because you don't believe me!

Just to make a point, that's not me you don't believe in, it's you!

Whenever someone tells you that you can't do something, that's them talking to themselves, ignore it and move on. It works the other way too: you should be stoked when someone does something amazing, not jealous or envious, and you definitely shouldn't let it take you off course! Cheerlead them and feel ecstatic that they just done changed the game for themselves, because it means you can too!!

Anyway, this reality check hack worked so well for me that I want to share it with you! Every time I begin to feel that horrible doubt or worry, or anxiety, or lack of confidence, or disbelief in myself, I amp myself up by proving to myself that whatever I am journeying towards is completely viable and more than likely someone has already broken the back on it.

I watch YT videos on the most amazing people, I listen to or read books about people's huge accomplishments, I research people like Tesla, DaVinci or some other absolute don, I read the new advances in technology from MIT or CERN. I reality check the shit out of myself! So consider the following...

There was a time that someone said: "I just came up with a way to cure tetanus, rabies and polio!"

There was a time that someone said: "I reckon I can build something that flies like a bird and can transport people from place to place."

There was a time that someone said: "I think this internet thing is gonna be big..."

There was a time that someone said: "We could use something circular to help us move stuff!"

There was a time that someone said: "If we cut the cornea with a laser and then screw about a bit we can make people see better!"

I could go on for ageeees! I love this shit so much!!!!

If you wanna super hack, then you can add a few of the following to your daily goals. There will be a time when I say: (insert some of your daily unrealistic goals).

Let's go back to the kid-mind. The difference between some of us and the list of legends I just mentioned, is that their obsession with their unrealistic goal/s never went away. They worked harder than anyone else and made it happen. They changed the world with their meagre 24 hours a day, often through adversity, and with nearly everyone they spoke to calling them crazy or tapped or telling them that "it won't work!"

'Everybody Is a Genius. But If You Judge a Fish by Its Ability to Climb a Tree, It Will Live Its Whole Life Believing That It Is Stupid.' – Albert Einstein.

We need to start growing a pair and listening to ourselves and not the opinions of people that don't know what is best for us. Have you ever heard something on the news or read it in a paper and then passed it on as gospel without actually checking if it is true?!

If you think about it, did YOU actually even take the time to question if you believe it?! It's time to stop feeling stupid and useless and it's time to start believing in yourself and fucking everyone else's opinions off – they don't know what's best for you, only you do!

What are you capable of? Your ideas on this will be different from mine, and that's cool! If your idea of super success is having a stable job, a mortgage, an okay car and the time to play Xbox in the evenings then cool, you do you! There is no wrong or right here, it just is what it is! You know what you want, and as long as it is ethical then you have my blessing to tell everyone else to do one if they don't agree with you!

Your opinions and beliefs matter more to you than anyone else! Doesn't for one minute mean everyone else is wrong, their opinions and beliefs matter to them just as much as yours matter to you. You don't need to change theirs because they are on their own journey. You just need to keep to yours! Kid mode is integral for our progression.

I want you to spend a few moments thinking back to your old thought processes, the ones with no limits. Ask yourself why you stopped thinking like that. What changed? I can guarantee it was a bunch of other people telling you a bunch of other shit, and that's it. Imagine if your whole life the news and media were telling you to go for broke, dream massive, take risks and be the best you – how would your life be different now?

# Exercise 1.1

There was a time when someone said... I used to write this down wherever I could until I didn't need the reminders. Set a phone reminder with this on right now, set it to go off 2 or 3 times a day as a reminder to make sure you remember that anything is possible, and so many people have already proved it...

___

Now, you know how people say one of life's absolute certainties is that one day you will die?! Well, let's make death our bitch and hack it...

___

## Summary

- Ex 1.0

What book would you choose if it was the only book you could ever read?

  – Why?

- Ex 1.1

Set an alarm

  – Make sure it goes off a few times a day to remind you that someone has already accomplished way more than you have

  – Make sure you read the alarm label each time and don't just turn it off

- Your mindset is the only thing preventing you from thinking like anyone else that you aspire to be. Make sure you read books, study information, and listen to all of your heroes daily to keep you juiced!

# Chapter 16

# Deathbed

So we just looked at what other people have once said, now we're gonna look forward to the inevitable future, to think about what we might say. Confused? Don't be, or do be, up to you, but I'll explain anyway...

You know how I mentioned you need to constantly reality check yourself! I can't stress this enough – think about all the distractions you have to deal with in your day-to-day. For instance, most of us don't just have one stream of correspondence.

Gone are the days where you write a letter, and also when you could only text or email someone. I remember when my burner phone, that was definitely not considered a burner phone then, could only hold 10 SMS messages and I would have to delete one to receive a new one otherwise the new one would just bounce!

Now, most of us have multiple email addresses across multiple accounts, that's without WhatsApp, FB Messenger, Insta, LinkedIn, Grindr, Bebo, MySpace etc. And I bet you don't set aside time to check them, I mean specific time.

Most of us look at our phone as soon as it pings or rings, with no regard for what we were doing before it started kicking off and doing its lid. I heard someone once relate owning a phone to having a hundred pieces of string tied to different parts of your body, and no matter what you are doing at any given time, no matter how important that thing is, one of the bits of string gets pulled and you can't help but notice it.

It takes your focus away from what you were doing, and for most of us, we haven't actually focused properly at anything since we've had a phone! Really, when was the last time you had a conversation without your phone interrupting, or watched a movie without checking your phone, or went for dinner and left your phone at home??

I get it! You need your phone on, what if you miss an important call or message?!?! I totally get that, and for those that know me well, I am always on my phone – but gone are the days of mindless, unscheduled traipsing through the internet. Now I know what I'm doing and it works – I'll put out a 'how to manage your phone' eBook or something when this is done to help you out.

Game time!

Answer the following questions quickly, just yes or no, no deliberation.

1. Do you ever unlock and check your phone seconds after turning it off and putting it down?

2. Do you ever pretend you are listening to someone while scrolling through your fav social media, knowing full well they know you aren't listening properly but you can't stop yourself looking?

3. Ever take your phone on a romantic date?

4. Ever take your phone to your kid's birthday party or check it while in the cinema?

5. Ever flip between Instagram and Facebook, then back to Instagram just in case someone has liked one of your pictures in the meantime?

6. Ever etc., etc.

If you answered yes to any of these, you're a slave to your phone! It's got you, man! Right where it wants you: useless, not anywhere near full potential, and unable to take control. I'm gonna tell you how to take control of this particular little geez later on, but for now, let's get back to reality checking.

What is a reality check? Dictionary says: 'a reality check is an occasion on which one is reminded of the state of things in the real world'. The thing the dictionary doesn't tell you is that reality checks are not only integral, but you have to figure them out yourself and find ways that they work for you. In the same way I explained you have to come up with your own mantras, you have to come up with your own reality checks! I'm gonna give you my personal reality check for you to use it at your own will, and I suggest you do. It's a goodun'! I would love to see what you came up with for yourself, hit me up.

So, picture this, and really picture it! Some of you will have experienced being on the opposite side and will understand the gravity of this. If you haven't experienced this yet, you more than likely will at some point, and it is such a strong thought process that if you have an ounce of heart you will be able to connect on some level.

This reality check hack is what I call 'deathbed'. Sounds serious, doesn't it...? Well it is, cuz so is your life!

We are going to put ourselves into a heightened state to help with this. To do this I very briefly need to talk to you about breathing. I am not going to force you into meditating or anything like that, (not that meditation isn't super beneficial or can be, it is just not for everyone) nor am I going to do some weird Hypno shit on you (I don't know how). I am, however, gonna get you to breathe properly.

Think about when you've been in a situation where you needed to calm down or calm someone else down. One soundbite that often comes up to help chill someone the fuck out is the advice: "Breathe... breathe." They're not telling you to breathe, you're doing that already, cuz you're brown bread if you don't! They are instead telling you to calm your breathing, and take deep breaths. Why? Because it alters your state.

Deep breathing relieves tension, stress, anxiety and a bunch of other wack traits due to its physiological effect on your nervous system. Being mindful about your breathing and controlling how slowly and deeply you breathe activates the hypothalamus.

Just in case you wanna know, the hypothalamus is connected to your pituitary gland in the brain even though it sounds like an awesome dinosaur. It sends out neurohormones that inhibit stress-producing hormones which put your body and mind into a state of relaxation, and in turn has a myriad of awesome benefits, one of which being it allows you to calm.

As I said, I'm not gonna go deep on this now because I want to keep on track, but I highly suggest you look into breathing techniques and how they can help you control your mood. But for this hack, you just need to be able to slow your breathing down. Now I have done the following with many people, and often it can result in the participant crying, feeling overwhelmed, and in a few cases has caused a very powerful breakthrough. You don't need the breathing to do this, but I really suggest you trust me on it and go for broke.

So, first I need you to calm your breathing – you cannot do this exercise while driving or operating machinery or anything like that. Best place to do this is lying down on your bed, but if you are reading this then familiarise yourself with the process, then lie down and go through the motions afterwards. If you can't do this now, then pause here and wait to do this when you can be somewhere comfortable, lying down, with your eyes closed, ideally at the end of the day when the lights are dim and you can be totally relaxed and in a place that you feel comfortable.

---

## Exercise 1.0

Let's go.

### Step 1
Lie down somewhere comfortable and close your eyes.

### Step 2
Begin to be aware of your breathing and count roughly how many seconds between your inhale and exhale.

### Step 3
Slow your breathing down by breathing in and holding your breath for as long as you can, right up until the point you need to suck in a new lungful, but not so long you start to go blue and freak out. Repeat this 5 to 10 times or until you start to notice you have slowed your breathing down.

### Step 4
Now allow your breathing to normalise – the fact that we slowed it down means that the normalised version of your breathing will be slower than your standard resting rate. The ideal amount I have found is 4 Mississippis for inhale and 4 Mississippis for exhale.

## Step 5

Once you have got into the flow of your breathing being much slower, we can begin – make sure your eyes are still closed.

I want you to picture yourself in a dimly lit hospital room. You are lying on a hospital bed in your own private room. It's warm and you have two big pillows behind your head. You are connected to a heart rate monitor and you have wires coming out of you and you're connecting to a drip.

You are weak, weak to the point that you find it a task to even shuffle around the bed to make yourself more comfortable and lifting your arm above your head is almost impossible. Your breathing is slow, long, and drawn out, but the breaths aren't too deep and feel weak. You know you are minutes away from your final breath on this earth. You are scared, anxious, worried, and numb. You are aware that each breath now really matters, but you are so weak that you can't fill your lungs properly.

Surrounding you are the one or two people that matter the most in your life. They are sitting on chairs close to your bed, holding your hands. This might be a parent, lover, friend, child, family member. They too know you are moments away from your final breath. Your breathing remains slow. You begin to feel it. Like a calm, dull, powerful wave covering your body. Your time is nearly up.

You know you will struggle to say anything, but you know you have to. It takes every last fibre and cell in your body to muster up the energy to speak. The person or people surrounding you are so important to you, and you love them so much that you want to tell them one last thing before you can't speak with them again.

Now take a moment, continue your slow, deep breathing.

Picture the dull lit lamp on your bedside table, and the flicker of greeny-yellow from the heart rate monitor. Feel the room, the worry, the sadness and impending loss. The grip of your mum, dad, brother, sister, son, daughter, best friend, lover, partner, husband or wife on your hand getting firmer, grasping at that very, very last time they can hold your hand.

Have you done enough in your life? Did you do the right things? Were you a good person? A happy person? A successful person? Did you live or just exist? You feel the wave again, stronger this time. You have moments left. What would you say to those spending your last moments with you?

Now I want you to slowly begin to come out of this, take as long as you need, but begin to open your eyes and take your mind off of your breathing. Take your time.

You can pause here for a minute if you need.

Now let's talk about the experience you just had. If you are anything like me, this would have been enough to wake you up and your brain should now be racing with ALL the questions! Did I do enough?! Am I doing enough?! Am I happy? Am I making others happy?! Am I a good person?!

---

For those of you that have experienced this already, I am completely sorry for your loss, and as hard as this is to think about, it is important, because it's real!

There are a few things that are absolutely guaranteed in life – and one of them is that at one point, you gon' die. I want to feel confident that when I am in this position, that I can smile to my nearest and dearest and tell them I'm fine, and really mean it and know that I've been my best me. Let's talk about what you would want to say.

So when that is really happening to you, what would you say? I guarantee the first thought that came into your head was either to tell them how much you love them or to apologise for something you did wrong or didn't have the courage to express until you knew you were going to die. Your words would be truthful, and expressive, and meaningful.

There is an amazing bit of footage you can find on YouTube of Randy Pausch, giving his 'last lecture'. The guy, the poor guy, was given only weeks to live, and with kids of his own, and a wife, he professionally, and with calm, talks about the things he realised were the most important in life.

Things he only realised after being diagnosed with a terrible disease that gave him limited time to survive. It is totally worth a watch!

His realisation of 'what's important' I guarantee you is different to the things we think are important from day to day. Our actions often don't replicate what's important. Being healthy, being successful, being a good role model etc. often fall by the wayside to make room for other menial and ultimately unimportant things like getting pissed off you forgot to take the bins out, or whether that person you don't really like likes you back.

So, I ask you, would you say it on your deathbed?!

For every time you freaked out about having no money, for every time you were worried, anxious, fearful, for every time you lied to yourself, for every time you did the wrong thing knowing it was the wrong thing, would you say it on your deathbed? It's a sure-fire way to work out whether you are wasting your thoughts and actions or not.

Here's a list of things you probably worry about on a day-to-day basis, and the same list applies to things you definitely won't think about on your deathbed:

Paying the rent. Paying the bills. Being too fat, thin, too black or white, too tall or short. Too ugly. Getting a parking ticket. Paying a parking ticket. Doing your tax returns. Finding out who the winner is of (insert generic BS celebrity show). Saving a few quid by getting the shitty wine you don't even like, etc., etc., etc., etc., etc., etc.

Fact is, you wouldn't worry about any of these things on your deathbed! They won't even pop into your head. Imagine it now – you've got a few moments left, you can feel it, the doctor has told you that you won't make it through the night, and your family, friends, nearest and dearest are there by your bedside. You are weak. You look at your mum, dad, brother, sister, best friend, partner, son, daughter... you call them closer so they can hear your frail voice: "Come closer, closer, I... am... so sorry... about that time I got a C on my GCSEs when I was predicted a C+." Or: "I... wish... I... had of... changed my ISP from O2 to Virgin because their sports package is better." Or: "I... know... I... never told you... this... but I once had a wank to some transsexual porn!" Or: "I am really glad I sessioned the whole first season of Narcos in one go."

Come the fuck on!!!! You know what you would think about on your deathbed. You would think about big things!!! Love and regrets. If it's not important enough to say on your deathbed, chances are it's not important enough to give your time to now. You wanna leave a legacy, right?!

Reality check! I know it sounds full-on, but one thing I am absolutely certain about is that we all die. I have no idea what happens after, but I know we all gon' die! Full-on is the only way. Go big or go home!!! Just do it. Do shit, get shit done!!! You got the same 24/7 as everybody else, what you gonna do with yours?!?!

I use this reality check most days! It is an amazing hack for getting you out of that funk you keep getting yourself in.

Pissed off because your day didn't go to plan?! Gonna think about it on your deathbed?! Fuck no! Weather is shit, gonna think about it on your deathbed?! Fuck no! That prospect didn't call you back? Gonna think about it on your deathbed?! Fuck no!

Can't get past level 984 of Candy Crush? Gonna think about it on your deathbed?! Fuck no! Failed your driving test? Gonna think about it on your deathbed?! Fuck no!

Stubbed your toe; the restaurant you're at has run out of your favourite starter; wifi isn't working at the coffee shop you are at; accidentally shat yourself in public in front of the person you were just about to ask out and then as you are trying to cover it up you slip on it and land face first in your own poo and as you look up the Google Street View van is taking a picture that will inevitably get passed around the internet of you covered in a face full of your own shit! Gonna think about it on your deathbed?! FUCK NO!

Cheated on your partner; missed huge opportunities; didn't spend quality time with your kid; forgot to tell your mum you love her... Gonna think about it on your deathbed?! Damn fucking straight!!!!

We gotta get our priorities right! Stop listening to the constant crap that everyone is telling you just because someone told them! It's not real!!! It's Chinese whispers and horse shit!!! History books only tell you the story of the person who had enough money or power to have the book written and published! Does not mean for one earth minute that it's true!

---

## Exercise 1.1

Journal, please. I want you to write down a list of ALL the things you do on a day-to-day basis that you would not even think about on your deathbed. And then I want you to write a list of all the things you would think about. If it helps you can just go over the last few hours of your day and categorise the shits you gave that you probably shouldn't have.

You are probably getting to the point where you are writing in your journal WAY more than you initially conceived. For those of you that are not, and for those of you that have not written anything, or don't even own a journal, this is the time to either start the book again with commitment or accept you are screwed and bail. Shit's about to get incredibly real...

## Summary

- Ex 1.0

Deathbed

  − See example

- Ex 1.1

Write down all the things you do daily that you would not think about on your deathbed

  − Go hard here, make sure you get as many things as possible

  − It will help to ask a friend or partner or family member to help you in case you have missed anything

- If you ain't gonna think about it on your deathbed, there is a high chance you don't need to worry about it now

- Everything you will think about on your deathbed will have a direct correspondence to an action or actions you have taken in your life.

# Chapter 17

# Your 10

# Commandments

Love it or hate it, the bible got some things very right! Tesla believed the bible was a multi-faceted instruction manual for life that helped him understand frequency and magnetism and force. Some people think it's an absolute crock, and others live their lives by it. I am not going to start a debate on the bible, but I do wanna extract something from it that is going to benefit you immensely.

In my opinion, the bible has saved as many lives as it has lost, it's on the spectrum, and further to that, its position on the spectrum is dependent on the person reading it, and they are on a spectrum too, which is constantly changing, remember?!

Anyways, now is not the time to blow the mind, it's time to blow up your life! (I've been told very specifically to not put emojis in this book but if I could I would have put the 'gag sick' one there to notify I am obviously joking at that cringe sentence, and while I'm at it, if you know me well you are aware that if I had been allowed to put emojis in this book there would be at least one per sentence, so it is probably for the best) : )

## The 10 commandments of the bible...

Here they are just in case you forgot them or don't know them.

1. You shall have no other Gods but me – handy, that! Cheers, Big G.
2. You shall not make for yourself an idol, nor bow down to it or worship it – Hmmm, I wonder why?!
3. You shall not misuse the name of the Lord your God – You shouldn't misuse anything really...
4. You shall remember and keep the Sabbath day holy – *Digs own grave*
5. Respect your father and mother – Fair!
6. You must not commit murder – Totally fair!
7. You must not commit adultery – Similarly fair!
8. You must not steal – True that!
9. You must not give false evidence against your neighbour – Damn straight!
10. You must not be envious of your neighbour's goods. You shall not be envious of his house nor his wife, nor anything that belongs to your neighbour – I couldn't agree more, envy is a timewaster.

So, the additions to the 10 commandments I added were my own opinions. You should have yours. But what's my point? Well, I believe, and I just want to point out for any of you that don't like people having opinions other than yours, which I should add is completely stupid and one of the best ways to stop growing or learning, I believe that the 10 commandments were not necessarily made for everyone.

Imagine, you are a top CEO, or football manager, or parent... You will always have a specific list of dos and don'ts that you expect your employees, team, or children to adhere to. They are things that make sense to you. How many times have you had a completely different opinion to someone else, whether it's how to run a business, how to run a football team, or how to raise a child?!

How often have you totally disagreed about the way someone else runs their game, but they still seem to be successful? Stop fighting it, you gotta understand that life doesn't have to be just right or wrong, well at least not in equal measure. Like I mentioned before, duality and spectrums exist, but I never said they had to be in equal amounts. Just because cold exists, doesn't mean you have to have cold showers throughout the summer just to make sure you can have hot showers throughout the winter. You also don't have to kill anyone to make sure you don't kill anyone, ya dig?!

Imagine the aeronautic industry if this was the case – 50% of planes would never take off, or have to burrow underground to keep the other 50% flying high in the air. Just because both sides exist, it does not mean you have to do them in equal measure. You can manipulate them to your advantage and live a better life. You hate your job but you love the weekend? Why not love the whole week?

To stay at the right end of the spectrum we have to do a few things:

**Thing 1:** we have to understand there is always the 'other' end of the spectrum, not just the section we are choosing to operate on.

**Thing 2:** we have to understand that to move to a different part of the spectrum, we need to change some stuff – do what you've always done, get what you've always got!

**Thing 3:** we need to use reality checks to keep our ass in line to really utilise the second step.

## Exercise 1.0

I want you to write your own 10 commandments. Initially, I want you to do this for an all-encompassing part of your life, but later we are going to look at the subcategories of our lives and write separate 10 commandments for them!

So, I'll tell you mine – there are a few things I've missed off that I consider to be just blatant common sense. I don't need to write out. "Thou shalt not kick a baby in the face," or, "Thou shalt not watch The Lord of the Rings trilogy every Monday for the next 6 years while spooning with Clive from the library."

So, here's my all-encompassing 10 commandments, and I have printed these out, written them down multiple times, put them on sticky notes on my car windscreen, yadda, yadda, yadda. Here they are, I'll explain them afterwards...

1. Thou shalt never lie to thyself!
2. Thou shalt always make time
3. Thou shalt always do the right thing
4. Thou shalt never sweat the little things
5. Thou shalt always keep moving forward
6. Thou shalt always listen and understand
7. Thou shalt never stitch thyself up
8. Thou shalt always think of the end game
9. Thou shalt always keep thy body and mind in shape
10. Thou shalt always reality check thyself

I have a different set of 10 commandments for each aspect of my life. I have 10 commandments with family, friends, business, motivation, health, and I also change and amend these, depending on what I learn (you gotta keep growing, bitches). I'll give you examples of these in a bit, but for now, let's run through my basic list.

## 1. Thou shalt never lie to thyself!

I realised a long time ago that lying to others is not as it sounds. Instead, it is always you lying to yourself. Like I mentioned before when people say "the world doesn't revolve around you", not only does your world completely revolve around you but only you have the power to change how it revolves. I mentioned I was writing my first book to a friend of mine I hadn't seen in a while. It was a childhood friend and we had a long phone call when he couldn't attend my stag do – definitely another book for another time (that I NEVER want anyone to read, and I definitely won't ever write)!!!

We hadn't seen each other for time but we were high school mates – since we grew up we usually only see each other at Christmas or when I go back to where I grew up to visit.

He asked me what I was doing, and I replied: "I'm writing my first book."

His reaction was, "Woah dude, that's hard, hardly anyone gets a book published, let alone makes any money from it." (Like monetary gain is the only obvious reason to write a book.)

Initially, I was taken aback by this, and in the same way people push their beliefs on others, more often than not based off of something some other tart said, that possibly has no education behind it. This guy has never written a book, and as much as I love him, I know he doesn't really read books either! But he had an opinion. An opinion that could have affected my masterplan, my confidence, and my future actions.

Previously in my life, I had listened to opinions like this and they had all affected me. "You should really do XYZ," or, "My dentist is great," or, "You really should mortgage a house," or whatever. THEY DON'T KNOW! Nobody does, we are ALL winging the shit out of it! FYI I could do ABC instead, your dentist is probably the same as everyone else's dentist – a pain-inflicting D-bag, and mortgage literally translates as 'death gauge', and I ain't owing the bank for 30 years to end up old and "yay, debt-free". But you do you. *Unscripted* is a phenomenal book – recommended read.

You are probably so used to being told what the 'best route' in life is that you may have to think hard to pick out an example, but when you start thinking hard and come up with an example they will start flooding in! Your whole life is made up of decisions based on what other people have told you; people that have had their whole life affected by what other people have told them.

I would never take my car for an MOT with an MIT graduate. Why?! Because unless they majored in mechanics they won't know how to fix my fucking car, no matter how clever they are on paper, or how much time they spent on the debate team. I also wouldn't ask my lothario mates that are single well into their 30s with drink and drug problems to give me relationship or parenting advice. Doesn't mean that they are dumb or wrong, but they will probably have an opinion that isn't as well deserving as I could find from someone that has 5 kids and owns it 'family style'!

I mentioned this previously, you gotta trust your gut/heart/ whatever you call it! If your intentions are good, your gut/heart/whatever will always be real to you. You gotta learn to trust it. We lie to ourselves because we have been brought up to listen to BS, and BS breeds more BS! We start not only BS'ing others but in turn we totally BS ourselves – the cycle continues. We gotta break the cycle.

This commandment, for me, was the most important. Every other commandment and life choice came off the back of this. It took me years to not only acknowledge I was lying to myself, multiple times a day, but to start remedying it. It was a long journey for me and I want to help you get there quicker than I did! I don't want you to lie to yourself any longer! Thou shalt not lie to thyself! Be real!!! Like hyperreal! Like actually real! You know when you're not if you think about it...

## 2. Thou shalt always make time

What do I mean by this? I mean make time for everything that is worth making time for! It's considered normal now to spend our evenings 'relaxing' after a hard day's work. We make time for the Embarrassed To Own apps on our phone, we make time for the porn we watch, the weed we smoke, the time at the bar, the gossiping, the time watching shit TV shows and the time to queue up at McDonald's. We make time to 'like' some sexy pictures on Insta but we don't make time real-liking our own partner enough to make them feel sexy. We make time to eat processed food and microwave meals but we don't make time to educate ourselves on why a new diet might be just the ticket. We spend time worrying and no time on solving. We spend time on feeling fat, and no time losing weight. We spend time on saving and no time generating more revenue. I could go on, you get the picture!

You need to make time for the important things. You are what you eat and you are who you hang around with, and this is also true of the time you spend! If you spend time thinking about quitting your job and starting a business doing something you love, but you don't quit your job then not only do you not have a new business, but you are still working a crappy job wasting your time thinking about how you could start a new business and quit your crappy job.

If you spend time thinking about asking 'that' person out that you've fancied for a while, and you don't do it, then you're still single and wasting your time thinking about the partner you don't have. If you spend your time thinking about the bills you've gotta pay, and you don't spend any time making new money, then you're broke as shit, worried, and you're wasting the time you could be making money thinking about how little money you've got!

You gotta spend time on the things that matter, not what everyone else tells you matters. The things you know deep down that actually matter, matter because they matter! Make sense?! You know you know!! Start trusting it. Just cuz your parents are your parents, or your friends or partner are your friends or partner, doesn't mean they know what's right, and it definitely doesn't mean they know what's right for you. You need to get your kid brain back. Anything was possible, and it still is, you just gotta cut through the shit! You changed, not the opportunities and possibilities! And if you changed, you can change back! Think about it...

## 3. Thou shalt always do the right thing

This sounds more self-explanatory than it actually is. You know what's right, you feel it deep inside, right?! We've established this! Thou shalt do the right thing. What is the right thing?! You know I believe you always know! I ALWAYS know! I know when I'm being a little bitch or a conniving dick head. Whether I change my actions because of this fact is an entirely different thing! I've made too many huge mistakes in my life.

I've lied, I've cheated, I've been addicted to drugs, drink, video games, sex, I've said one thing and done another, and I've overlooked opportunities because of my ego. I've been a certified ass hat for many years of my life. Like I said before: it's not your fault for the way you've been brought up, the situation you are in, the ailments you have or whatever else, but it's damn straight your fault if upon realising, you don't do shit all about it!!!

**4. Thou shalt never sweat the little things** (this is a category with some subcategories attached – lists within lists like the matrix, homes)! FYI I've never said 'homes' before, but it popped into my head and I the last time I heard it was on a GTA SA session so gotta show the love.

What constitutes a 'little thing'? Anything that doesn't warrant thinking about, or something you think warrants thinking about but really doesn't. I had to put this in my 10 commandments! It's so easy to forget what's important and then spend valuable time and effort on it. The repercussions are always completely detrimental. Here's a list of little things I used to sweat that I'm sure you will relate to. Think back to the deathbed chapter...

Paying bills, saving money, cleaning the house, being stuck in traffic, getting a parking ticket, the past, gossip, people that don't like you AKA haters, what other people are doing, making mistakes, the cost of a product or service, getting things 'right'.

I could go on for days! I'm gonna break this list down, but you can apply the general concept to pretty much anything in your life – STOP WORRYING!!! Remember how important your NOW is to make your future pop!

**Paying bills:**

Bills are one of life's guarantees, they are something that very few of us never have to think about, and no matter where you are at in your career, you gonna have to pay the man! I used to be scared to open my own mail; so scared, in fact, I would often put it in a pile to open tomorrow, and keep that rolling until I got paid, then open it, just to be safe! But in reality 'safe' just meant out of control. This is no way to live.

This is fear! Not the same kinda fear as having your left nut auctioned off to a sketchy 3rd-party deep web buyer, or being Mexican and having to spend a night at Donald Trump's house where all you can wear is a Borat mankini and a hat that says 'America Sucks' on it, but fear is fear. It affects our decisions, and unless it is used to our advantage, which in my case it definitely wasn't, it is an absolute killer! Anyway, you either run your bills, or they run you! One thing I learned the hard way was that everything is an opportunity. Lemme tell you my 'prison' analogy to prove this point.

Answer as quickly as you can...yes or no...

Would you ever want to go to prison?

I am guessing the majority of you said 'no'. I can't blame you. From what the media tells us, and the movies we watch, prison seems like a pretty horrible place. Now I am not for one moment saying that people don't have a really bad time in prison, but I am saying not everyone does. So more importantly, why wouldn't you want to go to prison? You'd miss your family, friends, lover, kids? Get assaulted, get bum assaulted, have no freedom, feel shame?

There's a bunch of reasons that you wouldn't want to go to prison. Well, I can tell you most of you are in prison now! I was!! For most of my life. The devil's best trick is making people think he doesn't exist.

But I bet you've never thought of the pros... There is an opportunity in everything. Either just watch Shawshank Redemption, or imagine this. You get put in prison, 10 years let's say. Long-time! But it ain't life. You finally have the time to study, the time to perfect a skill or skills.

The same rules apply in prison as anywhere else, you are in control of your actions. The confines may be different, but your actions are still yours. Let's say your prison warden is the person of your dreams. You get to know them, you fall in love with them. Game changer! Prison found you love, baby! Now let's take your average day. Is it phenomenal? The point I'm making is that being scared of something before you know what it is, how it could benefit you, or any other awesome thing is a waste of time, and a bit dumb.

Open the bills, pay the bills, spend your time you would usually fanny about worrying about the bills to work out how to make more money! Bills are now an opportunity to reality check you into the realisation that you don't have enough money!

## Saving money:

How often have you said something like: I just need to save up, or, I would love to but I don't have the funds, or, I am gonna save up and get it, whatever it may be. The worry about saving money needs to be flipped. It's not about how much money you save, or your outgoings, it's about how much new money you can bring in. If you want to buy a new car, not just a shit-heap, but the car of your dreams, the car you haven't even gone to test drive because you know you will never be able to afford it.

Your past money is past money. Your future money hasn't been obtained yet, and your now is spent worrying about the money you don't have. You need to flip that switch! Your now needs to be: get new money. There's more money in circulation than you could currently imagine.

Did you know, if you equally divided all the money currently in circulation in the world between every single person in the world, that everyone would be a billionaire? Yes, I said it right. There's that much gold coin in the world. Where's yours at?! Why aren't you getting your piece of the pie?! Well, the same reason I wasn't. And the same reason 99.9% of the population ain't got theirs either!

Saving is something you wanna do if you're stuck in the desert with one bottle of water. But this does not relate to your money. Your income needs to exceed your outgoings, not by a little, but by a lot! A penny saved is... err... a fucking penny!!! Spending our now working out ways to make new money allows your savings to take care of themselves. More on this later...

**Cleaning the house:**

Lemme ask you this, do you want to be a cleaner?! Next question, how much time do you spend cleaning each day or week?! There is absolutely nothing wrong with being a cleaner, it is a very noble profession, but I imagine the large majority of you never answered the 'what do you wanna be when you grow up?' question with 'cleaner'. It's a waste of your time.

Get a cleaner!! Your house has to be in order, it is a by-product of you being in control of your own life, but sweeping your floor, vacuuming, wiping down surfaces and taking out the trash are taking your now away from things that could make you enough money to employ a cleaner and leave your mind to focus on building your empire and not the dirty laundry.

The stress and distraction of waking up to a disgusting kitchen, cluttered desk, car, bedroom or kitchen takes our mind away from the important things. If you are one of those people that says "it really doesn't bother me", then I am telling you right now that you are not in control of your shit and it should bother you.

How often do you misplace things, then waste time and effort finding them?! Out of control. You need to know where your shit goes man! That's a slightly different story, but I'm telling you, spend your time on things that will make your life better. Cleaning is not one of them! Are you gonna think about it on your deathbed?! I think not...

## Being stuck in traffic:

This is a short one. Utilise traffic time! If you know your commute is often long and frustrating then it's because you are not using it to your advantage. When I first got together with my partner, she lived across the country; 3-4 hours' drive away to be exact. I used to drive to see her, so my round trip was often upwards of 8 hours just sitting in a car. God, I used to hate that drive. I would sit in the same position for hours straight.

I wanted to start making the journey worthwhile. I couldn't practice the drums, but I could practice vocals. I started using the time to do vocal warm-ups, practice, and song learning. I promised myself I would never do a journey again where I didn't get something positive out of it. I started listening to audiobooks. I started looking forward to the drive time each week. My 8-hour drive was now a 2-hour rehearsal and a 6-hour education. Game changer!! Use your time to your benefit. Everything is an opportunity.

## Getting a parking ticket:

We all hate parking tickets. They suck. Where I come from they are £35 and go up to £75 if you don't pay within 2 weeks. I would often leave my car on double yellows, unloading for gigs, or just to pop into a shop because I couldn't be bothered to park a mile away and walk. The worst I ever got was 3 tickets on the same day!!!

Idiot! Well, actually the idiocy didn't come until after I got the tickets. Here are my stages of parking ticket realisation: Anger, annoyance, freak out (because I was broke and didn't want to pay for them), acceptance. Upon acceptance, I would do one of two things. I would either pay to make sure I didn't go over the 2-week period before the price jumped up, or I would contest the ticket. Every now and again I would win the contention, and I would feel like a legend, and then waste my now telling whoever was near about my accomplishment!

Idiot!!!!

What I didn't realise then is the time and effort it takes to get out of a £35 parking ticket. Because at the time £35 was a lot to me. Nine times out of 10 it was the amount that would push me overdrawn, and then I would freak out about that. Believe me on this, if £35 is an amount you are worried about losing, you will struggle to make bare! You gotta change that thought process that you've been brought up with. Do you think Richard Branson is bothered about paying for a parking ticket?

**The past:**

It's happened, get over it and make your future better! That's it. Dwell on your past and your now is screwed, which in turn gives your future absolutely nowhere to go. That time you said the wrong thing, or told a lie, or cheated, or whatever (unless it's really bad, then shame on you!). All these things are part of life and growing up, even with the best intentions ever, nobody gets it all right! Learn to deal with the fact that you are transitioning constantly, and your tomorrow is waaaay more important than your yesterday!

**Gossip:**

Just stop it! If your life is that boring that you need to get involved in someone else's then you are by no means anywhere near your full potential. You know when there's a car crash on the motorway and the traffic grinds to a halt, and you realise that the only reason it slowed down is that everyone is looking at the wreck on the hard shoulder, and then you get past it and get back up to full speed. I hate that shit! Rubberneckers!! I've got too much exciting stuff I'm doing that I don't even think about looking!

I totally feel for the people in the crash, that's not what I'm saying.

I'm saying someone else's life will never slow mine down. Stop gossiping, stop being interested in other people's lives over your own. It will never get you anywhere. If you get excited about the latest celebrity scandal, or what's happening on your favourite show over your own life then you're wasting your time.

I don't mean don't be aware, that's totally different, you have to understand your surroundings, but when you start living your life, like really start living it, you won't have time to think about anyone else's. Sound selfish?! Nowhere near as selfish as wasting your gifts! Especially wasting them to watch some silicon idiot with no skill crying about their makeup!

## People that don't like you AKA haters:

We are gonna smash this hater thing later on, but here's a little bit... I know this one well. I spent the majority of my life trying to be liked. I hated it when I knew someone didn't like me, even if I didn't like that person! Crazy!!! Look, you gotta have haters. And not everyone is going to like you, or agree with you. But it's often only for a certain amount of time, and definitely not absolute. You would have had it before when you hated someone and then became besties or lovers.

Or loved someone, or thought you did, and then realised they were a total ass hat?! Or hated or loved an activity, TV show, movie or sport and then ended up feeling the opposite about it? Only the truthful can understand that it doesn't matter. What I mean by that is that when you start being true to yourself, you realise that you are you, and some people love it, and some hate it. In most cases, some love it sometimes, and some hate it sometimes. Spectrums. Think about your best friend or partner, or mum or dad, or kid, or boss. You may love them most of the time, but every now and again you want to kill them!

The other thing about haters... you need them! I've got a whole chapter for you coming up later on how important this is, but for now, let's crack on with your commandments...

## What other people are doing:

Why do you care about what other people are doing? They have a bigger house, a better relationship, they seem happier, they seem luckier, they are setting up their 4th business and you haven't even started your first... Etc., etc. The only reason you are thinking about what other people are doing is that you aren't obsessed with what you are doing! You can't get anywhere without being obsessed enough to make it happen!

When you are in full control of your ship you won't have time to think about other people's successes, just like someone else's crash, you'll drive straight past it. Doesn't mean you don't care, it means for the first time ever you are caring for yourself, and as a great man once said: "If you can't love yourself, then ain't nobody else gonna love you!!" I think it was Ru Paul just FYI (my missus used to watch his show, honest).

Cut the BS, other people's lives are other people's lives, they are not yours, we need you in control. Once you take control of your own life, people will start to follow you, not the other way around! The only positive thing you can take from other people's lives is to commend them for their successes! Don't be a jelly belly! If someone is absolutely killing it, tell them you noticed! Have their back, it's surprising what you can get out of being a cheerleader!

## Making mistakes:

I am gonna say this twice so it sticks: you have to make mistakes. Again... you HAVE to make mistakes!!! Perfectionism is another way of saying procrastination. You say you're making sure it's right but nothing is perfect and you're just wasting time.

What do I mean?! For every moment you are perfecting something, someone is getting paid and laid for putting out a lesser version. Why??? Because actions speak louder than words! You wanna ask the girl or guy on a date but everything needs to be perfect: guess what?! While you were checking your hair, breath or swag, someone like me was getting a BJ in the toilets! Oooooo!!! Not old me though! Definitely not!

We are told to aim for perfection. It does not exist! Again, IT DOES NOT EXIST!!! And as a side note, those people who told you to aim for perfection, I swear down they are not perfect!!

Look at the iPhone or any computer OS, or your car. There are bits that don't work, there are bugs, there are completely annoying issues. Issues you put up with daily AFTER buying the said product! You still bought the phone, or a computer or car.

Your partner has imperfections. Your kid, your job, your body all have imperfections. And on top of that, beauty is in the eye of the beholder! So your perfect is a trillion miles away from someone else's. You have to make mistakes!!! But the key is not to dwell on them, instead, we need to understand that they are an integral part of the growing process. Remember that kid at school whose parents had wrapped them in cotton wool, they grew up scared of everything and never took risks! Do not do this to your own kids.

Terrorism only works if you let it. I'm not saying give your kids a gun and some heroin and leave them to it, that's just dumb, but don't be scared of them playing at the park just in case there could be a paedophile around. You can't live in fear, and you must make mistakes. Learning from your mistakes is part of the course and it's worth getting used to it and enjoying it!

## The cost of a product or service:

Stop moaning about the price of stuff. When was the last time you moaned about the price of something? The coffee you had earlier? The last movie you went to see? The restaurant you took your partner to on their birthday? Well, that coffee was flown from the other side of the world to get to you, the movie cost literally millions to make, and your partner deserves it!!! How can you moan about the price of a cinema ticket but pay £5 for a pint of average beer?! Or £30 cuz you've drunk 6 beers?! Haha!

If you are running a business (your life), you must own the product you are selling (your life), you need to believe and be sure that your product warrants its price!

Again, we will talk about this later, but I want to point out now that you do not have to pay for something if you don't want to! Nobody is making you. Stop moaning!!! Think of it like this: you pay a cleaner £15 ph to clean your house, it takes 3 hours pw, so each month you are paying £180 pm to keep your house clean. For most of you listening, this will sound barmy! "Where the flip am I gonna get another near £200 to pay for this?!"

That's little you thinking! We need big, courageous, crazy you instead!! You are thinking about money, and I am thinking about the time. In the 12 hours pm you are saving from cleaning your own house, I am making 12 hours of calls and finding new business or writing a book, or playing more gigs, things that can make me bank! £200 pm is NOT bank!! You gotta be clever man! Flip your thinking, if it's not currently working then you gotta shift. Do what you've always done, get what you've always got!

## Getting things 'right':

This is similar to the making mistakes part of this list. Right is not a

189

thing! I mean, with regards to right and wrong then of course. But for what we are talking about, it's non-existent. Getting things wrong is sooo much better. You learn quicker when you get things wrong. Then you can make them right, or as right as you can. Real talk: you can never be right, just slightly less wrong!

Think of your favourite movie, I bet you there are mistakes in it.

It's still your fav movie! Some of my favourite songs have absolute clangers in them, still my favourite songs! My partner has loads wrong with her, haha, sorry cherub, but she is still my one and only! My kid is a moron sometimes/most of the time, but he is my life! Right doesn't work, it hasn't worked for you yet. I have a friend that is always 'right', and he's broke as shit, in a horrible relationship and he's lost all of his friends because of it, but hey, at least he is always right! Let's get some stuff wrong and learn from it.

---

I could add a bunch more to this list of 'little things' but I think you get the point now! Back to our main commandments!

---

## 5. Thou shalt always keep moving forward

You wanna go forward or backwards? It's that simple! You win a race by going forward. You gotta win your race, my dude! It's not a question, it's a statement! What do I mean by this? Well, if you cut your life into fairly obvious sections: love life, business life, family life, health etc. Do you wanna move forward with these or go backwards? Or even worse, stay stagnant?! Stagnant is the worst cuz it means you're not moving at all!

Anyway, you gotta move forward, transition, change and be malleable. I have to check myself on this one often, like daily. It's so easy to stagnate, especially with all the distractions we have to deal with on the day-to-day! Be prepared but never prepare! Anything can change in a split second, you gotta be ready to take that call and say yes, with no deliberation! Even when it seems like there is nothing to move forward on, I bet if you think hard enough you can pick something out! You gotta keep going! Constantly, always! Move forward while everyone else moves backwards or stands still and you'll find yourself leagues apart from your 'competition'.

## 6. Thou shalt always listen and understand

I mean really listen, and really understand. Understanding more often than not means changing YOUR way of thinking. To truly comprehend something you have to spend time and effort educating yourself. You cannot know stuff to a high enough level to have an opinion on it if you don't understand it, and you won't understand it if you haven't committed time and effort to it.

One of my old drum students once said: "How much do you charge for a studio session?"

I told him and he almost gagged (FYI it is industry standard, it was just a lot considering he was 17 and broke as shit). He then said, "What, even if you're just playing something really simple?!"

"Yup," I said.

He then said, "But even I can play really easy beats!"

I replied, "Yeah, you can, but I've been playing them for 20 years and you've been playing them for 3!"

We love to know what we're talking about! Even when we don't know – this ties in with 'thou shalt not lie to thyself'. Why would you wanna give someone the wrong directions to a place when they ask just so it seems like you know what you're talking about. Why would you say your dentist is better than theirs when you don't actually know!? Why would you tell me to support your political or religious beliefs when you don't know! It's not helpful, or clever! It's a dick move, dick!

Now relate that to things that affect you – if you have the symptoms of a serious illness, do you really want your doctor to lie to you about what it is just so they feel good about being a doctor?! Of course not, you want them to admit they don't know and refer you to a specialist so you can get your shit sorted! I know this is true because I used to be that guy! I would think I'd listened, but instead, while someone was trying to tell me something I would be thinking about how to get my point across – this isn't listening!

I also notice it when I am trying to explain things to others – you can see the cogs turning while they are trying to work out a way to prove you are wrong and they are right! Well, I don't believe both parties have to be split into wrong and right, I believe you can both be right, and enrich each other's lives if you just learn to listen and understand! You can always get something positive out of any situation; some take more work and dedication than others, but the way I see it if you're not getting something out of something, then why are you even giving it your time?

How many times does your partner, loved one or family member tell you something and you disregard it? It meant something to them, the least you can do is listen. More so, how many times have you figured something out for yourself a long time after someone had been trying to explain that very thing to you. You do not have to be the most intelligent person in the room, far from it, you have to be willing to learn, listen and understand.

When I employ people I never even ask them about what their GCSEs, A-Levels, or degree grade was. I don't care, it means nothing! Some of the most wise people I know are the most stupid on paper! Ya dig?! There is a humongous difference between intelligence, knowledge, and wisdom. And I want wisdom! Learn to listen. Here's an exercise you can do to prove to yourself how much you want to get your point across...

For the next 24 hours, refrain from saying 'I'. Bet you can't keep it up! We have been brought up to get our opinion across no matter what, because everyone else is trying to get their opinion across. Does not for one minute mean the opinion is correct! Hitler tried to get his opinion across FFS!! When we make time to listen and learn instead of forcing our own opinions (which may very well be completely wrong), we grow! And as another little hack, spend your time listening to people who are where you want to be, people that have already done it! Their knowledge and wisdom are more powerful than you can imagine!

## 7. Thou shalt never stitch thyself up

I don't know if this translates to all you guys across the pond, or in Oz, or wherever else you are, but in England, a stitch-up is an act of knowing full well you are doing something detrimental to someone and doing it anyway, usually for your own personal gain – in reality, this won't gain you anything.

This could be something kinda funny like swapping the salt for sugar – mini stitch-up, or something much more sinister, like swapping the salt for crystal meth – diabolical stitch-up!! Stitching someone else up is lame as hell unless it's really funny, then it's just really funny! Stitching yourself up though, man, that is a travesty!

Why? Because it's another form of lying to yourself! It won't get you anywhere! I reality check myself on this so often. Am I stitching myself up? If I get a phone call on the way to the gym and my friend says, "Dude, I'm at the bar, you wanna hang?" I know full well that my intention was to go to the gym, and if I go to the bar it won't be just one, I'll end up there till God knows when, but I say yes – instant gratification, ultimate self-stitch-up.

Snooze button on your alarm – instant stitch-up. Turning up for an appointment or meeting late – classic stitch-up! Look, man, these are not stitching others up, well they are but that's not the important part of this, they are stitching you up!

When you subscribe to a service on the premise of first month free, X amount thereafter, and you know you are gonna forget to cancel the subscription before they start wiping your account and you don't set a reminder to cancel the sub – are you stitching up Amazon Prime, or are you stitching yourself up?

When you choose to work a job you hate because you 'need' the regular income are you stitching yourself, or stitching the boss!? You, you big silly goose!!! When you ignore your to-do list just because it's the weekend – massive stitch! C'mon! The world will stitch you up enough times, all that luck that is out of your hands, that will happen regardless, don't do it to your goddamn self!

That's just crazy. Netflix and chill – stitch-up, it's costing you money, time, and prosperity! I'm not saying don't kick back from time to time, but you need to deserve it first! If you're going to watch the game but choosing the worst seats possible, with the worst view, just because they are within your price range, then you haven't worked hard enough to warrant even going to the game!

You need to be at the front, G! If you are going on holiday and choosing your hotel based on the fact it's all-inclusive so you will save money, I'm sorry to break it to you, you haven't worked hard enough to be taking time off. And for those of you saying, "I love a good all-inclusive," I bet you haven't smashed it in a 5 star+ after making 'nuff cash from hard work... Now not only are you stitching yourself up, but everyone else that's stitching themselves up has given you a precedent, and it's based on their own stitch-ups – mental!

You gotta be cool to yourself, and that means being true, doing the right thing, and it damn sure means not making your life any harder than it already is! Stop lying to yourself and others and take responsibility. Get rid of the stitch-ups!

## 8. Thou shalt always think of the end game

Like I mentioned previously, I have different sets of 10 commandments for different aspects of my life, and not all of these will apply to you. I am just trying to get you to understand you need to give yourself some rules to live by. If you don't, then you are trusting some trash puking idiot on TV to give you theirs!

Anyway, this one works for me! I need to remind myself of the end game. Why I am doing the things I'm doing?! You have to be ethical in your decisions. If you're talking about making your first million because you wanna get loaded and sleep with hookers then you are doing it for the wrong reasons. If you wanna make your first million because you want to start a charity, or help your ill nan or something like that, well then the hunger for money is fair!

I like watches, I dunno why, I just do: I went out for coffee with a dear friend recently and I was wearing a new watch. He said, "Shit dude, how much was that?!" And then went on to tell me how he thought watches were stupid because he had the time on his phone. I just like watches, what can I say?! We got into a massive chat about spending money and his opinion was that spending money on things you don't need is a waste.

I believe there is an element of truth to this, but this boils down to doing things for the right reason. This particular friend spends money on loads of things I think are waste but it's cool. I remember the first nice thing I ever bought myself. It was a black suit jacket that cost quite a bit more than my usual 'cheapest suit possible' jacket.

I had my arm twisted into buying it because another friend kept rinsing me on my dress sense. He would laugh that none of my clothes were tailored and at the time I thought he was an idiot for thinking this was important. One day he caught me at the right time and took me out to buy a jacket, promising me it would make a positive change to my life. I got the jacket, I wore it out of the shop and immediately I felt more confident. I'd never worn anything like it, it actually fit! It looked shit hot! I was getting smiles while walking down the street and that same day I landed a really big deal with a company I had been trying to close for a while. Now I am not for one moment saying this win was down to the jacket, it's a fucking jacket! I am saying though, that in the same way a new haircut, or clean car or desk, or new shoes make you feel good, it had made me feel good enough to feel confident enough to make a phone call I wouldn't have usually made. Now, this is all stupid unless there is a point, and there is. I give money to charity, but I can give more if I make more. Why would I want to help my immediate family, 2 people, when I could help them and another 50, or 500, or 5k or 5mil?!

The end game!

You gotta be true to the cause! I'm not saying you have to want to cure cancer or Alzheimer's just to start a business or buy a new jacket or watch, but it does help! If you are like me, and you want your family to be safe, happy, protected and healthy, then you base your life around these needs. You work to support them.

Your end game might be to help your local school, church or charity, it might be to get your confidence back, it might be to be healthier or to kick a drug habit. It doesn't matter how big or small the end game is but it has to be there, and it has to be ethical to you. I will go into detail later about investing in yourself, but now let's hit these last two commandments.

## 9. Thou shalt always keep thy body and mind in shape

This is a huge one! And before I drop the next couple of sentences I want to say this is NOT directed at people with actual diseases that prevent them from exercising, absolutely no offence is meant here.

You gotta be fit, body and mind! No excuses. I am gonna piss a lot of you off here, but I have been on the other side, and I know what I know! You cannot be truly happy if you're fat, and I mean your brain too, not just your body. There, I said it. Hear me out. I am not saying you can't absolutely kill it if you are overweight – some of my favourite people are chubsy-wubsy.

What I am saying though is that unless you are choosing to eat unhealthily and not exercise for a completely warranted reason (is there one?!), then you are not in control of your body and mind. Would you want to be a billionaire and super successful in business if your relationships always fell apart and you had a drug addiction?

Or, you are an amazing parent, but you don't have a penny to your name. Or your body is in the best condition it can be, but you don't have any confidence. If you can't choose what you eat, and when you eat it, then you are not in control. I weighed 20 stone when I was 15 years old, for those of you that don't work in stone, then another way of putting it is that I was a fucking fatass! I didn't realise how unhappy I was until I got trim.

If you have never been healthy then don't be a hater and tell yourself it's not better, prove it to yourself. Get healthy, eat well, and look after yourself and then have an opinion. It will change your life! There is SOOOO much research into the benefits of healthy nutrition and a strong body – see for yourself online.

## 10. Thou shalt always reality check thyself

I don't think I need to explain this. It's kinda an all-encompassing commandment. If you are aware and mindful of yourself, your surroundings, and your goals, then you will be on track, way faster than if you don't. Ever taken a wrong turn? It takes longer to get where you're going, you still end up where you were going, but it often causes a whole new bunch of issues.

Take a wrong turn on the motorway with hardly any fuel, the petrol station was just off the exit you just missed, then you're gonna run out of fuel. Then your car is stuck, you gotta call RAC or AA, you gotta wait, it ruins your plans and makes you angry. Why did you miss the turning? Cuz you weren't paying attention! Pay attention! It's your life after all. If you don't pay attention to it, hardly anyone else will...

So, these were my standard 10 commandments. Did they help you? I'd absolutely love to hear yours! Hit me up and let me know!

If you wanna start small then try 3 commandments, or 5. But aim for 10!

The more you write your commandments out, the more they will stick in your mind and you'll start living your life by them. Post them on your social to help others too!

Now we have spent a lot of time so far writing things down. What we are doing here is investing in our future, and I wanna go into detail about this now...

---

## Summary

- Ex 1.0

Your 10 commandments

  - Write overall commandments that you feel are integral to your life

- – Make sure these commandments are beneficial to everyone and not just yourself
- – You can change your 10 commandments as you progress through your life

- It is integral to reality check yourself, it is easy to be distracted and autopilot off course

- Use your commandments to earth you and keep you on the straight and narrow

- Don't be afraid to print them out and stick them on your fridge or wall or whatever. If they are good your nearest and dearest will follow them.

# Chapter 18

# When You Point

# The Finger...

You will probably have heard this expression before: when you point the finger, there's 3 pointing back at you! I love this expression, and I live my life by it. For those of you that haven't heard this before, or it doesn't make sense, just make a classic finger-point hand gesture, with your thumb towards the sky and your index finger stretched out as your pointing tool.

You'll notice your three remaining fingers are all focused directly at you.

A gorgeous physical depiction showing that every time you blame someone else for something, there is probably a high chance there are a few reasons you may be wrong, or at the very least not 100% right.

Real talk: knowledge is power, well, it's potential power! I am sure you can all think of those super horrible moments when we realise we are wrong. Even worse, when you know full well you are wrong and don't own it. That's a different story for another time but while we're on it, don't do that! It's hyper lame and makes you a stinky butt poopy face.

If you think back to our two types of luck and eradicate the one that is actually just luck, you're left with the luck that we create for ourselves. You can create this kind of luck by learning, pushing yourself, working at yourself, investing in yourself, and admitting that there's always a high chance there is often more to a situation than initially meets the eye.

Who do you think is luckier? The guy or girl that sings in their bedroom or shower or the guy or girl that starts performing in front of people?! Even if the latter singer is way worse than the former, they will still have a much higher likelihood of 'making it'. You can't get good at anything without first being shit at it.

You can apply this basic analogy to anything! Have you ever said or heard anyone say one of the following?

1. Dieting doesn't work for me
2. I'm just no good at (insert skill)
3. I would but...
4. I'll do it later/tomorrow
5. It's easy for them because...
6. I just don't have time
7. 'So and so' made it impossible...

I could go on but the list started making my tummy churn! When I quit smoking I kept telling myself, "Ahh better not quit today, I've got (insert event) next week, and I find it hard not to smoke at (insert event), so I'll get that out of the way and then stop after."

Like I said before, don't make decisions that aren't going to be for life. They need to be life changes and not diets or whims. You can make tweaks as and when you need to, but commit from the start and tweak later! Just start!

So STOP pointing the finger. Most of the time when we have a dispute, or difference of opinion, we are never absolutely right or wrong. Spectrums! Without having the complete understanding of the other person's argument, experience, and life you will never see it even close to how they do, and vice versa. Instead of using excuses and diversion tactics let's get down to the real problem behind why your life isn't where you want it to be... you.

I totally understand that some of us are dealt the shittiest of shitty hands and sometimes life is completely unfair, heartbreaking and tragic. But no matter what trials and tribulations you have had to overcome, they have all happened, and now we need to look to the future to work out what we need to focus on in our now.

Like I've said a bunch of times, we need to take responsibility for ourselves.

Nobody else will trust me on this! When we point the finger it is our way of passing the buck. If you think about it logically, why would you even want to waste your precious time blaming someone or something else? Either step up and fix the problem or shut up and crack on with your own shit.

We all know someone, or multiple people, that don't take responsibility for their own lives. Problem is these people are surrounding you too, and that's without the media getting involved and forcing you to believe that it is okay to moan about things without fixing them, especially things that really don't matter. Do you actually really care about most of the things you are expelling energy on?!

It's worth taking the time to work it out:

## Exercise 1.0

Here are some questions for you, and as always, answer honestly and without too much deliberation.

1. Are you aware of when you moan, point the finger, or blame?
2. Can you think of the last time you moaned, pointed the finger, or blamed?
3. Can you remember a time when you completely believed something and then found out you were wrong (and did you admit it...)?
4. Do you notice when a friend, partner or family member is wasting their time on issues that really don't matter?
5. Do you have an excuse for why XYZ didn't work for you?

If my knowledge of humanity is correct, there are some of you that not only didn't answer those questions honestly but even worse, as you are hearing me call you out on it you are still not willing to admit to yourself the problem might just be you and take responsibility! Even though you know you are being a dick. I hate that! I have spent so much of my time on earth being a dick, so I know how you feel.

It's a waste!

For those of you that did answer those questions honestly, YEAH!!! GO YOU!!! You are one step closer to your new life. For those of you that didn't, and are aware that you are being a dick, you can start to remedy this immediately by saying out loud, right now: "I am a dick."

I promise I am not asking you to do this cuz it is funny for me – I mean it is, it really is, but on the real, it will be the benchmark for future progression. Go on, do it. Shout it out if you want, it will help! Plus you will probably smile to yourself afterwards, which is nice.

Right, so we need to set not playing the victim as a life goal and not just something that gets forgotten. It needs to be added to your daily goals. Make one of your goals something like: "I always take responsibility for my actions and always try to understand other people's points of view, and if I don't, then I acknowledge I am a complete dickhead face."

Once you begin to notice people with 3 fingers pointed back at themselves you will start to hear it everywhere! It is like a vicious virus. It has plagued our world, but unlike a virus, it is immediately curable with a simple change of mindset. You can start this now! Commit to taking responsibility for your own life and stop being a martyr to everyone else's.

Cool things that happen when you stop pointing the finger:

1. You will begin to feel like less of a dick, which sounds funny, but is actually an awesome feeling!
2. You will begin to see things differently and for the better.
3. You will free up phone-brain storage space which you can then fill up with stuff that actually matters and moves you forward.
4. You will begin to come across to people like a winner – you will not believe how quickly you can change someone's opinion of you by taking responsibility. It's crazy!


One specific story comes into my head while I am thinking about all this: I was tutoring a troubled student once. He had been taking the course below the one I ran. It is aimed at the same age but is the B option for students that didn't do too well in school, meaning they couldn't get straight on to the course I was running (I disagree with this process FYI).

I noticed this kid while he was on that course, and overheard him playing the drums a few times across the year. He had the potential to be really good, as does everyone, but it was so obvious that he was not happy, or being pushed, and ultimately had no idea what he was doing. His grades and attendance always reflected this, and he was close to being kicked off the course multiple times throughout the academic year. All of his regular teachers would vex on him in the staff room and say he was a lost cause and a rubbish student.

In true 'Good Lee' form, I saw this as an opportunity to help. My first meeting with him was when he wanted to move up onto my course. The process to do this is that a prospective student has to have an interview/audition with the course leader in which they will be asked questions, asked to perform, and also show their current work or qualifications.

On my way to the interview, one of my then-colleagues said: "Oh God, good luck with him..." Let's call him Bradley for ease of explanation. "...Good luck with Bradley, he's one of my level 2 students and he is a nightmare."

For me, this was a green light to see how I could help. I am always early (early is on time), and his interview was meant to be at 10am. It got to 10:10 and he still hadn't turned up. I waited 5 more minutes and then left the room. My next interview wasn't until 11am so I went to grab a coffee from the canteen.

I saw him chilling with his mates. As I clocked him, he had that sorry look on his face – you know the one, a mixture of realisation that he had missed his interview, embarrassment that he had been caught, and cog-turning thought processes of how to get out of this immediate situation he was now in. He was living up to my colleague's initial "good luck with him" statement, but why was he acting like this?

That college has some of the best equipment and studios in the whole country, and I would have killed for that when I was starting out, so it couldn't be that. He had support (or I thought he did) from the other lecturers and staff, so it couldn't be that!" What could it be? I figured it must be something else and I wanted to find out what so I could work out a way to help.

I asked him to come for his interview even though he had missed his slot and we sat down and chatted. He was shy but it was very apparent right from the outset that he had been dealt a shit hand in his early years, and following in the footsteps of most people, was blaming everyone else for it and had given up. I asked him where he wanted to be in 5 years. It took me a while to get him thinking bigger than, "Err, a job in music I guess," but after some careful prodding, we managed to ascertain that he would love to be a YouTube drummer and in a touring band.

He was reluctant to admit it because, as with all of us, not only had he previously spent minimal or no time thinking about his future, but more importantly, he deemed it impossible so not worth contemplation. We got stuck in and I helped him write a 1-year plan and you could literally see his eyes lighting up as we spoke about 'how to' and not 'why not'.

Now, this wasn't all to do with the fact we were talking about a passion he had now starting to seem possible, but also the fact that someone was interested in him and willing to cheerlead. I asked him why he thought previously that these dreams he had were not worth giving his time, and he responded like nearly every one of my students does on a first meeting: "It's too hard, I won't succeed, I'm not good enough, I don't have time," etc.

This is finger-pointing at its worst. Man, it's bad if you're pointing the finger to get off the hook of some hairbrained thing you done did, but it's really bad if you are pointing the finger at yourself, and the remaining three fingers are pointing everywhere else – it's messy and confusing, and ultimately makes you feel like shit, and then you give up.

I worked regularly with Bradley, and by the end of the first 2 weeks he had not only taken the steps to begin making his dream a reality, but he was implementing massive amounts of action to get there. At the start of the year, nobody wanted to work with him because of his previous track record, but after a month he was being asked to be in bands left, right and centre. He went from hardly attending classes to never missing a class. He went from turning up late to sitting outside the classroom 15 minutes before the lesson practising with his drumsticks on his knees. He went from doing nothing, no promotion, to posting 4 or 5 videos a day on social media.

He bugs the shit out of me, this kid – I get a text message from him 3 or 4 times a day asking for new things to do, and advice. What an absolute legend! He is only 18 now but he is on the path to dominate the industry he is going into. The rest of our faculty couldn't believe the change, and after getting to know Bradley better I found out his home life was hard.

He had no father figure and he helped look after his mum by working in his free time and giving her the money he'd earnt for rent and groceries and shit. The kid is a don! And all it took was a little bit of cheerleading to help him to stop pointing the finger and start just getting on with stuff.

The thing about the finger point is that it's always about stuff that has already happened and never about solutions. So how similar are you to Bradley? I asked you at the start of this chapter to think about how often you point the blame and ignore responsibility. This should be blatantly obvious now and you will be noticing others partaking in the blame game all over the shop.

So how do we move forward? Well, with action of course. We need to change the way we think and take responsibility. One of the most apparent things I've noticed about the super successful is that they are always learning, and will always own their shit. They haven't got time to point the finger because they are either too busy reppin' their own lives, or they are immediately figuring out solutions to the problems they face. We all screw up – own it, fix it, move on!

---

Here are some examples of things that constitute a finger point and I'll go through these after I've listed:

1. Well, I would have but...
2. It's not that easy for me...
3. They always get... and I don't
4. The traffic was bad...
5. I'm ill...
6. I'm too tired...
7. I'm broke...

Again, I could go on, but let's tackle these – I'm sure you can think of a bunch more.

## Well, I would have but...

But what?! But you didn't, or haven't, or won't! The obvious thing to put after this sentence is an excuse, and by now you can probably guess how I feel about excuses. They take time and energy and guess what? They do sweet FA for your life.

## It's not that easy for me...

Why?! What is different about you? Let me talk to you about easy and hard. And just as aforethought, I hate when people say "it's too hard", or "it's really easy". You know the difference between easy and hard?! Commitment and work. Everything you find easy now was once almost impossible – you learned it, spent time perfecting it, and now you can do it. It's that simple. If you say something is too hard, what you are really saying is "I haven't worked at it enough to make it easy", and similarly, if it is easy, then you have spent a commendable amount of time on it, be proud of it, and then use your knowledge of it to help others!

## They always get... and I don't

*"They always get opportunities that I don't."*

*"They are in a better position than me."*

*"They just have it easier."*

*"They don't have the same problems I have."*

Blah, blah, blah, blah, blah! Stop whining! Use these people to work out how they got whatever it is you want, learn from them and catch them up, then work harder than them and overtake! Be an inspiration, not another problem!

## The traffic was bad...

AKA you didn't leave early enough! You know that traffic gets bad – leave earlier! Manage your time and control your actions. Chances are you are only ever late when you didn't control the situation. Is it that the traffic was bad, or you had forgotten to wash your shirt the day before and then ran around the house flapping to find a clean one and now you're late?

Or you didn't do your kids packed lunch the night before and then woke up to realise you don't have enough food for them and have to last-minute shoot to the shops in rush hour to get them lunch?! Or any other standard bad time management episode you may frequent.

I used to work with a girl that was always late, her reason being that she didn't drive and always had to get the train. She refused to get the earlier train as it was a couple of quid more expensive because of the time of day. She would always turn up to work flustered and behind, and it threw everyone else off too.

I asked her about it one time and suggested she took the super early train, which coincidentally was cheaper than her late one, and way cheaper than the rush hour one, and she said: "Yeah but then I'd be at work an hour before everyone else with nothing to do!" Baby, there's always something to do! Freeing up an hour in the morning she could have done an uncountable amount of awesome shit and not only get more done in her power hour but also stood much more chance of the boss noticing and giving her the pay rise she always moaned about not getting.

## I'm ill

Don't get mad here. I am NOT talking about actual diseases or illnesses. I am talking about the dreaded cold, or tummy ache or similar. A lot of people snoot when I say this, but I believe you get less ill the busier you are. I haven't taken a day off in years! And remember, it's not just taking a day off from work, it's taking a day off from your life!

When I started changing my diet and exercising daily, I got ill less. I actually think that the media have a huge part to play in this – they tell us when to get ill and then sell us a product to fix it. It comes back to the 'you are what you eat and you are who you hang around with' analogy. If I watch TV at Christmas, every other advert is screaming flu at me, and the brain is a powerful thing, remember!

I'm not saying people don't get colds and tummy aches, but I am saying you can almost eradicate them, or at least remedy them much quicker if you are in control.

I know if I eat a whole box of chocolates I am probably gonna have gut rot the next day. Dig?! Just read up on the power of placebos and you will get an idea of what I am talking about! They work!!!! Fooling your brain, or programming your brain to deal with minor illness in a different way works! If I get the initial signs of a cold, I eat better, exercise more, and work through it. Worst that happens is I feel a bit rough for half a day. Try it next time.

## I'm too tired...

Your fault! Be in control of your schedule. Are you too tired to come into work because you woke up that way, or because you went to sleep that way?! Exercise and diet help immeasurably here too! Organise your time to ensure you don't feel sluggish. The planner from the '24' chapter is an absolute killer when it comes to this!

## I'm broke...

Yup, been there! And said that! This is not an excuse that holds any weight, even though it really can feel like it does. If the thing you are doing or meant to be doing is important, then you will find the cash for it. Plus, and I'm sure you can relate, I have been part of so many mardy pub chats where someone is moaning about the fact they are broke while nursing a pint that cost £5.

When I started noticing MY finger-pointing, it really got me thinking. I spent a lot of time coming up with exercises and hacks that would help me to blast this utter waste of energy and free up my time, and also to ensure my thought processes were beneficial to me. So here's a little hack that worked a treat for me.

---

## Exercise 1.1

Years ago, I went through a huge Arnold Schwarzenegger stage (I realise how that sounds). It was at the height of his career and as I imagine most Arnie fans do, I tried to replicate his voice and push out any of his many catchphrases whenever the opportunity came up. Problem is, I can't do his voice very well, and with too much time on my hands (and often way too high), I spent a long time practising them. That's the sort of shit I used to do! However, now being a producer as opposed to a consumer, the following hack came to me.

I was spending time looking through YouTube to find some of my favourite Arnie quotes, but the process was arduous. I would have to remember the quote, then try and find the clip with it in, and sometimes fanny about navigating the clip to find the exact quote so I could practice my Arnie voice. More so, this was double annoying because to perfect it I had to keep skipping back on the video, and more often than not this would end up with an advert playing while I waited to get back to my mission of perfecting my Schwarzenegger impression!

One hazy living room and a little while searching on Google later, I came across the Arnie soundboard. It's basically a click and play section of different soundbites from Arnie movies. All the classic catchphrases and sayings and all you have to do is click whatever one you want, and sit back and chuckle. I just checked, and it's still there. Google 'Arnie soundboard', just don't waste too much time on it.

Anyways, this got me thinking about my own soundboard – do I have one, and if so, what would the sound bites be? So let's run the hack –

grab your journal, and write down your standard, go-to responses to the following questions. Then to stack this hack, hacky-stack, I want you to write next to each of your standard responses, the very best responses you can think of.

Knowing our answers to obvious questions before they are asked, we give ourselves a mini cheerlead and boost of confidence and energy where we would usually just auto-pilot rubbish and negative responses. I'll go through them afterwards. Let's begin.

1. How's it going/how are you/how's your day?
2. What are you up to?
3. Why were you late?
4. Why didn't you finish (insert task)?
5. You look tired!
6. You got plans at the weekend?

In true style, I'd love to see how you answered these – hit me up! Let's go through the standard answers:

### How's it going/how are you/how's your day?
You may have answered something like: "not bad", "yeah alright thanks", "okay ta" or something similar.

### What are you up to?
You may have answered something like: "not much", "this and that", or something similar.

### Why were you late?
As mentioned before, something like (insert excuse to do with the car, traffic, pet etc)

## Why didn't you finish (insert task)?

You may respond to this with some form of excuse or finger-point like, "because so and so didn't do what they should have..." or, "this, this and this," or as I hear it now, "blah, blah, blaaaaaah."

## You look tired!

Something like "yeah well the kids/my partner/my work blah, blah, blah" etc.

## You got plans at the weekend?

And you might respond to this with: "nothing much really" or, "just chillin'".

If you answered with any of my guesses to the above questions, then not only is this not your best you, but it's also how everyone else hears you! Both need changing, and quick!

Here's how a great response would sound:

## How's it going/how are you/how's your day?

"Absolutely amazing. Thanks, you?" or, "Always great thanks, you?"

We will look at this in detail in a later chapter, but try this at your next opportunity and notice how the other person reacts.

## What you up to?

Well, if you are smashing this book like I know you are then you will be buzzing just thinking about responses to this! Your excitement of actually having a purpose in your own life will be enough to spark a much more meaningful conversation.

## Why were you late?

Now this one is slightly different, as it is calling you on your BS. Our primary reaction when someone calls us out is to either lie and come up with an excuse or get pissed off. By agreeing with the questioner, and coming up with an immediate solution and they will have nowhere to go and you can then turn the situation into a positive.

Something like, "You're right, I am late, I guarantee it won't happen again. I was so caught up in writing the book that I lost track of time! How can I make it up to you?" or similar will go down a treat.

## Why didn't you finish (insert task)?

Whether it's your boss, partner, family or friend asking, you can use a similar answer to the above.

## You look tired!

Again, this can seem like someone 'getting at you'. Own it, and make it positive. Something like: "I know, I haven't been in control of my sleeping pattern and I am going to do everything I can to nip this in the bud, in fact, I'll set a reminder on my phone to go off at 7pm tonight to remind me how important it is to control my sleep pattern so I make sure I get to bed on time."

## You got plans at the weekend?

As with question 1 or 2, you should hardly be able to contain yourself when you get asked this. If you haven't got anything exciting going on at the weekend, guess who's fault it is.

---

We need to stop this mindless small talk we have with people, and turn it into an amazing conversation or nothing at all! A few things will happen when you start being aware of your soundboard, of what you say and how you say it. Especially if it is auto-pilot responses. Zig when they zag, mother flipper!

So, this whole playing the victim finger-pointing shit is slowing you down. Use the notes you made in your journal to affirm how you perceive yourself and how others perceive you. Remember, you are completely in control of what you say to others, and how you say it. Take pride in yourself and keep in mind that only dickmunchers pass the buck.

So we about to do a murder...

---

## Summary

- Ex 1.0

Answer dem Qs

  - Be honest!

- Ex 1.1

Soundboard

  - Come up with the best responses possible

  - Drill your responses

  - Notice the difference to people's reactions

- Take responsibility. Everything is your fault, and even if it isn't, stop bitching and fix it

- Only butt holes point the finger

- Being right means sweet FA and will get you nowhere, owning your shit will.

# Chapter 19

# Kill Your Ego

I've been waiting for this chapter.

Man, the feeling I had when I started killing my ego lives with me to this day. To understand how to crush our ego we need to understand exactly what ego is, and why we would wanna kill it.

The dictionary definition is Ego – a person's sense of self-esteem or self-importance.

If we psychoanalyse that, you can think of ego as a mediator between your conscious and unconscious brain, enabling the level of identity you feel. So what does this mean, and why would we want to kill our self-esteem, self-importance, or identity? Let's revisit the understanding that absolutely everything is on a spectrum.

Ego is the same, except it is one of the few examples that is negative at both ends. At one end we have a big ego, or egotistical. The reality here is that you are a complete wanker, completely self-absorbed, entitled, and wrapped up in your own shit with no care for anyone else.

On the other end of the spectrum, is no ego. Having no ego, i.e. no self-esteem or self-importance, lack of confidence or lack of self-belief can be just as damaging.

You have to understand, when I say kill your ego, I don't mean losing your self-respect, self-esteem or self-worth. Quite the opposite! I mean kill the ideal of ego. It's no good no matter how you look at it. Instead, we need to replace it with similar ideals that actually work to our advantage.

Remember that the majority of what we believe was told to us by people that believed the majority of what they believed because they were told by people that... You get it!

What do you think of when you shake someone's hand? An impossible question to answer without asking some of your own questions back, right!? Let's look at the hand-shake. And to keep it simple, let's just use 3 different variables, we won't take into account the cleanliness, height, age, odour etc. of the person shaking our hand. All we will use are different grips: super strong, matched strength, and super weak (AKA floppy or wet).

If you are like me, you would have had an immediate reaction to either the super strong, or super weak, or both. We've all had them, the overly confident, my-dick-is-bigger-than-yours super-strong handshake, or the wet, limp, I-can't-even-look-you-in-the-eye, super weak thumbing-in-a-softy handshake. In fact, I bet you can think of people you know that have one of these two handshakes. You can also probably think of people with a bloody lovely, non-imposing handshake.

Think of the handshake spectrum like the ego spectrum, one end being the super-strong, and the other end is super weak. Just to make it easy to visualise, the super-strong handshake is a massive ego (which weirdly enough usually means a total lack of confidence, and is a paradox as it exists at both ends of the spectrum) and the super weak handshake is no ego at all. Like I said before, most of us will be all over the spectrum for different reasons: you won't talk to a stranger but you are happy to fart in front of your husband or wife, for instance.

You are really confident when you are playing a sport on a video game but you'd never dream of joining the basketball team (for whatever dumb reason, like you think you're too old or something). You are uber-confident with reading but not with writing. I could go on forever. Anyways, the point is that ego does not help anything, unless you completely understand it, kill it, then replace it with new brain hacks that allow you to take control back!

So, how do you kill your ego? First, we need to find out where your limits are. There is no right or wrong to this and all of you will have different limits. No problem. For instance, you may feel anxious about going for a job interview but you're more than happy to attend a fetish sex party, or you don't mind showing your tummy but the wheel-of-fortune arms are a no-go, or you don't like people seeing you eat but you burp in public with zero fucks given.

You may not like what is coming, but I absolutely guarantee you with 100% certainty that if you do what I suggest in the next few minutes, your life will be unimaginably better. You will have begun to unlock your full potential, and you will feel more alive and freer. This is no BS. I am so certain of this that I will put my reputation on the line to vouch for it. I firstly have to put in a disclaimer though, which I'll explain in a min, so you understand some of the things that are going to happen if you begin this process.

## Disclaimer to killing your ego:

1. People will talk shit about you (haters) or try to convince you to stay where you are (cynics).
2. People will question what you are doing.

3. You will realise some of your friends and family don't actually have your best interests at heart.

4. You will feel VERY scared and doubtful at times (it subsides).

There are a few more things I have noticed on this subject, but not big enough to worry about now, so lemme' explain these 4 points.

## 1. People will talk shit about you (haters and naysayers)

There is a chapter on this coming up, but for now, all you need to know is that when something changes, everything has the potential to change. Think about something you chose to do that other people laughed at or ridiculed you for, ultimately spending their time and energy focused on you. You may have even noticed this happening just off the back of you mentioning to someone you are reading this book. Just trust me, I've been there, and I promise you can put your trust in me until you got your own back.

## 2. People will question what you are doing

Similar to the above, people will not understand that you are making changes, just remember this: when someone tells you you can't do something, they are not telling you, they are telling them! You can do anything, babe!

## 3. You will realise some of your friends and family don't actually have your best interests at heart

True, it hurts, to begin with, but when you get your head around it you will realise it doesn't matter. This does not mean your nearest and dearest don't love you or want anything other than the best for you, it just means they haven't committed to themselves and in doing so will not understand your choices enough to support you in the best way. They will instead want to give you advice based on their findings in their own lives, or more likely, advice based on what the media, their school, or others have given them, that is by no means necessarily valid or helpful.

**4. You will feel very scared at times**

Yup, it's gonna happen, you are gonna have to jump off the cliff a few times as of yet, I'm not gonna sugarcoat it, I'm just gonna tell you the truth. Embraced fear is always followed by immediate gratification, success, or happiness. We will look at this in detail later.

So, let's kill your ego. Oh, actually, before we start, and this is quite a hard one to come to terms with: you have to be completely honest. Like, completely.

Throughout this book, I am going to show you things to help with this, but there is a point when you will need to 'come out' and take the dive yourself. I am gonna say this once, and I hope it rings home: we always know when we are lying to ourselves, always, we just don't acknowledge it.

---

# Exercise 1.0

Grab a pen and journal. No phones, this one has to be written out in your handwriting. Some of you will want to do this in a private room so nobody looks over at what you are writing. That's cool for now, no problem. I need you to spend a moment going deep. Some of you won't have done this for a while, if at all, and it is really important that you actually commit otherwise this won't work effectively.

I want you to close your eyes and think about the real you. Not what other people think of you, not what you want other people to think, but the real you! It could be that you are unsure of your sexuality, or that you are fascinated with poop, or that you are really unconfident but you act like you're not.

If you are allowing your real you to come through, then you wouldn't have had to think, you already know (you just might not be ready to own it and write it down). It might be you don't love your partner anymore, or you want a divorce, or you hate your job, or you have a phobia of snakes, or you like cross-dressing, or you want to be an artist but your parents are both barristers and want you to follow suit. It doesn't matter what it is, it is there, it has always been there, and we need to use it.

Suppressed energy is strong, bro! It's like antimatter! You, if anything like me, will have multiple things that came up; they feel a bit naughty, like a secret. Write however many of them you have down on the paper and read back what you have written. Now stop for a minute.

This was step 1.

You are probably thinking that I'm going to try and hypnotise you or some other thing, I promise I don't know how even if I wanted to. I believe in taking control, not putting your control into someone else's hands. I will never ask you to do something you don't want to, but I will give you the option to take control of your own situation. That's why I'm here!

So, you can probably see where step 2 is going. Before I go on and tell you to do what you know I am going to tell you to do, I want to stress this point... you HAVE to do this. Not for me, or anyone else. As I said, I won't force anything on you, but you do need to do it if you are going to be your best you and fucking dial your life.

So, and I promise this is easier if you don't dwell on it and just get it done, you need to come out with it, whatever it is. To yourself first. Then to whoever else. If you secretly want to write a book, you need to start telling everyone you are writing a book. If you want to be a crossdresser or split up with your partner, or you're lying to yourself about being confident, whatever it is, you need to own it. It's you! It is literally you!!! It is the you that you have been fighting, more than likely without even realising, for your whole life.

***

As soon as you admit, you can commit. The old admit and commit! Think of it like this: you have spent most of your life committing to someone else's set of standards, which they got from someone else. You've gotta be yourself! But first, you have to learn how. And it all starts with us accepting that we need to reset and start again with this new power, the power of being ourselves. Wanky, I know, but I don't care, and neither will you when you know what I'm talking about.

Scared of snakes, you gotta go find a snake and pick it up. I'm not joking. Whatever it is, you gotta strap up and take control. It is the only way! So, for those of you that just had the "oh fuck, I just can't, I just can't" thought process thinking about snakes, or spiders, or losing weight, or starting a new business or telling your homophobic dad that you're gay – you can, you just haven't yet, but when you have you will have!

There is one uber important word in "you can". Which one is it? It's 'you', motherfucker! YOU. If you are reading this then you probably haven't ever died. And if you haven't died, then like me, you have no idea of what really happens, or doesn't when you do finally pop your clogs. By using the most basic of assumptions, that the worst that could happen is you die, and it is a 50/50 as to whether that is better or worse than this life we are living now. So just suck it up already and pick up the snake! What you are doing hasn't been working! I know, because I hadn't been working correctly for the first 27 years of my life!!! I made all the mistakes, ALL of them.

I do this exercise with students, and the worst part of this process is that when you do finally come out and admit who you are, nobody actually really cares. Ever had that friend at a party, they've had a couple Patróns and they finally decide to come out as gay, and apart from the gossipy life-wasting D-bag reactions, everyone else is like: "Oh yeah we all knew, nice one mate, fancy another tequila?"

For those of you that have a serious worry on this, especially if it is something you really struggle with because of pressure coming from somewhere else, then I've got one thing to say to you: that sucks, and it breaks my heart when we end up in those kinda situations, but you have two options: 1) Exist in their ideals, or 2) Don't give a fuck and run your game.

You cannot live life in fear, that is not a life! Be proud of yourself and shut the haters down, or even better, enjoy the free promotion the haters give you and carry on being a legend!

I can't stress enough, you need to jump off the cliff today, not tomorrow or next week, don't build yourself up for it, just trust me and don't look back! I have jumped off the cliff a bunch of times now, it never feels easy, but the benefits are second to none.

When I started writing, I knew I had to put my money where my mouth was, so I quit my job at the college (which I had done for 7 years and was 'secure' income), ran full force towards the edge and jumped. Of course, I had ALL of the negative thought processes – What if the book is not good? What if people don't like it? What if people hate it and write bad, nasty things about me?

What happens when my parents read it and find out I am a recovered drug addict? What if I can't survive off of it and my wife leaves me and my kid hates me? I could go on. Same thing when I set up my third business, asked Hannah to marry me, took on Cal as my own son, had my first communal shower at the gym etc., etc., etc.

The longer I thought about these things the further I was from the cliff edge. Fortunately, I have been implementing my hacks for years now and this particular situation, as terrifying as it was, was just another cliff to jump off. And cliff jumping is fun as hell once you get used to it. Look, the reason I am being so full-on here and asking you to absolutely crush one of your biggest fears is that I have experienced it first hand, and it is arguably the most important part of this process. Rumi said: "Your task is not to seek for love, but merely to seek and find all the barriers within yourself that you have built against it." This is so true. The thing he didn't mention is where these barriers come from, and how detrimental they are if you don't break through them! They are built up over years and years, since childhood, when our brain is like a sponge and just sucks in as much data as it can. But ask yourself this: What if it is the wrong data? Is there a chance nearly everything we have been told is incorrect? The ego is yours to kill though, even if it wasn't initiated by you.

After pushing students to commit ego suicide, I have witnessed them do amazing things, from quitting the job they hate to starting a business, to telling their parents they are gay/bi/trans, to quitting drugs and drink, to asking someone they really like out on a date, to asking someone they really love to marry them – I've seen all of these first-hand and the feedback has been monumental! You know how I said earlier that you always know! This couldn't be truer right now! You know what you need to do, but can you do it?

The reason I said just go for it is that the longer you deliberate, the higher chance you'll listen to your neg voice and not go through with it. Do it, do it now!!!! The rest of this programme will not entirely work, well, definitely not to the level it can, if you do not complete this step, completely.

This is really important for your progression and if you do not do this now, you will more than likely not complete the programme, and I can't let you do that. I know what will happen if you commit so you need to do this. Don't give up now, we are coming up to the good stuff...

Scared of water, learn to swim. Scared of heights, book a skydive. Scared of dating, jump on Tinder. Scared to tell your kid you love them, do it! Scared to join pole-fitness, suck it up. Scared to commit to your future? Well, what can I say? It's your future whatever you choose to do, but right now you have the opportunity to change it, in mammoth ways that you won't have yet experienced! Do it! Do it! DO IT!!!!

My huge cliff dive, well, the first huge one, was moving to Brighton – 200 miles from my friends and family. Maybe doesn't sound like much in comparison to fighting a phobia of snakes, or asking someone to marry you, but I was working at a job I hated but was very comfortable, I had a long-term girlfriend, and my friends and family, although supportive, did not want me to go! I came to Brighton to study drums and make new connections and contacts. I was petrified! I talk about this move more in my blogs but I can tell you it was, at the time, the hardest decision I had ever made.

Other things I cliff jumped with were splitting up with my partner of 8 years, quitting my full-time job of 7 years to pursue a career I could run myself, taking on a step-son, asking my now partner to marry me, admitting I had a serious drug problem, dealing with said serious drug problem, I could go on. They never get easier, but they always get more rewarding.

So, back to you. Please do not continue with the book until you have taken this step, but do not leave it too long! It feels like there is never a right time to do something scary, but with that mindset, the time will never come, and the quicker you do it, the easier it is – RIP OFF THE BAND-AID NOW...

Welcome back! If you didn't do what I asked you, I get it, but as much as this feels like the hardest thing you may have ever done, you need to do it. If you did, then you have no idea how happy I am for you – I'm literally beaming ear to ear just knowing how it feels and now you feel it too! So, while you're absolutely buzzing your Ts off with adrenaline and positivity, let's move on...

## Summary

- Ex 1.0

The real you

  - Think about the real you, and allow whatever you need to get done surface
  - You know what it is you need to do so don't fight it
  - Now get it done
- We have been taught to fight our true selves our whole lives and conform to the standard
- The standard doesn't work for 99.99% of the population
- Living with the real you is the only way to live, if people don't like it then don't worry, they have their own shit to deal with.

# Chapter 20

# Consumed

Like I mentioned, I have been consumed by so many different things in my life. Sex, drugs, work, relationships, diet, music, fitness. Some of these are not good things to be consumed by, and if we are thinking about our spectrums, everything can consume you in a good or bad way. For example, being consumed with healthy living is good, depending on the level of consumption.

Exercising once a day and having mostly good nutrition will keep you in great mental and physical health. But if you go full-force obsessive consumption at the gym, say you did a 9-hour HIIT training session or 300 bicep curls in one go, you would more than likely end up tired, injured, and not wanting to ever go to the gym again. Healthy obsessions allow us to get better and unhealthy obsessions just screw us over. There is huge harnessable power and energy in obsessions, but to be consumed by the wrong thing can be cataclysmic!

What you are consumed with is the problem, being consumed is not.

# Exercise 1.0

Journal please, babes! I want you to draw a quick mind map, or brainstorm or whatever it is called now, with your name bang in the middle of the page. It will work even better if you draw a picture of yourself, so it looks like you, but your name will do. Then sign it. Draw a circle round it and draw lines to everything you are consumed by in your life at the moment.

Don't worry if they are bad or good things at the moment, but do make sure you get as many as you can. So just to make sure we are on the same page we need to understand consumption.

The basic definition of consumption is the action of using up a resource. Again this can be positive or negative. But once a resource is gone it's gone, right?! Things that most of you will be consumed by on the day to day are:

TV, internet, work, family, friends, vices, sleep, diet, and hobbies. There are some other obvious ones but let's roll with these.

You know me well enough by now that I don't have to point out which are positive and negative, and also, which parts of them are positive or negative. For instance, work can be totally negative if you are working a job you hate, or totally positive if it is your dream job and you're killing it. Or going deeper, you may have your dream job but your sex life is shit or non-existent because of the hours you are putting into your job.

Once you've finished your mind map, and everything is laid out in front of you, all obvious like, I want you to stick a tick next to the healthy obsessions, and a cross next to the unhealthy ones.

---

We need to work out how much of your energy is being expelled on unhealthy obsessions, things you do all the time, things that consume you and leave you broke, or sad, or unhealthy, or tired! And then we can replace them with things that consume that are awesome!

The thing to note here is that the amount of effort it takes to go on a porn binge or have a cocaine habit, or session a Netflix season in one go is not the problem, in fact, it's the solution! Whaddya mean? Well, let's say that we all have 10 energy points in a day, just to keep it simple. Let's say a task like having a kid takes up 2 points, running a business takes up 2 points, eating and sleeping takes up 2 points, and any hobbies or positive activities takes up 2 points – you're left with 2 remaining energy points.

The amount of effort and time you put into running a business or raising a child is not only necessary but also never quite enough – there's always something else you need to do or something that doesn't get finished. But what about those remaining 2 points?!

For example, it's Friday, you're in the office or at your job and you've got that Friday feeling and you spend from mid-morning right 'til 5pm secretly on your phone under your desk making plans and sorting out what you are gonna do to spend your hard-earned cash from that week.

You keep checking your phone to see if Molly has got back to you about which cocktail bar to hit up and all of your focus is on that. Well, there goes your 2 remaining points. Controlling the focus of our brains and being aware of the long game doesn't come into these spontaneous impulses unless we force it to.

If you are a drinker, or a smoker, or a porn-junkie, or a junkie-junkie, or sex addict, or a Netflix binger or whatever, then you know where I'm coming from – it takes your time, your resources, and your effort, not to mention a fat chunk out of your 24!

I remember when I finally quit a VERY bad habit (the details are not for this book but I will write about it in the future) I had all this energy and was overwhelmed with what to do with it. My thought process' first reaction to this was to go back to the thing I had quit and breaking that habit took time (and still rears its head on occasion) but I know what happens when you succumb to it!

All those years lost for what? What the fuck are you gonna do with 7 seasons of The Wire, or a bunch of one-night stands you can't even remember, or every single cigarette break you took?! It won't get you anywhere but it's got you locked! I realised after killing my demons that it wasn't the fact I was consumed that was the problem – it was what I was consumed with.

So we need to harness that energy and move it from the bad IGMF to the long game activities that are necessary to create a great life.

---

# Exercise 1.1

I want you to go back to your mind map and next to where you stuck the ticks and crosses I want you to write a percentage. I want the percentage to reflect the amount of effort per day you put into that activity, between 0% and 100%. If you are one of those people that says, "I'm gonna give it 110%," then don't, because you can't! You should end up with well over 100% i.e. Activity 1 = 70% Activity 2 = 31% effort and so on.

Upon completion, I want you to work out how you can fit your list into a total 100% and draw a new mind map, just like before, only this time the things you put down have to be good, and they have to add up to 100%, otherwise, they won't fit in the day. Welcome to the new you! We are gonna talk about how to stay in this state and shift your focus away from the bad shit in a few chapters, but for now, we gotta build some shit...

# Summary

- Ex 1.0

Mindmap

  - Draw yourself or write your name in the middle of the page
  - Draw lines connected to everything you are consumed by in your average day, these can be good and bad

- Ex 1.1

Mindmap 2.0

  - Revisit your previous mindmap
  - Add percentages next to each activity that are relative to how much time and effort you spend on each activity
  - Now jig all percentages to fit into a total of 100%
  - Now draw a new mindmap
  - Win

- Your mindset is the only thing preventing you from thinking like anyone else that you aspire to be. Make sure you read books, study information, and listen to all of your heroes daily to keep you juiced!

- You cannot fit more into a day than you can fit into a day! You have to prioritise and act accordingly

- You need to be consumed by all of the positive activities in your life, and prevent the negative activities from gaining traction.

# Chapter 21

# Lego

I love Lego! I love it because it can be whatever you wanted it to be, well, within the parameters of Lego. I started on the big stuff, when I was super young; they called it Duplo in the UK, not sure what it was abroad. I remember feeling super grown-up when at the age of 5 or 6, I was given my first proper Lego, the one where each block wasn't the size of a small country.

The pieces were more intricate, and I loved it!! Then, after a few more years, I remember getting bummed out when I'd think of something to build and the little square or rectangular blocks didn't allow for my vision. No matter how hard you try, you totally can't make a realistic vagina with square Lego pieces – and it hurts your manhood, no matter how much lubrication you use!

Then they brought out Lego Technics, even more intricate and adaptable, capable of much more interesting builds than the standard Lego, often with motorised parts, still impossible to make realistic yaya's, but cool AF regardless!

Why am I talking about Lego? Well, I'll tell ya!

If you had every single size and shape of Lego, and you were given a YouTube tutorial of how to make whatever you want, and unlimited time, then, in theory, you could build anything, right? What if I told you we don't need Lego. What do I mean? Well, Lego has to be created for you to be able to play with it or use it – it has to exist. Our own future, success, happiness and everything else has to be created too, but by us. Another story for another time but you should always aim to be a creator and not a consumer...

Anyways, for example: worrying. Worrying about the future, the bills you gotta pay, your rent, your family, your health, your pets, your career and all those other things you worry about... They haven't happened yet, but by giving them our time and brainpower we begin to manifest them. I want to be straight here too, I do not believe that just by writing stuff down or thinking about it loads will make it magically appear or come to fruition, but I do believe the thoughts we choose to spend our time with allow us to notice way more opportunities that in turn can get us that much closer to our goals.

How often have you watched a doc on Netflix and then thought loads about that particular thing, even if you hadn't previously? If you watch a documentary about paedophiles, you way more likely to worry for your children's safety than if you had just watched a doc on how golf balls are manufactured, get me?!

What we choose to think about can massively affect future decisions and actions, which could end up in either positive or negative results. Don't believe me? Go visit your sick nan or granddad in their home, or go and chat to a homeless person, or watch a film on poverty and try not to at least think about it for a while afterwards.

Let's explore this a bit with an example. So let's say I watch the paedophile documentary, I go to bed that night upset and worried about my children's safety. I can't sleep, scheming of ways I can keep my children away from any danger. Over the following months I tighten the strings on my kids freedom, calling them in earlier than the other kids, stopping them from going to scouts or guides, or whatever extracurricular activities they want to be a part of just in case the adult running them is twisted, all the while reminding them to be safe and not talk to strangers.

Long story short, the kid grows up a super introvert, scared of certain situations, and misses opportunities because of this, and furthermore passes down the same terrorism BS to their children.

Let's flip this example and say that by being overprotective as a parent I actually manage to prevent my child from being in danger in a particular incident that may not have been averted without my worrying. Fact is, we can't prove what the real repercussion is of this example, but this is not the point I'm making.

I'm suggesting that your brain is more than capable of thinking something up and then letting it manifest into a life-changing new you, whether it be bad or good, or both! Now imagine I hadn't just watched one documentary on paedophiles, but I chose to watch them all, read about them, and research them every waking moment of my life, like I was consumed by them – it's gonna exponentially exacerbate the situation.

Let's look at another example of this, and one that is way more relative to the new life we are creating! Just as a side note, you're fucking dialling it at the moment! Thank you for going deep into this book! Go you!

So let's say you have picked up a book, let's say it's called something like *Do Shit, Get Shit Done*. The book is all about life hacking, self-motivation, and positivity to reward success! You notice it on the table in the dentist's waiting room. You find this kinda shit funny and stupid but the only other available read is a boring newspaper so you reluctantly pick it up and start flicking through the pages for something to do while you wait to be called in. You read some of it, get the gist, and surprisingly and reluctantly get a bit hyped.

In the time you are waiting to go in for your check-up, or extraction, or whatever, you read some super insightful paragraph about seizing the day and being confident, and it rings home. The dentist's assistant calls you in, and as you look up you realise they are your perfect potential partner! Usually, you would cower under the aura of a beautiful person who was just your type, but with the little buzz you got from the book you think: "F it, #YOLO," ask her out on a date, she agrees, you get married and have kids and live happily ever after!

Sounds slightly unrealistic, right? Fair. Obviously, you haven't watched any films starring that soppy twat Hugh Grant... But imagine if you immerse yourself in sheerly positive media and nothing else: books, conversations, web searches, seminars, blogs, vlogs, forums etc. as opposed to the complete crap we are all subject to in the form of TV, radio and ads! Do you think you would be a better person or a worse person?

I used the crack den analogy earlier, and it's so true. You are what you eat, and you are who you surround yourself with! But there's more to it than that! It's YOUR Lego!!! You can begin to create the situation, by living it. Now please don't be mistaken, when I say living it, I don't mean riding the wave that already exists, I mean creating a brand new one, bigger and more powerful than the others! Don't be the wave, be the fucking water... and the gravity moving it, not just the surfer on top of it hanging ten.

The surfer has to follow the wave, one false move and they wipe the fuck out! I wanna control the surfer. I wanna control the waves. I wanna control the ocean. I wanna control my life! I got so sick of someone else telling me when to pick up my board and when I had to stay home! I can pick up my board whenever I fucking like! Full disclosure, I can't surf. I hurt my bum really badly once when I was 14 and tried surfing.

So we need to build the wave, first within ourselves, and then moving outwards onto everyone else. Two things happen when you start to create the wave. Firstly people will ridicule you, laugh, doubt, naysay and hate. Secondly, you will begin to doubt yourself, and that inside voice we spoke about earlier, the naggy one, will make you want to quit. Ignore it, it's a dickhead.

To understand this, I need to spin you a yarn... Imagine you are thinking about one of the following, hopefully, you can relate to one of them... Joining a class, like yoga or pilates, or a football team, or any sports club, or you want to ask someone on a date, or you want to cold call a prospect to source some new business, or you have an interview for a new job...

You will have experienced one of these things before, and without a shadow of a doubt, you will have experienced one of the following emotions or feelings while deciding on whether to take action. The things you would have felt are our good friend 'fear', which in turn leaves us with our other good friends 'no confidence', 'anxiety', 'doubt' etc., etc.

So, picture this, you are thinking of joining a yoga class, or asking someone out on a date. Fear, which you can guarantee will rear its head every time something with the potential to be really awesome presents itself in life, is the feeling directly before something amazing happens. I'm gonna say that again; it is one of the most important sentences in this book.

Fear shows up directly before something amazing happens!

Say it with me: **Fear shows up directly before something amazing happens!**

Every time!!!

You can all probably think back to a time that you had worried crazily about something that turned out to be absolutely fine, in fact, you probably do this daily. And you are fine. This is a Lego brain. Build it and they will come. Or more to the point, build it and you're right effin' there! You have to learn to live with and ultimately embrace fear. It is your friend.

237

You have probably heard the following acronyms for fear: false evidence appearing real, for everything a reason, future events appearing real, false expectations about reality, future events already ruined, and my personal favourite, face everything and rule!

Fear will never ever go away, it is part of the way we work. It comes in different forms, and this is what people don't always realise.

Form one is the fear that gets us the fuck outta trouble – walk into the house, lion in the sitting room, fear, adrenaline, shut the door quick, run away, don't get mauled by the lion! This is what I call original fear. This type of fear has allowed humans to live after ending up in dangerous situations.

Think about if this was the only kind of fear though: if our ancestors had run away from everything whenever fear hit, we would not have constructed buildings, sailed oceans, connected with other people, had pet dogs, tried eating fish or pineapples, pushed our body through 'the wall' or whatever else.

The other form of fear is what I call evolving fear and it is the form of fear that allows us to run into danger and push hard. Don't get me wrong, I am definitely not saying try and spoon with the lion you just found in your living room just because it's dangerous, or try sailing an ocean in a bathtub full of scorpions and aids needles just because, but you can if you want to, people have done MUCH scarier things before.

If you think for one minute that all those people you have heard of weren't more often than not petrified as shit and winging it then you are completely wrong: Gandhi, Christopher Columbus, Rosa Parks, Warren Buffet, Malcolm X, Jim Carey. If you have heard of them, then they were completely shit scared multiple times, but they did it anyway and now you know their names, and they've left a legacy.

Now before you get the wrong idea, I definitely do not mean you need to be a trembling mess to make big things happen, that's not good for anyone. Instead, you need to learn that fear is not a reason to tremble. It is a sign to move forward, with gusto and great force. How do you know when it's okay to walk across the street? The traffic light goes green. Think of fear as a green traffic light. You don't have to be reckless, you need to be courageous.

Just because the light is green, doesn't mean you should cross the street, but sometimes the light is red and you HAVE to cross the street regardless because something overrides it, say like a really sweet puppy or child that's run into the road...

Start telling your brain that fear is here to help. Your mind is Lego! Fear is one of the most incorrectly used emotions we have and it unlocks the key to your happiness and success. Well, it does when you learn to harness it.

I can tell you this, the feeling of fear is within us, it will never go away, in the same way, laughter doesn't leave when you hit a certain age (farts are ALWAYS funny!!), fear will always feel the same, it has to, cuz it's fear! It fits within the spectrum of fear, it might be a little fear or a huge fear, but it's fear, and it feels the way it does. You have to learn to use it to your advantage.

How do you know when you're hungry? Your body tells you! How do you know when you're tired, or thirsty, or horny, or bored? Your body tells you, it gives you signs. The thing they don't tell you about fear at school is that it is your body's way of telling you to do something. Evolving fears anyway. We will come back to this in more detail later, but right now we need to start learning how to build our future, with the power of our own supercomputer, the brain!

Let's go baby steps on this first of all...

I want you to use the big Lego, the huge one where you can only build very basic structures. We are going to start by building a positive with our big Lego. This won't get too hippy, don't worry!

# Exercise 1.0

I want you to grab your journal, you are allowed 3 pieces of big Lego. You have to build something. Each piece of Lego has to be a different thing, with the last piece of Lego being the ultimate goal. Again, we'll start simple so let's pick something nice that affects someone else positively. I want your Lego to be a tower, really nice and simple. In your journal, draw 3 Lego squares, one on top of the other, with the bottom one on top of a line, which represents the floor, cuz we need to ground our structure.

We are about to build a positive structure that will benefit a person of your choosing. The positive thing we are going to do is to write a really nice thing about them and link other people to them via social media. This is a phenomenal way to build and strengthen bridges and meet new contacts, and more importantly, doing something nice for someone you like or love is dope.

Choose someone that deserves your time. I'm gonna do this exercise too, right now. I am choosing two of my dear friends who are moving to China after being in Thailand for 4 years. It is a huge move for them, and totally awesome! They both have Insta profiles so I am going to use this build to help them out by telling my network about them and linking my peeps to them. Here is what I just posted:

'So tomorrow, 2 of my dearest friends and one of the most amazing couples I know (and probably in the world) are making a completely 'jump off the cliff' move! They have been living and teaching in Bangkok for the last few years and are now moving to China to continue their journey. I can't tell you how much respect, love and admiration I have for these two (who might as well be one – pop the question moff *ahem*).'

They are wise, clever, super hard-working, and they are taking massive action to make sure they are in control of their lives instead of their lives being in control of them! These two are a testament as to how to own your own life and a constant inspiration to many. You can follow them on Insta @_wanderlost and @hellmoth.

I love you both (I love you slightly more moff but only cuz I've known you longer, Rachel will overtake pretty soon, sorry!)

We all love you, and I can't wait to have that first Skype when you have settled in! Owning life like a pair of absolute dons!! Good luck tomorrow (you don't need it) and lemme know when you get there safe! All the best!

So, this was my end result. Really simple I know, but we are gonna go full mental on this in a bit. I designed not only the outcome, but I designed the idea, how I wanted to execute it and built the idea from the ground up. This is a much more literal exercise to the very first one I asked you to do right at the start of this programme! So, my build looks like this.

## Primary block

Create a foundation. This is where you create your initial idea; the sky's the limit with this but the simpler it is, the fewer bricks you will need to stack on top. This is such an important step as it's literally the first block, the foundation or seed, and the stronger it is, the easier it will be to stack more bricks on it. Make sure this is an awesome idea no matter how small it is!

## Secondary block

The build. Now you have your foundation, you next need to start the build! Once you know what you are building, you can begin to grab your tools. In this case, all I needed was an internet connection and a phone. If my build was something else then I would use this block to gather the tools I need to complete my whole build.

## Action block

Execution. This is the final block, the block that counts, the action block. In the same way, your Lego house isn't finished without the roof, as is your build – it's not finished without the last piece, otherwise it's just waiting to be finished. The action block is where all of your planning (time) and building (energy) come to fruition, and you are left with a creation.

---

Let's take this literally. I want you to think of as many different 'builds' you have left uncompleted, with leaky roofs... Two questions:

1.   Why didn't you complete them?
2.   Where would you be now if you had?

The answer to number 1 will be different from your answer before you started life hacking. Before you would have said things like, "I just didn't have time," or, "I was unsure it would work," or some other bullshit! You can't answer like that now, so why didn't you complete them?

Well, the answer to that is actually not because of the reasons you gave, but instead that you wasted time giving reasons instead of just finishing – diggit?!

Now you know that I wanna take some time to think about the answer to question 2.

Where would you be now if you hadn't made those excuses and actually finished all the things you started? It's like an awesome movie that has you captivated right from the start and keeps you guessing the whole way through, only for the credits to roll at the 'end' without there being any resolve. Frustrating as fuck!

'Lego builds' will totally help you with this in future. I speak to so many people that have felt completely dumbfounded after putting serious amounts of time and effort into something, but with no reward! More often than not the reason is that they didn't have the action block. The action block is the reason you are doing something! It's the purpose! If you are putting loads of effort into something but you don't know why, then you are building a house with no roof, and nobody wants a house with no roof!

Like I said at the start of this programme, you gotta have a purpose, otherwise literally what's the point. Are you making the world better? Are you making the world different? Are you doing anything at all? If you ain't moving forward then you're a sitting duck, and sitting ducks are good as dead! Let's get mo' purpose...

---

## Summary

- Ex 1.0

Build your first Lego
  - Draw three blocks, one on top of the other
  - The top block is the goal
  - The middle block is the build
  - The bottom block is the foundation
  - Choose a goal and create it (foundation block)
  - Now build it (build block)
  - Now execute it (action block)

- Repeat as necessary with any other goal to establish a clear and succinct path
- You can build anything you can imagine
- You have to construct a strong and grounded foundation to build a solid structure.

# Chapter 22

# 1YP

Let's get practical. In this chapter, I will explain how to write a 1-year plan, my way. I have been told by many different people to write 1-year plans, 5-year plans, 10-year plans before, and they never worked. As with everything else, I got hyped in the initial stages, on the odd occasion I felt gassed enough to actually write a 10-year plan, and then it teetered off and before I knew it a few months or years had passed. They don't work.

Well, that's not entirely true, they can work. Well, they completely work, but the standard way to write an X-year plan has pieces missing, it's like a puzzle without the very last piece, which is arguably the most important, and in this case, it absolutely is the most important! Let me show you how to absolutely smash the back doors of an X-year plan.

I am going to explain this for a 1-year plan initially, but the same rules apply no matter how long or short your plan is. For those of you that have never written out an X-year plan then the main premise is that you write out a goal that you want to hit in roughly this order:

The 1-week goal, 1-month goal, 3-month goal, 6-month goal, 1-year goal, with each goal being slightly bigger than the previous, working up to the big 1-year goal in increments that are realistic and manageable. FUCK THAT! That's for little-thinking mother flippers. We are making our life amazing, not realistic. Realistic is what everyone does and it ends in old age and normalcy. Realistic is what your nan does when she plans dinner around toilet breaks if she remembers to make dinner. You're not there yet so I need you to be unrealistic! Like supercharged, cray-cray, rule-bending unrealistic! We'll come back to this...

So let's say your big 1-year goal is to save for a deposit on a house (I'm not suggesting you do, check out *Unscripted* by MJ Demarco, recommended read). Your 1-year plan may look like this:

1 Week – Start to put 'going out' money into a piggy bank

1 month – Save £1,000 from not going out

3 months – Speak to a financial advisor to help balance books

6 months – have £6,000 saved

1 year – have £12,000 saved to put a deposit on a house

This is a lame plan! It won't work and for a bunch of reasons. Lemme' tell you why:

1. You know when you are writing it you probably won't stick to it.
2. You are not thinking unrealistic enough, by a long shot, and failing on unrealistic is 100 times better than failing on realistic!
3. You are missing the most integral part of the plan, which I'll explain in a minute!
4. There is absolutely no structure to this plan.

So, here's how you do it.

**Point 1:** You know when you are writing it you probably won't stick to it.

The plan will only work if it is attacked daily. This means you need to marry it with your daily goal setting, and now your Lego blocks. How's that going by the way? Sleeping better? Waking up more excited? Getting more done? Lemme know how you're getting on.

You should always hit things from more than one angle, and with massive amounts of action. If you want a deal then you need to call 10x or 50x more people than you initially think to get someone to bite. We'll come to that later too!

The only way you will stick to something is if you do it every day! It has to be a life choice and not just a diet! You have to commit to changing your life, not just changing a couple variants just for a little bit.

**Point 2:** You are not thinking unrealistic enough, by a long shot!

Your long-term goals, as with your daily goals, have to be what you would currently consider unrealistic to give you any chance of making them realistic and normal to you. Stuff is only realistic to you if it is realistic to you, ya dig?

Do you think that Mark Zuckerberg now thinks it's unrealistic to make billions of dollars a year? There was one point he probably did think it was, but it's realistic for him now. You need to be the same! Same 24 hours a day and same 365 EVERY year.

Ever had building work done on your house, or known someone that has? It ALWAYS takes longer than the builders quote you for! Why? Is it because they are trying to get the job and then charge you more when they are already in your yard? Possibly, but it more likely is that they haven't thought big enough and taken into account the unexpected huge problems that always arise and need troubleshooting on a job. Think big, or sink big! The old think or sink!

**Point 3:** You are missing the most integral part of the plan!

This is the most important part of a 1-year plan, and the bit that is missing in every single X-year plan I have ever seen. They are all missing RFN, or Right Fucking Now. They plan for the following week when they more than likely won't be in the same mindset as they were when they initially wrote the plan.

I found this out one day when I was at uni. My tutor told me to write a 3-year plan. At the time I was 20 and all I was thinking about was my band doing really well, and at the time I couldn't have thought of anything bigger for my main goal than playing a 500-capacity venue in Brighton called Concorde 2. It seemed so unrealistic that I used it as my main goal. God knows what would have happened if I'd written 'Wembley Stadium', or 'Red Rocks' instead!

Anyway... I had written a bunch of X-year plans before and never stuck to them. I reluctantly took my tutor's advice and started another one. I was in a proper peppy mood that day and upon finishing the plan, I decided to crack on with it right away. Here was my plan...

1 week – Organise rehearsal for next gig

1 month – Be playing at least one gig a month in town

3 months – Finish writing album

6 months – Have album recorded and push it

1 year – Play Concorde 2

Looking back at this, it is super rough around the edges, however, that never matters if you get started on the work immediately, and if you're persistent and tenacious you will figure out the issues as and when they arise. In true form I started with a bite-sized, manageable task to be completed by the end of the first week: organise one rehearsal.

I was in an 8-piece band and rehearsals could be tricky to organise as all of us had different commitments, so I figured that this was a good starting place. As I said, I was feeling peppy AF that day and I just wanted to get on with my plan so I added an extra title in, above 1 week, that said 'right now'!

Next to right now, I wrote, "Message other bands on Myspace (I'm not old I'm not old I'm not old) to make new connections and grow our network."

I immediately got on my computer and started messaging people; the hours seemed to pass crazy quick and before I knew it I had worked through the day and into the night without even thinking to stop for food. I had a bunch of different conversations going on with different bands of a similar genre AND I had been so excited about some of the gig swaps they had offered that I had rung every member of my band to tell them the news.

While I was on the phone to each of them I organised each one to rehearse the next day, and I could sense they could feel my excitement and energy. Even the ones that would usually be a pain to organise were committing to a late rehearsal the following day even though they had early work. This never usually happened with that band, or most bands for that matter, hahaha.

Then one message came through from a band who were doing way better than us, saying, "Thanks for the love brother! Loving your tracks and totally up for some gigs if you wanna support us." I eagerly typed back and after a couple of back and forths this came through: "We've actually got a gig at the Concorde in Brighton next month and the main support had to pull out, would you guys be up for it?"

Now I know what you're thinking, and I can't prove either way if this would have happened anyway, but one thing we both know for sure is that absolutely nothing would have happened without taking action. You don't get anything without taking action! You wanna go out for dinner, you have to get dressed, travel, order! You wanna ask someone out, you gotta go up to them, speak to them, offer them a drink. And God forbid you wanna win the lottery, you have to go to the shop, buy a ticket etc.

Just in case you're wondering why I said God forbid: playing the lottery means you are out of control, it's the same as X Factor or the like; missing out the work to get the reward is lazy and stupid, and you won't be able to harness the power if you do win. It would be like winning a prize to fly a fighter jet without any previous experience or knowledge of piloting an aircraft = CRASH AND BURN!!!

It turned out my 1-year plan was completed in just under 2 months! And the only reason this was different from previous efforts was that I started it immediately! Your plan will not work if you do not put it into effect immediately! Think of it like this: you super fancy someone, you're standing at the bar mustering up the courage to go ask them out on a date, and while you're plucking up the courage, some absolute G jumps in your place and gets the date. Speed is everything! When people say slow down, chill out, relax, you deserve the rest, don't listen, cuz it won't get you anywhere. You can do that on vacation when the goal is completed. Speed wins the race.

I know when I'm proof-reading this book that I will have that voice in my head saying, "You need to change that, or do this different, or check your grammar and spellings." I never listen to that anymore (as you can tell from my grammar and spellings), cuz while you are perfecting your book, I'm selling my one with mistakes in it. Speed and courage.

Don't get me wrong, you have to have put the initial effort in to do something well and care about it, but there is a cut-off point where you have to take the leap and just do it! Let's get back to our date: you're standing at the bar and looking at the person that you super wanna ask out, but your hair is a bit messy and you're in a shirt with a stain on it from where you just spilt your coffee and you convince yourself that they won't want to go out with a messy-haired stainy-pants!

That thought just cost you a prospective partner or friend, or business opportunity. Here's how I would handle that: "Hey, sorry to interrupt you, I just thought I'd let you know that you're SO pretty that while I was staring into space trying to think of a way to come ask you out I spilt my coffee all over my trousers! Wanna go for a glass of red wine so I can really put my washing detergent to the test?" That's a really rubbish line I just made up, but it doesn't matter, a conversation started and you can figure out how to not sound like a twat later. Speed and courage and risk.

**Point 4:** There is absolutely no structure to this plan.

I have mentioned this so many times now, so I won't go on, but when you write out your plan you need to make sure it fits into your schedule. One of the biggest reasons that shit never gets done is that we have the idea and ignore all current commitments.

Problem: You wanna join the gym but you don't get in from work until 7pm and you're always too tired.

Solution: You either need to wake up earlier, or get a different job, or replace something else in your schedule to allow gym time. Na'mean? You can't just have the idea without understanding you will have to make changes or sacrifices to your current situation, so definitely take this into account when you begin a new venture. This does not mean give up on the idea of a new venture because it doesn't fit your current situation, that is staying inside your comfort zone, and you know how I feel about that.

What it does mean though, is prioritising and being on top of your schedule with the understanding you have to move things around to accommodate exciting new ventures is integral. Einstein seemed to be able to create intricate visual diagrams in his mind that explained his theories, but in the most simplest Lee-form, you can think of your schedule like one of those sliding puzzles, you know the ones, where you have to not only shift each piece to the correct spot on the board, but you also have to move other pieces that need to stay in the puzzle but are currently in the way of the piece you wanna reposition. If any pieces don't need to be there, you gotta get rid of them because they are just taking up your space and not allowing you to freely navigate the rest of the puzzle.

Think unrealistic and get started straight away. You got this!

Now your thought processes should be beginning to work for you as opposed to against you: "I'm gonna make a 10-year plan to get my dream career, and I'm gonna have two 5-year plans and five 1-year plans to keep me on track. To strengthen this strategy I'm gonna use my 24-hour planner to keep my day-to-day in check, and my Lego builds to deal with each part of the journey."

This may feel like a bit to take on, but it is actually only a bit to take on cuz you don't currently run your ship like this! You know why you're rubbish at ballet or mechanics or speaking a foreign language... cuz you don't do them. That's it!

Like I said at the start of the book, this is all down to commitment and you! Nobody else can do this for you, so I need to remind you how brilliant you are, and take the time to give you some feedback!

Obviously, I can't do this 1-on-1 with you, unless you book in for a 1-on-1 session, but I can give you a few bits of overall feedback, and I want to take this opportunity to do so now.

If you have made it this far, even without trying most of the hacks I've explained, then I commend you. Really! It takes effort to get a few hours into a book, and here you are, and you've made it this far! For those of you where this is your first experience with this kind of life hacking or any kind at all, I commend you! A lot of these exercises take courage and initial blind faith, and if you have even tried one of them to avail then you should take a moment to smile to yourself and feel powerful.

For those of you that have already gone deep and trusted me and have implemented these first few techniques, then fucking A, dudes and dudettes, you are crushing it!

I can pinpoint and remember exactly how it felt when I first started letting go and putting effort into me and investing in myself. I know how you feel and I'm so proud of you and excited for you, like, literally buzzing thinking about what success stories you are going to email me with or post for your network to see! This shit, in this book, done saved my life! I know what it can do if used respectfully and for the good, and for those of you feeling what I'm talking about, let me know – hit me up with your videos, posts, comments and suggestions. I love seeing what you guys have done!!!

Also, I'd love to know how you are getting on with supercharging my hacks – have you come up with any extra fine-tuning I haven't thought of? Share, share, share if you have! I wanna know. You guys are fucking awesome, and we are only just getting into it! There is some serious life-affirming game-changer shit coming up so prepare to work. I want you to take a rest now, only for the rest of the day, but it is important, you've been working hard, and we need to rejuvenate now. See you tomorrow...

## Summary

- You need goals, and your goals need a plan
- The plan will not always go the way you want it to, which is why you need to spend time strengthening your mindset too! It's not what life throws at us, it's how we react
- Start the first part of your plan immediately
- If you wait for the 'right time' you will always be waiting, because the right time never comes.

# Chapter 23

# Haters, Cynics, and Cheerleaders

For those of you that rested up, shame on you! Ain't no rest here. We need to get cracking. More is more in this case. Slam this book and then read it as many times as you can. My favourite books I have read or listened to 5+ times. True story! Get involved.

For those of you that ignored me and carried on cuz you're hungry, I'm talking to you! FUCK YEAH! Work harder! Hahaha, anyways, I'll stop roasting you now because we need to talk about people that will roast you even more than I will, how to deal with them, and how to use them to your advantage! Let's talk about two of them right now, and we'll come to the other one in a bit...

The hater and the cynic. Two very different kinds of people, one is good for you, one is not! I guess most of you will be thinking: "Wtf?! Surely they are both bad for you?" ...Lemme' 'splain (sorry, was just sick in my mouth too but I've never been able to put 2 apostrophes back to back before) <there's a chance that I wasn't meant to use apostrophes like that cuz' my grammar is bad> {there's even more chance using different types of bracket like this is worse}.

When I was lecturing at college we would have an induction day at the start of each academic year. I always had to do an introduction to the course and take questions from the new students. Each year I would waffle on about a bunch of shit but every year there were 3 things I seemed to always bring up without fail.

1. "I only have one rule on my course: don't be a dick! Encompassed under that are things like: be on time, don't make excuses, don't be negative, don't smoke weed in college toilets (AKA don't get caught smoking weed in college toilets) or put dead rats in the air conditioning units etc."

2. "I will never tell you off, or shout at you – if you work hard I will give you all my time, and I will bend over backwards to help you. If you slack, I won't say anything, I will just stop helping."

3. "If any of you have hot parents, please shout me their numbers and I'll make sure you pass the year with distinction!" (This backfired once when I ended up on a date with Maurice.) Note to self re hitting on students' 'parents' – always make sure said students understand that by parents I mean smokin' hot mums!

And just in case you're worried, obviously the first two are not things I would say! One ride I can never get on is the 'opportunities that people miss out on, even when you push them to go for it' train. I am a full-time musician with loads of decent accolades and contacts, and these kids have chosen to come to music college, saying things in their interviews like, "I love music, I want to work as hard as I can at it," or, "I will do whatever it takes to be a professional musician," and then not following through or doing any work!

However, there are always a few students that go above and beyond, and this particular year there was a band of them. I spent my free time helping one of them especially. I was blown away by this guy's commitment at the young age of 17. He was entirely professional, super hard-working, and exceptionally driven. He now works for me, I should add.

Anyways, when this band started playing together, they were in the studios rehearsing at any given opportunity; they came in on their days off, they were in before everyone else and left after everyone else. I called them all in for a tutorial about a month or so after they started working together and said: "Guys, I couldn't be more impressed with you, you have done everything I have asked of you and more. I need to tell you though, it won't be long before the rest of your year will start bitching about you, talking breeze, and saying harsh things, and you have to not react or let it take any of your time. It's gonna be hard, especially as you are so young, but this is an integral part of being successful and happy."

About a month passed and a few of the band members asked to see me for a tutorial. It turned out everyone had started bitching about them. One of them was pretty much in tears about some of the things that had been said, and the others were either hurt, disheartened or angrier than someone licking wee off a stinging nettle. All of which are emotions and feelings that won't help.

Now think of any famous person you know, any! Bring them into a conversation in a group and some will love them, some will hate them, and some will not care. In order of importance for your success is haters, lovers, don't-carers. Just let that sink in.

You would imagine that lovers would be the most important, right?! Don't get me wrong, they are super important. In the previous example, they are the ones that will come to shows, buy merchandise, and push your music on their friends. They will also show support and be there when you need them to be.

The hater, however, will spend more time and effort promoting your band, absolutely FOC, with more energy, effort and drive than pretty much anyone else. But how, and why? Surely if someone is writing bad reviews on your social or talking shit about you at the bar, that is bad for business? Nope, not if the business is good.

The reason Hitler got a bad name is that he was a horrible prick. In fact, you could sing his praises from the rooftops but his actions always precede him and not only would nobody listen to you, but they would probably hurl abuse/whatever projectile was nearest directly into your stupid face.

Now if it's someone like, I dunno, Buddha, or Michael Jordan, or Princess Diana, it doesn't matter how much bad press is spread about them, their actions will always prevail. And in turn, the bad press can attract other people that didn't previously have an opinion to at least check them out and ultimately come to their own conclusions.

You need haters, man! It means you're actually doing something worthy enough of someone else talking about you. Think of all those conversations you've had with friends or family where you were totally sold on something and whoever you were talking to totally disagreed. Either way, you still know the person. I bet you've had raging arguments with your family or friends, or both, and you still love them and want them to succeed. And more so that makes you a lover, but why? Because you didn't talk shit about them to anyone else.

Let's say your mum and dad are absolute C-words when they've had a drink, and one particular night they do something proper lame like come home toe up and wake up all the neighbours and take a dump on the front lawn while singing 'We Will Rock You' at the top of their lungs! You are gonna grill them for it, and get angry at them and hate them for a moment. But as soon as a neighbour calls around your house calling one of your parents a C-word, you stick up for your fam! See, lover, not hater. Hater would agree with the neighbour, well, in fact, hater would have been talking shit and spreading gossip before the neighbour even got round!

A really good way to judge if you are on the right path is noticing when people start to talk shit about you. Let them, enjoy the fact they are talking about you and don't waste your energy on them. Let them be your free marketing. I have loads of people hating on me, bring it on, I love it!

For every hater I have I get 10x the amount of lovers. And the funniest thing is, and obviously, I can't show you for legal reasons no matter how much I want to, I have had people talking absolute shit about me before, like proper horrible untrue rubbish, and then as soon as I started doing well they came asking for help or sucking my dick.

The other thing to mention is that when you break out of your old life into your new life, these guys will start coming out of the woodwork, and they WILL try and stop you. Do not let them. Think of them like the 100s of annoying bits of string I mentioned at the start of this book that confuse and distract you when they are pulled. Do not let them take you away from your mission or goal. That's how they win and how you lose momentum. To summarise: you need haters.

So what's the difference between a hater and a cynic? Cynics are harder to deal with, much harder to deal with. Cynics come in two obvious forms – cynics you know and cynics you don't. They both have the potential to completely ruin your life in a super negative way and will have already done so plenty of times. I need you to be able to spot them so you know what to do when they approach.

Cynics you don't know: Usually people on the TV, or news, or radio that spout absolute bollocks about things they don't know. They often have absolutely no experience in what they are saying. Usually, they have been brainwashed by the same shit from other cynics and then just regurgitate that onto other unsuspecting people.

An example would be when a politician talks about education or the NHS without having ever talked to a teacher or nurse about the real struggles those services go through. Often, most of us subconsciously hear this regularly from the media via adverts or the radio being on in the background.

Think about it, if you actually pay attention to the ads in between TV shows then they bounce between extremes: you're eating too much or you're not eating enough, you're too fat or too thin, you're working too hard or you're not working hard enough... but don't worry, we can sell you a cure for it! Man, it's enough to drive you crazy, and for most of us, it already has. Let's break out.

The cynic you know: These are more often than not family members, friends, and close acquaintances. Ultimately people that love you and want the best for you. They have all the advice for you based off of mostly bad advice they were given by the cynics in their life. It's a horrible cycle that you have to break out of to then start another cycle that works.

The biggest problem with the cynic you know is that their sway is monumental for a few reasons: you respect them, you love them, you care about what they think, you'll have to hear about it if you don't do what they want you to, they can make you feel guilty etc. – you get the picture.

Think of it like this: if some random person came up to you in the street, let's call them Maurice Sippycup, and asked you to quit your job because it was upsetting them that you weren't spending enough time at home with your family, chances are the most action you would take (other than telling them to piss off and mind their own business) would be to think about what they said and either agree or disagree. If you agree with them, there is a very, very, very small chance that would snowball into you actually quitting your job.

If your mum, or partner, or nan, or a best friend drops you the same home truth, it is much more likely that you will actually consider making the change, and at the very least you will think about it more. And more importantly, its effects on you will be deeper. Fact is you were given the same information about the exact same issue, but one has much more gravity.

You see and hear this every day with politicians, the fact is you are drawn towards one specific political party, but you only listen to the positives about that party to solidify your decision to support that party. If your whole family and friendship group support Party A, it is much harder for you to support Party B – not impossible, just much, much harder. You go to a restaurant and you really fancy steak and a margarita and the 3 people you're with order salad and are teetotal... it's definitely not impossible to stick with your first choice but it is definitely much harder. NB: If you want steak and a margarita, order steak and a margarita!

With this in mind, it is one thing supporting a different political party or ordering different food, it is an entirely different thing going against the grain and telling your network that you are changing your life. It's not that they don't want to support you, or that they don't care, quite the opposite. But they won't understand because they haven't experienced the huge changes you are about to make or are making!

Even if you tell them you are listening to self-help audiobooks or joining a new club they might laugh or question it. As I mentioned earlier, you can test this by telling them something huge, well, huge for them, like, "Hey Mum and Dad, I'm starting a new business and quitting my job and I've just taken a 100k business loan for the start-up."

The response you want from that, especially from your close network is something like, "Fucking A, kid! I know you can do this, you're a complete G! Do you need any help with anything?"

So, haters we need, cynics we don't. Don't worry, I'm not gonna ask you to cut ties with your friends and family, but you do have to understand that the more cheerleaders you have, the easier the transition is. And you also have to remember that to start living this new life you are gonna end up with new friends and acquaintances and people to spend your time with: do what you've always done, get what you've always got. A HUGE bonus of this is that when you start moving forward, everyone else will want to follow: be the wave and not the surfer...

This definitely does not mean ignoring your current network or being a dick to everyone you care about. But as I said before, you have to make a change to accommodate change, and this might mean taking a step back from your close group, at the very least to reassess. You are what you eat and you are who you hang around with!

Cynics get all of our emotions going. In the same way, a child can manipulate a parent to get something they want by being relentless in their sales pitch, a parent can tug on your heartstrings and use guilt or pressure to make you feel a certain way and ultimately change your path of actions, or make your home life so unbearable that you can't think straight, or bully you into seeing things their way.

You have to make sure you are prepared for this, it will happen. If it's not your parent or family member, it will be your friend or work colleague. It will be someone, and they will try to push their beliefs on you because that's what they know. It's often all they know! So remember, the hater will do you well, the cynic will not.

So how do we get rid of our cynics if they are people that we frequently spend time with, care for, and can't help but listen to?! Well, the way I did it was to begin to back up my whacked-out ideas before I released them to anyone. Do the work first and prove the result.

For example, if you want to take a loan out to further your career then do and make it work before asking for approval. So instead of, "I'm thinking of taking out a loan, Mum and Dad," you can say, "I took out a loan and used it for XYZ and now my business is flourishing," or similar. The difference in response here is immeasurable. I have been on the other side WAAAAY too many times. I've started things with the best intentions and hyped everyone up, then lost interest when the hard work began and then felt stupid and lame when I had nothing to show!

It's all about showing and not telling. The cynics you know in your life genuinely want what's best for you but they are often wrong. Proving yourself is the way to remedy this.

One prominent fact I have noticed about the super successful is that it takes mammoth amounts of courage to move out of mediocrity. If you want a super successful marriage you have been courageous all the time: the initial date, meeting their friends and family, the proposal, the decision to have kids, raising kids etc. You have been super courageous, and in turn super successful. Same thing with a job, or uni, or anything new that you do! You have to fix up, jump in, and get cracking, otherwise it doesn't happen!

So why if you can be super courageous with stuff like that is it so hard to be courageous with yourself and your own goals?! Like I mentioned earlier, courage is different from stupidity, but often it looks the same to the 99%. However, it looks completely different when you're in the know. I can spot it a mile off now. But that's not the important part, it's the '99%' bit!

The reason most of your immediate network don't understand when you start taking risks and being courageous is that to them it just looks stupid! And when something looks stupid most people won't give it the time of day, so even when you try and explain why you are doing what you're doing it falls on deaf ears. They aren't hearing what you are saying and the cycle continues.

Then they make you feel bad, or even worse they make you question yourself, and then the anxiety kicks in, your confidence goes south and you either give up or attempt the thing anyway but with reduced levels of certainty, which will always end up in failure, limited results and/or take extra time and energy.

You have to be certain, or as near as damn it to have the balls or tits to make a huge decision like taking your first loan out for a personal venture, or asking someone out on a date, or fighting a phobia you've had since a kid.

Imagine Mike Tyson going into the world championship fight and the cornerman says: "Mike, I can't see you winning this fight, my dude, I think you're going to lose, I mean, damn, look at him, his arms look like tree trunks and he has that 'I'm gonna kill you' vibe that you just don't have. Maybe you should give up now and just forfeit so you don't get really hurt!"

This alone may not be enough for Mike Tyson to doubt himself, and in some cases may even make Mike more driven to succeed. But now picture this, it's not just the cornerman spattering these negativities, but instead, the whole crowd starts chanting, "Tyson's weak, Tyson's weak," or similar. Now it is a lot harder for Mike to ignore this. Now imagine the limo driver, on the way here was telling Mike the same thing, and in between sentences the guy on the radio was saying the same thing!

You're Mike Tyson, well, you have the opportunity to be, and your network is the crowd, and the referee, and the cornermen, and everyone else! Think about what you would be wanting them to be saying.

Let's talk about cheerleaders.

Imagine every time you woke up in the morning feeling groggy and like you just wanna hit snooze that someone was there just giving you a little push, in a really soothing but affirmative voice (kinda like your mum or nan or that chick from Sister Act – "C'mon baby, you got this, let's get up and start the day off right," or something like that).

It would be easier to get up! There is tremendous power in telling yourself what to do and how to do it. Think about when you need to pull yourself together after something bad has happened, or you're feeling down, and one of your mates says, "C'mon friend, you can do it." It helps, right?! This is entirely why you get more from a personal trainer than just trusting yourself at the gym...

These amazing people are cheerleaders and they are imperative to your growth and new life. Weirdly enough the best cheerleaders are the cynics you know, but not while they are being cynical.

We all need cheerleaders and positive surroundings to push us and keep us on track, even when our doubt-monkey comes into play. With this in mind, you need to stay as far away from negative situations and people as possible. You wanna be a shit-hot basketball player, there's a point you're gonna need to hang around with other shit-hot basketball players. Same goes for anything. You wanna be an exceptional mechanic, you gotta start hanging around with exceptional mechanics. Same goes for musicians, artists, business-people, swimmers, engineers, physicists, nurses, and everything else.

Do not be the big fish in a small pond, you won't learn shit and you'll be the first one that dies when the water goes bad.

The awesome thing nowadays is that you don't even have to be in the same room as your cheerleaders just to be surrounded by them. You can literally sit in front of your computer or phone with a hard line direct to some of the most amazing people alive in the world right now. You can get video meetings with some of them, or mail them for advice, or buy their books, or watch their seminars, or listen to their podcasts, or stalk them and 'accidentally' turn up at their favourite restaurant...

When I was learning the drums I absolutely immersed myself in other drummers and musicians. I literally spent hour after hour, day after day online or at gigs or on forums just speaking to the best, most wise, exceptional people, drawing as much information from them as I could. You can do the same! And even better, whether it's a quick clip on YouTube or an email response from someone you admire, it will be that confidence boost that helps you find the courage and energy to pick yourself up when you are about to give up, or the kick up the butt to get started.

You know the difference between success and failure? The successful kept going every time they failed! That simple. If the boxer keeps getting up, no matter how many haymakers to the face, they will win the fight if they get up one more time than the opposition. It often only takes that one more time. But the kick in the winky is that you never know it was 'just one more time' until you have done the 'one more time' and can then reflect that it was indeed that last effort that got you there.

More often than not it is the help of a cheerleader that will push you the extra little bit. Ever had a personal trainer? For those that have, you know exactly what I'm talking about. They get more out of you. So does a great teacher, parent, friend, lover! A great way to prove this to yourself if you don't believe me is to cheerlead someone else!

Just try it: next time you experience someone that is about to give up on whatever it is they are about to give up on, no matter how small, see if you can convince them to carry on. A great example of this would be something really blasé and mundane, like, the washing up or taking the bins out or making some toast or popping to the shop.

Next time you see your nearest and dearest umming and erring about doing a little job, try and pep them into doing it. Something like, "C'mon, let's just get it done now, you'll feel better when it's done and I'll make you a cuppa while you do it so you get a little treat when it's finished!" Make sure you say this meaningfully and NOT sarcastically and make the reward obvious! Baby steps...

You can only get so far on your own.

You need cheerleaders, and you need to cheerlead. Did you know that the majority of small start-up businesses fold in the first year because the director, AKA the only person working in the company, will not expand or pass jobs on to others! You can't do shit on your own in this life. It takes your network too, and the bigger your network, the higher your likelihood of success.

Cheerlead others and surround yourself with people that cheer for you, and if you can't find enough of them IRL then stick 'em in your ears and in front of your face via the internet, documentaries, seminars, YouTube, Instagram, or whatever else!

What do you do when your friend, partner, kid or parent is upset? You do whatever you can to help them out! But why wait for something to go wrong to put that positive energy into it? Imagine what happens if everything is going well and you push someone to do more! A great teacher will always get more out of a student than a student will do on their own because the teacher pushes them. It's the same with PTs, head chefs, managers or whatever.

Are you getting your push from anyone? Who is pushing you to be your best self?

You need as many as possible, as often as possible! I would love to be able to spend 365 with each of you and give my full 100% but I can't, so when you can't listen to me then you need someone to take over.

Or just listen to me constantly. That will work too for the time you are on your own (until you go completely batshit crazy), but what about home life, work-life, or any other time you read?

How do you turn your close peeps AKA your close-5 into cheerleaders? FYI your close-5 are the 5 people you hang around with the most, the ones you spend your time with and listen to. Unfortunately, they may more often than not be cynics or average-folk.

Obviously, your close-5 will help you when you are down or need advice or need to make a tough decision, that's a given. But we need them supercharged and pushing you forward the rest of the time too!

## Exercise 1.0

Grab your journal. A line down the middle of the next fresh page. One side: cheerleaders, the other side: cynics. I would make you do a third column for haters but like I said, let them get on with passing your name around and give them zero of your time or energy. I must stress, I want you to choose people at the opposite ends of this particular spectrum! So if they are just meh cheerleaders or not too bad cynics then leave them out.

Under your cheerleader side, write out everyone you know that cheerleads you no matter what. The ones that have always got your back, and always make you feel good when you hang out with them. This may not be your best friends, so think hard and make sure you pick the people that are best for you, even if it's a friend of a friend or an uncle you hardly ever see.

Now write all the cynics in your life on the other side.

For this to work effectively, I want you to put as many on each side as possible. To give you an idea the average total of names written down tends to be between 8 and 25.

Now if the cynic side outweighs the cheerleader side, you need some movements! In fact, for every 1 cynic, you need about 3 cheerleaders to counteract their nagging, nausey, grey, wanky bullcrap. Kinda similar to if you just drank bottled juice straight without diluting it with water.

Most of you will have more cynics than cheerleaders. But even if you had more cheerleaders than cynics we still need to add a multiplier! For you guys with more cynics, here's the hard truth: this needs to change. Something to note is that when you start being crazy awesome all the time, and most of you will have noticed this already, others begin to follow. Interesting, eh!? Anyway, you cynic-heavy motherfuckers, let's sort this out. You must dump them cynics, well at least dump the time you spend with them until you are where you need to be.

They are slowing you down. They are like rust on a car. You wanna spend ages taking the rust off, or you wanna replace the car?! Sometimes we wanna spend time taking the rust off, but for now, we are gonna replace the car!

You guys with more cheerleaders – well done! This would have been mostly a conscious effort so great job, now we need to 10x it!

So, whatever side of the table you are on – more cheerleaders or more cynics, we can apply the same little hack. We are going to hyperdrive our current cheerleaders by taking immediate action and we are going to reverse and topsy-turvey our cynics. Let's deal with the cynics first and get them out the way!


*How to Deal with the Cynics in Your Life*, by Lee James Bridges.


Chapter 1:

Stop spending time with cynics.

The end.


Get it? Got it? Good!

It's that simple. You're in control of your actions, right?! So just stop giving them time, don't listen to their shit, and if they bring it up and ask why you are not spending as much time with them then make it very clear that you are starting a new life and you need to be surrounded with positive people.

You don't have to be a dick about this, just be real. If you are indeed changing your life for the better, you will have to hit this subject at some point and make a few changes anyway. Does not mean you will lose friends, quite the opposite, but sometimes you gotta be selfish to move your life forward.

You don't even need to call these cynics up to explain what you are doing, just make sure you aren't being a self-righteous cockmuncher about it. Just start focusing your time on the important things. That's it, just stop hanging around with them!

As for the bad boy cheerleaders! We need to supercharge these people! They have the power to help make your life awesome beyond your wildest dreams, you need them. And you need them in tippy-top condition, and they need the same from you!

---

## Exercise 1.1

So, immediate action please. I want you to call, not text or email, all of the cheerleaders on your list. ALL OF THEM! No excuses! Even if these are the people you haven't spoken to in a long time. Some you may have not spoken to for over 10 years but they just inspire and push you through their social media presence or something, doesn't matter. If they made the cut, give them a holla.

The way I want your conversation to go is something like this (but make it your own, obvs):

"Hey (insert name), how are you? I just wanted to call you to let you know that you are one of the most positive people in my life and I wanted to acknowledge and thank you for this! Your words and actions since I've known you have really helped me to begin to start smashing my own life and I am super grateful! I am currently making some huge life changes and I wanna see and hear more of you! If there is anything I can do to repay your inspirational lushness then just let me know!"

---

This will be a proper feel-good call for both of you! Why? Well firstly, people love being told they have been helpful, and even more so if you word it correctly and execute what you are saying with conviction and genuine love and meaning, you will make this person's day! Which in turn will make you feel great and buzzy.

And if you're on top of your game they will probably say similar back. More often than not it will be stuff you didn't even know they thought about you – maybe something cool you did a while back they never found the opportunity to thank you for! Secondly, and this is great, they will cheer you on more. They will talk to others about your phone call and pass on how you are getting on! Win squared!

This is you working to increase your relationships with the best people in your life! And this is a great springboard too! The number of times I have made calls like this and then later that day or week I get a message or phone call or email fixing a problem I may have mentioned on the phone.

One that springs to mind is when I called a dear old friend of mine I hardly ever see now, I had a similar conversation thanking him for getting me through some of my neg times and he asked me how I was doing with my band at the time. I told him we were doing really well but wanted to do some gigs on the mainland in countries we hadn't played before, like Switzerland, France, Belgium, Holland and

Germany. I didn't ask any favours, just pumped him up for being an amazing guy.

Two days later he got at me with a bunch of contacts for different promoters in the previously mentioned countries! The absolute legend had spent his own time helping me and my band out just because. No other reason. Now I know what you're thinking. You think it's because I said nice things to him and then he felt like he owed me something. Well, that is a little correct, but the main reason and the one that is of the most use to us is that I reminded him of my mission at the time, I made him aware and he could see how excited and hard-working I was and he wanted to help.

I could have been anyone. Think about it, how many times have you gone above and beyond and bent over backwards to do something amazingly nice that took effort and energy and time for someone you hardly know? Ever had that mate that brings his friend or partner to your birthday party or wedding or whatever social gathering, and nobody knows the person, but they get you the most thoughtful present or card and your best mate doesn't get you anything!? Why? Because they wanted to make a lasting impression but your friend feels like they know you well enough to have stopped putting in effort = you have probably stopped putting in effort with your friend too!

Cheerlead the shit out of awesome people and see what happens...

That's enough on haters, cynics and cheerleaders, for now, I'm sure you get the point. Now we need to get super practical again, and I need to teach you one of my most powerful techniques. I want to share it with you, and I want you to share it with everyone else...

## Summary

- Ex 1.0

Cheerleaders and Cynics list

  − Line down the middle of the page

  − Cynics on one side, and cheerleaders on the other

  − Make a comprehensive list for both sides

  − Replace cynics with cheerleaders IRL

- Ex 1.1

Give props to your crew

  − Call EVERYONE on your cheerleader list and give them props

  − Make sure you don't expect anything in return

  − Do not miss anyone out

- You need haters, let them do their thing and don't waste your time on them

- You need cheerleaders; give them as much of your time as possible and surround yourself with them as often as possible

- You do not need cynics.

# Chapter 24

# Burst Training

Welcome to burst training. In this chapter, I am going to drop you a goldmine hack that is the fastest, most efficient way of learning anything physical, and you can also apply the techniques to mental things too. This is dynamite if you want to absolutely boss a skill and get it shit hot as fast as possible! A bold statement I know, but you will see the proof within 1 week, and in most cases a day!

Before I explain how to burst, I need to tell you how I came about the idea, and I can't even begin to tell you how much this hack changed my life! This is more than a game changer and I am hyped to tell you about it so you can tell your friends and pass the knowledge on.

As you know, I'm a musician. I started playing the drums at the age of 14 because I was fat and had no self-esteem and what better way to stop people noticing you and go under the radar than by playing what most people consider to be the loudest instrument! That's a different story for another time...

I started playing and within a few days, it was all I could think about. I always loved music but I had never previously thought about taking up an instrument. I wouldn't shut up about it, and within no time I convinced my parents to let me have a drum kit in the house – idiots, hahaha! They gave me one caveat: to prove it wasn't just another fad,

I had to take regular lessons, and work towards doing my 1st grade. Upon completing this my dad said to me that if I saved half the amount of money it would cost to get a beginner kit, he would match it and give me the remaining half towards it = LEGEND.

I later found out my parents were absolutely broke and believed in me enough to help a brother out. At the time I had just started working in a cafe, a really shitty greasy spoon, and I asked for every extra hour they had to start saving for my first drum kit. I worked and worked and worked and went to weekly lessons and listened and played at any opportunity. I wanted the kit more than anything.

Long story short, I got to the amount I needed, my dad matched it, and I got my first drum kit. I played whenever I could. My friends used to come over and sit in my room while I played, I'd sit in lessons at school thinking about nothing other than being a musician. It was all I wanted to do! There are some super funny and amazing stories from this time of my life that I will definitely tell you another time...

Fast forward to 7 years later and I had moved to the south coast to go to music university. I managed to get in without any A levels or C+ GCSEs (even though I was told this was impossible). I was so serious about my music career. I lived, breathed and ate music but where I came from there were hardly any musicians that felt the same. Upon moving to Brighton, finally, I was surrounded by similar minds. My housemates were all drummers or singers or guitarists or bassists and we spent all of our time scheming on music.

One day we had a guest tutor at uni, an exceptional drummer by the name of Pat Garvey, you should check him out, absolute don (he was also the gorilla in the Cadbury's advert playing along to Phil Collins if you remember that)! One day after a lesson I asked him if he had a few minutes to impart some wisdom.

He asked me how often I was practising, and what I was practising. I told him I was doing about 2-3 hours a day outside of uni. I remember feeling fairly smug when I said this as I knew I practised more than most of my peers. He immediately shut me down. "That's not enough," he said. I was like, saaaay whaaaa?!

He asked if I would practice more if I could and I replied, "Yeah, of course, I just don't have the time." God if only I knew then what I know now.

He said, "Well then you need to make time." He asked me what I did on an average day. I told him and he replied, "Well you need to get up earlier then! If you wake up at 6am you can get in a couple more hours of practice per day." 6am!!!???

I only saw 6am from the front side after a night out. How the hell could I stay up till 4am smoking weed and wanking if I had to be up 2 hours later at 6am?! Does not compute. He told me that my priorities were all wrong and if I wanted to be a professional musician I had to start taking it seriously! I thought I was, but God was I wrong. I will explain why in a minute, but this turned out to be fairly bad for me.

I went back home after that conversation with Pat and started practising more, immediately, mainly through stubbornness. I didn't want anyone thinking I wasn't serious so I started going to bed earlier, and waking up earlier, and practising more. Now the thing about drums, which is true of pretty much everything, is that you get out what you put in, but doing anything repetitive will eventually cause a problem.

Usain Bolt does not train for his sprints by sprinting for 8 hours a day. Surgeons don't train for heart surgery by holding a scalpel in their hands for 8 hours a day, and world record eaters don't train for competitions by eating hot dogs 8 hours a day. Like I said before, if you want bigger biceps, doing 8 hours of bicep curls a day, every day, will just end up giving you serious issues, for a plethora of reasons: fatigue, injury, boredom, arms exploding etc.

In drums, we have these things called rudiments. Think of them as the alphabet: you can't speak words without knowing the alphabet. They are the basis for everything you can play on the drums, much like dancers have fundamental moves. Mathematicians have numbers to be able to do the simplest of addition, right up to completely complex sums, but without the foundations, you can't do either. You cannot play anything on a drum kit that isn't one of these rudiments. Rudiments can also be used as warm-ups. Once you've got them down you have these fundamental exercises to warm up with.

So for 4 years, I practised my rudiments. And I practised them hard, 3-4 hours a day! I knew this was the case cuz my housemates and peers always commented on it. I hated it. I had to force myself to do it each day, and often I would get a few minutes in and my brain would drift and I'd just hit autopilot for the following 2-3 hours.

Now don't get me wrong, this really tightened up my game. My drumming got better, faster, stronger, and in turn, I felt more confident as a drummer. This was all well and good until I started to notice problems with my wrists and arms. By the end of the 3rd year, I had a mixture of tendonitis, carpal tunnel, RSI and general aches and pains. It got so bad I had to stop playing for months and every time I picked up anything in that period, it immediately hurt and then played on my mind.

If you've ever had to stop doing something you love because of injury then you know how I felt. It crushes you. Completely. I was not only depressed all the time, but I also went from specialist to specialist to try and get it sorted, and on top of that I had to cancel gigs with different artists I was working with, which not only makes you feel like shit because you wanted to do the gigs, but loses you future work because some motherflipper jumps in your grave and takes your work. I spent all my money, and I mean ALL my money on different treatments, and I wasn't bringing much in because I was missing gigs. Chicken egg like a mofo!

I tried everything, from physio and chiropractic work, acupuncture and meditation to considering chopping off my hand with the machete I bought from a market stall in Colchester when I was a kid. I tried it all. Even worse than the constant pain though, was what it did to my mind. I would wake up in the night having anxiety dreams and spend most of the day thinking about it cuz everything reminded me of it. The mental detriment far surpassed the actual physical pain.

After all the treatments, and a few years of feeling down and done in, I went back to my local GP. My usual doctor was not there so I saw his replacement: this 60-70-year-old guy, big bushy beard, wise eyes. He looked badass for some reason despite his age. I explained the situation and he took a pause, looked me dead in the eye, and said: "Jesus! Grow up! So your hands hurt, what did you expect? You hit things for a living with wooden sticks, of course you're gonna do yourself damage. The best advice I can give you is to get it out of your head and play through it with the understanding one day it will stop you playing completely, but DON'T waste your time now worrying about it when you could be doing something you love."

I left the surgery kinda deflated and a bit pissed off that his advice was such but I was desperate so I took heed. After a few days, the problems started to become bearable. In hindsight, a lot of the issue was manifested in my own mind. I started playing again, and I'm still playing. One valuable lesson here is that the mind is stronger than anything else. You just have to read some real-life tales of people that have been right through it and come out the other side to prove that point.

The point I'm making here though is that the main reason I suffered RSI was the amount of time I was sat at my kit going through the motions. I got repetitive strain injury from repetitive straining, duh! Problem is, working hard and working smart couldn't be more different. One question I always get asked, and this one kills me cuz I know how it feels, is when people are working soooo hard to reach their goals, but they aren't getting anywhere. I know it first hand from many a venture.

I'm sure you can relate. This one is the hardest as you really can put your all into something and get nothing out of it, and in some cases get detrimental results like I did with my wrists. I worked my dick off on my drums and it resulted in me not being able to play my drums! Pat Garvey wasn't wrong, I did need to take my profession much more seriously, and he completely opened my eyes to what amount of effort is necessary to succeed, but the necessary effort has to be thought out, clever, and smart. It needs to work for us as much as we have to work for it. I know now he didn't mean just play incessantly every day, he meant network, listen to music, get my finances right, don't go to sleep at 6am, etc., etc.

After this whole experience, I realised that I didn't have to put myself in the hospital to get the results I wanted. Well at least I figured there must be a way, and just so you know, there is ALWAYS a way. I put pen to paper and tried to come up with a way to get the results I wanted without doing myself damage. The realisation I ended up with was much bigger than I ever thought possible. My intention was a way to get better at drums without hurting my hands, but what I worked out is something I now use every day, numerous times, to get shit hot at whatever I want to get shit hot at! Burst training, bitches!

So now you know why I wanted to come up with this, but now you need to know how.

Like I previously mentioned, I was always fat when I was an 'iccle pickney, but when I got to about 18 I finally decided to take control of my body and slammed the gym, changed my diet, stopped smoking weed and dropped from 20 stone to 12. I finally started feeling good. I lost the weight before I started uni and was now on a regimented gym schedule 5 days a week. When I moved to Brighton I started enjoying the uni life, staying up late and drinking and eating badly. I didn't put it all back on but I was aware I was being unhealthy. Everyone else seemed to be doing the same though so I didn't feel bad about it. NB: just because everyone else does, definitely does not mean you should. Sheep follow the herd...

Fast forward some years and I started seeing my now wife, and within the first year, I had done the classic and got comfortable and fat. She did the same. We were like 2 Jigglypuffs. FYI being fat makes you feel like shit whether you think it does or not, and it slows your progress right down, again, whether you think it does or not. There is so much proven research on this, don't kid yourself.

After I proposed to her I found myself joining a gym again. It wasn't the same as when I was 18 when my only responsibilities were to go to a job I didn't care about and then go home, still living with my parents. Now I had a job course leading at a college, a music career, a step-son, a fiancée, and a more demanding friendship group. I had less time, much less time. When I went to the gym when I was 18 I went every day after work and spent 45 minutes doing cardio, and Mon/Wed/Fri I did an hour of resistance training afterwards.

When I started the gym the second time I had all these extra responsibilities. Even if I woke up earlier I still didn't have time to do 45 mins cardio every day and then 1 hour of weights 3 times a week. It just couldn't happen with my then-schedule. At that time I had very specific goals and unfortunately, gym time was not at the top of the priority list (even though exercise always should be).

So here's what I did.

One day I was reading up on different types of gym training and this thing called HIIT kept coming up. I'm sure you've heard of it, but for those that haven't lemme explain. HIIT stands for high-intensity interval training. In short, it means working at your optimum for short amounts of time with small breaks in between. This makes your heart rate go from 0-60 and back to 0 in no time at all and causes you to burn more calories in less time, and as a bonus, you will keep burning calories throughout the day.

The first time I heard this I was blown sideways. *OMG*, I thought, *I can do a 45-minute cardio session in 10 minutes and get better results.*

I know what you're thinking. "That sounds too good to be true." It's not! It's completely true. But I won't lie, it's hard work, like, one of the hardest! To this day I stand by the fact that I would rather do 45 mins of kinda pushing it cardio than 10 mins of 100% effort HIIT training, or AMRAP, EMOM or Metcon.

One reason being is that because you always have to give 100%, even if it is for short amounts of time – your 100% is always your 100%. Think about it, pushing yourself to your absolute limit, even if for a few moments, is gonna be harder than sorta pushing it for 45 mins. I got to thinking and realised that with a few tweaks this concept could be utilised for pretty much anything.

Something that happens when you get a bit older than early 20s is that with each month that passes you have more responsibilities, and loads more unexpected problems. Whether it's moving out of your parents' and paying rent, council tax and bills, running a car, having a serious relationship, kids and dealing with your parents getting old and needing help or whatever else. Life gets more full-on. I noticed that when I started doing well with my music. I didn't have time to practise because I was living the job.

Instead of having free evenings to practise I had gigs and sessions. These were upkeeping my skills but I wasn't necessarily learning new techniques. In fact, I wasn't learning anything other than gig experience. I'd gotten complacent and was just going through the motions. I still had a hunger to get better at my discipline, but I literally didn't have the time if I was prioritising the other parts of my life. Remember the slide puzzle analogy?

Going to a rehearsal studio for a few hours a day wasn't possible cuz I had a kid, a wife and a job to pay the rent. This was not even taking into consideration all the standard bad luck or life throwing me any curveballs. I needed a way to get better, to keep learning, but I needed it to be more than efficient, I needed it to be a ninja!

One day I was in rehearsals with a band I was working for. I had recently seen one of my drum idols doing this crazy technique where he had two drumsticks in one hand and was owning his high-hat. I desperately wanted to learn this technique but I knew it would take some hours in the studio on my own to get it perfected.

After about 1 month of first seeing this specific technique I sat at the kit one day and I could do it. I couldn't believe it. I was made up! I racked my brains as to how I had managed this in such a short space of time without putting in any specific or coordinated effort! I thought about it and soon realised that every time I sat down at the kit, whether it be on a gig or in a band rehearsal, or while waiting for my class to turn up for a lecture, I had been attempting it, mostly for about 30 seconds at a time.

In one 3-hour rehearsal I would sit there doing these little 30-second bursts without too much thought. After a month these bursts had amounted to a few hours of practice. Now the important thing here is that they were regular and often. Little and often is better than one big push, if it's worth doing... eh?!

In that month I must have accidentally practised this technique 100s of times! And now I could do it. Granted, it was rough around the edges, but I could do it! This was without any structure or general awareness of what I was doing. Think of it in the same way as brushing your teeth or some mundane task like that. You do it for little increments of time each day, but over the years you get sooo good at it that without even noticing you are a grandmaster of picking up the brush, applying the toothpaste, running the tap and scrubbing your teeth. You didn't mean to get good at it, but through regular short bursts, you turned into a badass tooth brushing assassin! Now imagine the power of this if you focused, and instead of brushing your teeth we were talking about something you are passionate about.

Burst practice.

There used to be a show on British TV, I think it was called 'Faking It' or something like that. The premise of the show was that one person would have to learn a skill that was completely alien to them in just 1 week, and at the end of the week, they would have to showcase said skill in front of industry judges while competing against 3 other people, all of which were professionals in the chosen field.

The interesting thing was that 9 times out of 10 the charlatan won! The judges genuinely believed the fake was a professional just because of the massive action they had put in that week. Thing is, that person would take the whole week off and just focus on the task at hand and most of us can't just take a week off to do whatever, so we have to fit our learning around our current obligations. Great news! It's entirely possible and totally not that hard!

Introducing Lee Lee's burst practice! So here's how you do it... But before I give you the steps I should explain that if you want to get the most out of this it has to be aggressive and you have to take advantage of the little gaps of time in your life you didn't previously use!

Remember your 24 planner from chapter 10? That you are using regularly now?!

Now is the time to go full nutter on it and break it into smaller time segments. Start with one block a day and see how much time you can make by cutting your hour blocks into half hours, quarter hours, and if you wanna go complete fruit loop then break it into 5- or 10-minute slots. Burst practice will be most effective 3 or more times a day, for a minimum of 1 or 2 minutes at a time. I know all of you can find 3+ minutes per day...

# Exercise 1.0

Choose a thing. This really could be anything, the power of burst practice applies to absolutely anything and allows for easy progress tracking.

Be aware of the fact that you are learning one specific thing, try not to convolute ideas, do one new skill at a time and do it until it's done. It's like riding a bike; once you've learned it, it won't get forgotten, as long as you've done it to the point of muscle memory and understanding, and you can add a bunny hop after you learn to ride. It would be dumb to try and learn both at the same time. Make sure you can do one thing correctly before stacking something on top of it, you don't want a sketchy foundation Lego brick to build on.

For those of you that are thinking, "But you said stack stuff up and practise more than one thing at once." Well, firstly, great retention skills! And secondly, I did say that, and I still mean it, but for the specific purpose I said it. In this instance, we are gonna focus hard on one thing and you can stack after. We spoke about this in the 'know thyself' chapter: sometimes you need 'this' and sometimes you need 'that'! As a side note, this is why I take little bits from every religion and not just one. Pick your battles, man! Some shit works for some shit and doesn't work as well for other shit; do not be closed off to new ideas and ways of thinking. Adapt and transition constantly.

So, here goes...

**Step 1:** Practice the skill as slow as physically possible. Just to put a point on this, whatever you think is slow is more than likely way too fast. As humans, especially nowadays, we cut corners, and cutting corners is not hacking, it's cutting corners, it's not getting the job done properly, and it always shows at some point.

Burst practice only works if you spend the initial amount of time needed to make sure the skill you are learning is as near to perfect as possible. When it is, then we speed it up. To make sure this is the slickest most efficient it can be, film your very first attempt, and film the next day, and following days until it is as close to perfect as possible. Ask a friend to be sure. For example, if I wanted to learn how to do the 2-step, or how to make an awesome sales pitch, I would do it slowly, super slow the first few times. Slow breeds understanding and I can't stress this enough, if you can't do it well slowly, you definitely won't be able to do it well fast. I am gonna say this one more time as it usually takes a few times to get it through: what you think is slow is more than likely not slow! Check yourself and make sure it is SLOOOOOOOOOOOW.

Doing something fast is sloppy if it's not good! You need control for this and you have to commit to getting it right so then you can speed it up. A more important point to make is that there is a speed where even the most novice of people can do anything.

Imagine if I said that you needed to learn one of Mozart's symphonies in a month. Initially, your thought process, unless you are an accomplished classical pianist, would be, "Not possible." However, you missed the important question: "How fast do I have to play it?"

Fact is, if you could learn it one note at a time, with a minute in between each note, and you had a tutorial video on YouTube that you could play and pause at your will then immediately the task goes from impossible to totally possible. Now consider there was no time limit, and you could play through the piece, still with 1 minute in between each note. Then each time you played it you decreased the time between notes. First 55 seconds, then 50, then 45, right down to 1 second. Now it sounds like a piece of music, and your muscle memory is so ingrained that you don't even need to look at the sheet music!

In this instance, slow is the new fast! It gets you there quicker, and when you get there it's not just better, it's closer to perfect than previously possible! This is step 1, and it is integral you don't get big-dick syndrome and start running before you can walk.

Make sure you track your progress by filming what you are doing and comparing it between takes.

Do NOT screw this step up.

Sacrifice today so you don't have to compromise tomorrow! Take time on this and get it right, do not advance before you have done this.

The thing that is a hyper-nause if you take the tact of "well it won't work so I won't waste my time bothering". This is another 'trust Lee' time! You will not regret it and I can 100% guarantee you that if you do this correctly that you will save so much time in the long run. How can I be so sure? Ask any of my students! When I started implementing this at college with my students I had the previous 5 years of teaching to compare it to. The students that committed to burst practice not only advanced up to 80% quicker than their peers, but they also developed a much more coherent understanding of their chosen skill/technique, and more so, they could execute said skill 10x better than their peers that didn't commit to burst training.

So, I trust you will get this right and have self-control. To make sure you know when to move onto Step 2, you can follow this checklist:

a) Can I do the thing I am learning without thinking about it?

b) Can I half the speed of the thing I am practising and feel confident it is correct?

c) Does the filming of my first attempt seem light years away from my most recent attempt?

Done? Coolsies! To Step 2.

**Step 2:** Once you can do the thing you are learning uber slow, you can start to burst! Again, do not make the mistake and run before you can walk, it doesn't take long at all to do Step 1 but you MUST do it properly and completely! If you slack on it or go too fast this will not work! Remember all of the hacks in this book are about the long game and not the IGMF!

As a rough metric (and this will alter depending on the intricacies of the thing you are learning and your current understanding of that skill or discipline), if you commit to 3 lots of 3 minutes a day, by the end of the fifth day you will be ready to begin bursting. If you want to be double sure, then do 7 or 9 days, but no less than 5!

As soon as you have your new skill down super slow, you are going to practice it in bursts. To make a point, and I have researched this on literally 100s of people including myself, by doing this thrice per day for 5 minutes, within a week you will be noticeably better, within 2 weeks you will be killing it, and within a month you will be able to say you are a pro at whatever it is you chose to do. For all you cynics out there saying this is impossible, I'll make you a deal: record yourself doing your chosen skill for a month, every day, just like I've explained, and if you are not 100% satisfied after a month I will not only refund you for this book, but I will personally phone you up and apologise.

Lastly, this is specifically for solo ventures. What I mean by that is you won't be able to call yourself a professional guitar player in one month as many different skills are integral to learning guitar and becoming a master at it, but with this technique, you will be able to get to a professional level at playing an E chord, or similar.

Then you can spend the next month on other chords, progressions, strumming patterns, voicings, feel, changes etc. and add one skill at a time. Plus, each time you add a skill your burst training will be easier and quicker to master because you will have a process down. Within a year you will be able to play all the chords, but you will play them so much better than anyone else that has learned for a year with conventional methods. There isn't a skill I have come across that this has not worked with.

## Exercise 1.1

So, let's burst. We will start with 5 minutes, an amount of time anybody can free up! You are going to burst in 30-second increments, with the first 10 seconds being as slow as you can possibly do – just like in Step 1 (depending on the skill, this will usually be 2-3 times round). The remaining 20 seconds will be going from 0-100%, with the last 3-5 seconds being almost impossible to keep up with. Then you repeat the process until your 5 minutes are up.

That's it, there are only 2 steps. Now for those of you thinking your chosen skill won't work with bursts, for instance, things that aren't sport or training orientated, like asking someone on a date or something like that, then you are kinda right in the same way you can't learn all the nuances of guitar with this method, however, the mini skills you need to ask someone on a date are entirely burstable.

But for things you don't need to do at light speed then you can just cut out Step 2 and practise super slow. Learning lines, shaking hands, walking or skills like this will all progress phenomenally if you practice them suuuuuuper slow!

Lemme know what you are bursting, add videos of your first attempts and where you're at now! Share, share, share!!!

See you in the next chapter!

---

## Summary

- Ex 1.0

Pre-burst practice

  - Choose an particular skill (you can't choose tennis but you could choose serving)
  - Practice the motion as slow as feasibly possible without speeding up, ideally for a few minutes a few times per day
  - Once the motion is near perfect, you can begin to burst

- Ex 1.1

Burst practice

  - Practice gradually going from ridiculously slow to as fast as possible in short bursts, ideally for a few minutes a few times per day
  - Repeat until mastered

- Slow and controlled ALWAYS beats fast and uncontrolled
- If you think you are going slow you are most likely not going as slow as you could be
- Winning at life fast is possible if the process is correct, make sure you get the process correct.

# Chapter 25

# Progress Report

Do you think of your life in different eras, or sections, or parts? You will have often heard yourself or someone else saying, "I remember when I was young I used to..." or, "Oh yeah, I used to be into football but I much prefer video games now," or, "I used to be so much healthier."

Fact is, and remember our spectrums, this is your whole life. This is not your half-life, quarter-life, $1/10^{th}$ of a whole life. It's your whole life!!! It's all yours, and nobody else's. Your transition is happening whether you like it or not, you're getting older but are you getting wiser? Are you getting more experienced? Are you where you want to be? Are you financially stable? Are you hitting all your goals? Do you even know what your goals are? Is your current situation bleeding you dry? Are your partners, family and friends happy? Are you happy?

Life is undeniably hard, but how much harder are you making it for yourself? I was making my life impossible for myself, for a long time! If you have any destructive vices then you're making your life harder. If you're overweight or unfit then you are making your life harder. If you are going to sleep too late or waking up too late, guess what... You're making life harder!

It's instant gratification that screws our long game and stops us thinking ahead!

Why in the hell would you want to make it any harder than it is already anyway??

If you had to run a marathon, would you buy yourself trainers 2 sizes too small and stick a tiny stone in one of them and fill the other with itching powder just for shits and gigz?! Of course not! You gotta be real, not with me, or your parents, or friends or family (well you do), but waaaay more importantly you gotta be real to yourself before anyone else comes into the equation!

If you can't be real to yourself then what do you think is happening when you are telling others about your life?! It's not real, it's not true! You gotta stop lying to yourself and break the curse. We are surrounded with bull shit but it is our job to realise it is just bull shit and not to let it get in the way of our mission. This book is all about changing your life, transitioning to a better version of your life, 2.0, baby!

Notice I said changing your life, not having a different one. You can't have a different life. You got this one so let's make it count. You have the potential, power, ability, skills and passion to move it from the beta version to the all-singing, all-dancing, loaded on steroids version. You gotta choose life: your life!

You are either on top or you're not, there is no extra space in 1st position for more than one person, and this is true of your life. There is only one position for you to take. Which one you gonna choose? I don't wanna end up in second, third, or even worse stuck on the start line with no fuel of my life and you shouldn't of yours.

Only you can choose to live your life, nobody else can; they will act like they know what's best for you, but they don't. Remember, YOU know, every time! It's time to check your progression...

Remember the questions I asked you at the start of the book in the 'Commit' chapter? Let's see how much you've changed so far...

As before, answer all of the following honestly...

## Current you

(% between 1-100)

1. Happiness
2. Productivity
3. Confidence
4. Fear
5. Anxiety
6. Self-esteem
7. Doubt
8. Belief in future
9. Friendship group
10. Diet
11. Fitness level
12. Self-control
13. Overall

## Future you

(% between 1-100)

1. How confident are you in your current abilities to smash your future?
2. How committed are you to your future?

3. How fearful of your future are you?

4. Are you ready to make a change?

5. Do you want to take control of your life?

6. Do you want to be healthier?

7. Do you want to be fitter?

8. Can you picture your life being much better than it currently is?

## A little bit about you (up to 3 for each)

1. What are your best traits?

2. What are your worst traits?

3. What are you amazing at?

4. What are you terrible at?

5. What are your favourite activities currently?

6. What are your least favourite activities currently?

7. What things do you want to change in your current life?

8. What things do you want to try (small)?

9. What things do you want to try (big)?

10. Who is your biggest inspiration?

You should have not only have answered these with higher scores and more positively than before, but will also have found you answered much quicker and with a much higher level of certainty.

Don't worry if they still aren't where you want them to be, there's still time to get them near 100%!

Now I want you to go back through these questions and write down what you need to do to make your percentages higher. To help structure this better you can use a Lego build for each answer, and keep it super simple, 3 bricks! I'm gonna be real with you, my answers to all the above were between 90-100% throughout my 20s, but it wasn't until I started working on myself that I realised I was completely lying to myself, and in actual fact, if I compare them to how I feel now, they were all more like 10-20%. You never know 'til you know, ya know?!

Let's say you run a 100-metre sprint in 15 seconds, and the previous year you could only do it in 20 seconds, and the year before that you couldn't get off the start line. If I asked you how happy you were with your time in the first year I'm sure you would be bummed out as you didn't even finish. If I asked you in the second year you may answer 100% as completing the 100 meters in 20 seconds feels like it's 100 times better than not getting off the start line. If I asked you in the following year (where you have shaved 5 seconds off your time from the previous year), your 100% is now not 100%, cuz you bested it!

Shaving another 5 seconds off this time would be a MASSIVE accomplishment, right?! Most people can run 100 metres between 15-20 seconds. Only a very small percentage of the population can do it in 10 seconds! That's the 1% you always hear about! It's the upper limit of our ability after strict and clever practice and self-improvement! Being in the 99% is a piece of cake in comparison to being in the 1%. Until you spend time in the 1% and realise the 99% is horrendous, scripted BS and nowhere near as fun, rewarding, and amazing as being in the 1%.

Fact: The 99% don't trust what the 1% are saying, even if they haven't spent time there to be able to compare.

Join the 1%, even if it is just for one part of your life, just so you can see how it is and then choose whether you want to apply it to the other parts of your life too! I'm currently working on getting loads of parts of my life up into the 1%!

If we all smash this together then 1% could turn into the 10%, and then one day the 100% where everyone is killing it, happy, and successful. Make it your duty to be the absolute best version of yourself.

Your life is in transition, constantly; this is why you have to stay outside of your comfort zone and keep changing. Don't be afraid of change, embrace it and make it work for you.

How many times have you caught yourself saying, "If I'd have just known YouTube was gonna be huge when it first came out I could have been one of the first to upload videos and now I'd be riiiiiich!" or you have watched Shark Tank or Dragons' Den and you'd already come up with one of the ideas that are being pitched but never followed through with it, and now Peter from Epsom is getting an investment from that one that looks like he is an actual potato. It could have been your investment!

Stop living in the past, you gotta embrace the fact that everything is changing with every moment that passes, stop being behind, stop getting stuck on the start line! Choose your life, not someone else's! So you missed out on being one of the first YouTubers, or you had a great idea that someone else took to market first. Stop bitching! Why do you think they took it to market first?! You think it was just a coincidence? Nah, fam! It was hard work, courage, and commitment!

And this, my friends, is exactly why we don't get what we want... we don't work hard enough, we lack courage, and we don't commit to the required level! I've done it, you've done it, Usain Bolt's done it. Remember, it's not your fault being dealt the hand you have, but it is entirely your fault if upon realising you don't do sweet FA about it!

Take responsibility and commit. Commit to your life! It's yours, and as far as I know, it's the only one you got! Use it, do not let it use you! Same with tech! Own your phone and don't let it own you. Same with your relationships, business, health, vices... own them, do not let them own you!

This is gonna be a hard pill for some of you to swallow, but it's true! And even if you are fighting it, you know deep down that it is true, I know you do.

None of the following will be easy but fuck someone else making the rules for your life! If you know you are in an abusive relationship or some absolute waste of breath is treating you like anything other than a queen or king, and you know it's abusive and you're being treated bad, your fault, bail, no matter how hard it is! If you're in a job you hate and you know you need to quit but you haven't because (insert excuse), your fault, bail! If your diet is shit and you know it, your fault, change it! If you know you lack confidence, your fault, sort it out! Do something! ANYTHING!!! Just start!

I know some of the things I'm saying will rub some of you up the wrong way and I definitely mean no offence, but I would rather die trying than give in! Take responsibility and commit to a better life, your life. You think I'm preaching?! Damn fucking straight, I wish someone had have told me how real you need to be to yourself to get what you want in life! Everyone sugar-coated it for me as they did for you. The TV is constantly puking on you, the radio is constantly puking on you, the cynics are puking on you so for the sake of Dawn French's tits, don't puke on yourself! Balls, I said 'puke' again, didn't I?!

I need you to flick the switch to 'unstoppable mindset' now, and I need you to completely understand that it's time to stop pointing the finger and bitching and time to really take control and start living your best life! The more successful you are, the more people you can help, and now you know this I believe it's selfish and a waste of life not to take action.

I know it probably pissed you off when I said 'abusive relationship – your fault'. I get it, it was hard to write and harder to read back, but I believe it! When I used to get bullied, pretty hard at some points, the worst thing I did was run scared! Same with 'terrorists', they only work if you sit tight and hope it blows over! They are all bullies, and bullies need kicking in their fat stupid faces! And the best way to hit 'em where it hurts is to fight back and to be more successful than them.

Fucking take charge and start swinging (with your fists, not at a key-swapping party, although you can do that too if you wish, it just might not help this situation). Choose your life and I promise you there will be people like me to help you when you need it. Choose life and I swear you won't have to do it alone. Choose life and I guarantee you will never look back. Fuck the haters, fuck the cynics, fuck the bullies, and fuck the negativity and waste! You got this, and if I'm right then deep down you know you got this!

Let's go...

## Summary

- Take 1 minute to reflect on your transition so far and notice the difference between your mindset now, and your mindset when you started
- Understand that your actions are caused by you, and you can change them or pre-empt them.

# Chapter 26

# Selling Yourself and Totems

In this section, I am going to explain why it is so important to learn how to sell yourself, and exactly how to do so. I'll also get you to buy some jewellery. Selling is something that everyone has to do, like it or not. Whether it be selling your kid on joining an afterschool club, selling your partner on giving you oral sex, selling yourself on joining the gym, or literally anything else. Not only do you need to do it, but you need to be an assassin at it!

You can't put these things down to chance because in true DsGsD style we do not put anything down to chance. We control and dominate! I realise 'control and dominate' while using the example 'selling your partner on giving you oral sex' sounds a bit rapey, I didn't mean it like that. You know what I mean. Er... anyway, if you guys are still struggling to force out that last bit of self-doubt, or racka' confidence, or low self-esteem, then this chapter will attack it full force in the easiest of ways.

Selling does not always mean monetary exchange. It basically just means getting what you want in exchange for something, and that something could be anything! You're chilling with your mates and someone needs to do a shop run and you can't be bothered, so you have to sell your buddy to go instead. Similarly, you want to watch Friends and your partner wants to watch the Super Bowl and you only have one TV and neither of you want to leave the living room, one of you is gonna make the sale! Now, these are just small little day to day issues that some of you will come up against, but what about the real sale: your life! To really get stuck into this we are gonna have to start the sell yourself process and to do that I need to ask you some questions.

When was the last time you bragged? Like told someone how fucking awesome you are and sold yourself? Now ask yourself the question, how many times have you had the opportunity to tell someone how amazing you are and not done it? For those of you thinking: "Bragging is for dicks!" Well, it's not bragging if it's true...!

---

## Exercise 1.0

Grab your journal... We are going to elaborate on an earlier exercise.

Write down 5 things that you are fucking awesome at, and then write down 5 things you are absolutely rubbish at. You have 1 minute to do this, and it is imperative that you don't take longer than 1 minute to do this. Go! (insert Rocky Theme).

---

The first time I asked you to do this exercise you would probably have struggled to fill in the 3 good traits, and probably had more than 3 bad traits to write down. I wanted you to do 5 this time to prove a point. Those of you that have been listening on a deep level and working hard at your transition will have found this version of the exercise so much easier, even though there were more answers to fill out.

Like I said before, you need to know what you are good at and what you are bad at so you can figure out what to double down on, and what needs work. A maze ain't a maze if you've got a map. You have to know yourself. It really is a huge step with regards to reaching your full potential. Soon as you know something, you can manipulate it, change it, make it better or worse, richer or poorer, happier or sadder, faster or slower.

So to elaborate on our previous exercise we need to add some actions to this list. We need to make our pros work for us, and we need to be able to work on our cons.

---

## Exercise 1.1

For each of the 5 pros that you just wrote down, I want you to write a percentage next to them relative to how much you are utilising that skill. For instance, if I wrote 'shit-hot drummer' as one of my 5 pros but I wasn't playing the drums at the moment in my life at all, I would write a big fat zilch next to it. If I was uploading daily drum videos to my Insta and it was getting me work, which amounted to about 20% of my income, plus the added value of free promotion, then I might write between 30-50% next to it.

And if I was drumming 8 hours a day, and it was getting me TV and radio sessions, huge worldwide tours with massive artists, making me happier than anything else and bringing in a few mil a year, I would write 99% next to it (there's always room for improvement).

This is for your pros, we will come back to them in a moment. Next to your cons, I want you to write a percentage next to them based on how much effort you are putting into fixing them! For instance, if I wrote down 'lack of confidence' for one of my cons, and I wasn't doing jack to remedy it, I would write a big fat zilch. If I was attending weekly self-help classes, or reading this book for an hour per day, I would write between 30-50% and if I was immersing myself in self-help techniques, going to groups, investing in a mentor, reading and listening to beneficial material every day I would go for 99%.

Let's go back to the 'our brain is a smartphone' analogy. Now let's consider that you have a smartphone that can do all the things a smartphone can do, but you have to programme and build the phone as opposed to it coming user-friendly all built in a box! The odd one of you would be able to do that. For most of us, we wouldn't have a clue.

The potential smartphone is there but it is unusable because we don't know how to make it work. Oh the frustration! If you're like me then you just want the thing working.

I never shop at IKEA! Why? The quality is absolutely atrocious (I used to love their meatballs though), and more so I have to put whatever I buy together by my shitting self! I enjoy the odd bit of carpentry as a hobby but I don't want to build my own crappy table or bed. One of the primary reasons I don't want to build the thing myself is that the instructions that come with IKEA furniture, and also pretty much any other companies that offer similar flat-pack furniture, are completely unreadable to me.

I get confused with them really easy and I always end up figuring out a better way for myself to understand it. Fact is, IKEA doesn't know how my brain works, or yours, but they pump out generic instructions that will make sense to 'most' people. I am not most people! If they wrote the instructions based on how I like instructions to work, colour coded and simplified, then a bunch of other people wouldn't relate, and before you know it everyone in the country would own a half put-together crappy table or bed. This is not good for anyone! It's the same reason school is fucking stupid for about 98% of the population.

Point is, terribly put, we need to write our own instructions, especially when it comes to our own life. Nobody else can write your instructions! You have to figure it out yourself through trial and error, mistakes, and learning. Everyone else will try and sell you their instructions, their manual, their ideals but they are not yours. Yours are yours. Of course, some will work for you, and that's when you take them and keep them for yourself. But for the most part, you need to figure out your own based on what works for you!

Why does it work for you? Can you make it better? You gotta learn to be self-critical, analyse yourself and be reflective and evaluative so you can finetune your own manual and get the best out of yourself. You don't want to be a half put-together crappy table now do you?!

So, back to the point, you need to brag, but only if it's true. Why do we feel embarrassed to say "I'm awesome at..." whatever it is you are awesome at? I'll bet you my last pound that you feel okay to talk to people about what's gone wrong for you, but you feel weird AF about telling people how awesome you are. It's not bragging if it's true! Get this firmly stuck in your head.

Doesn't mean you have to wear a t-shirt that says 'I'm awesome at XYZ' like a complete bro, and I definitely do not mean be an entitled ass hat, but I do mean be able to talk yourself up as and when you need and don't shy away from selling your best attributes.

If you can't sell yourself, nobody else will, apart from maybe your mum or your life partner, but that's nowhere near enough, and they kinda have to. Think of all the times you've spent serious effort on something and then not done anything with it because the doubt kicked in. Is it good enough? Am I good enough? Will it work? What will people think? Screw that, it only matters what YOU think! If you

DO SHIT, GET SHIT DONE

know for a fact you do something better than everyone else, then that's your thing, babe, use it!

There is a distinct difference between words and actions. Saying you're the best at something and not being able to prove just means you're a dick. Keep in mind the haters and cynics and I bet you that the majority of your actions are based on what you think 'they' will think or say.

We will get to these in detail in a few chapters, but for now I just want to give you some mini-hacks to get you going. These hacks are all based around killing the doubt.

You need to absolutely know what you rock at, minus doubt. What do I mean? Well, think back to anytime you were doing something you're good at but ended up doubting yourself. How did it feel? It felt like you weren't good even though if you thought about it with logic you would know you are super fucking awesome at said thing, you just didn't feel awesome at it at that particular time.

With this in mind, it doesn't count if you're judging your abilities in a state of doubt. Doubt don't count! The old doubt don't count. If you felt confident at it at one time then you know what's possible. We need to eliminate the doubt! I know this feeling soooo well! I've had crippling anxiety singing to an audience or playing drums in the studio, or giving a lecture or speaking publicly. The feeling can't change, in the same way fear feels like fear, doubt feels like doubt. So it seems we can't change that, but we can control it, well more than we think at least. And again it is down to awareness.

You can do this with any state but let's use doubt as we are talking about it. To be able to control your doubt, you need to:

# Exercise 1.0

**1.**

Realise you are in a state of doubt, and that it is just another state. Think of it like one of those science experiments at school where you change the states of water. From water to ice to water to gas and back to water. Bear with me on this one (as if you aren't constantly bearing with me throughout this book). Imagine if someone bet you all your money that you couldn't prove how to change the water from one state to another.

For instance, they say, "Can you change the state from ice to gas?"

You say, with an impending winning smile slowly lurking onto your face: "Yes, of course, I would heat it up to melt the ice and turn it to water, then heat it up further to boiling point to turn it to gas." An easy bet to win, right?! And one you would definitely take!

Now would you make the same bet if you weren't told what state the water started in, and what state it needed to end up in? Of course not! Waaaay too risky. This is true of us and our states, or emotions. If we don't know or aren't aware of what state we are in, then we have no chance of being able to affect it and follow the instructions to change it to the state we want. How do we make sure we know we are in a particular state? (Remember you can do this with any state, but doubt is a good one to start with, anger and worry work really well too)! Well, I'll tell ya...

Remember in the movie 'Inception', the amazing film with that total babe in it, The Rock I think his name is?! Total babe has what he calls a 'totem' which he uses as a tell. His totem of choice is a spinning top that will keep spinning if he is in a dream, and will fall over (due to gravity) if he is awake. He uses this totem to know what state he is in.

So we need a totem!

Something that we can use to make us aware of what state we are in. I want to make this as easy as possible so our totem needs to be familiar and easy to keep with us. I want you to use a piece of jewellery. If you don't wear any jewellery whatsoever then this is gonna work better for you, even though I know you are screwing your face up at the idea of buying some bling! Ignore that, trust me!

I'll quickly explain the reason this will work slightly better if you never wear jewellery: your totem, once chosen, will not only be a reminder for your mood or state of mind, but also a reminder that you chose to take action to invest in yourself, and in turn, the feeling will be stronger, and stronger is good when we are transitioning. Also, it will be a talking point amongst your network ("Oh my god, that's a gorgeous watch, I didn't think you wore watches?!"), which is another opportunity to let them know you are making moves! Don't fret though, this will still work for you regular jewellery wearers!

So if you need to, I want you to shop for a piece of jewellery, this can be anything from a ring, necklace, chain, bracelet, anklet, watch or similar. If you are really diggin' your heels in about this, you can invest in a trinket, something like a zippo or coin or a talisman or whatever. The reason I suggest jewellery first and foremost though is that it is always on you and more often than not visible.

If you take the trinket option you will need to keep it in your pocket at all times! Choose something that makes you feel good, and if you wanna stack this then get the motherfucker engraved with something awesome like 'never give up' or 'don't doubt yourself' or anything that reality checks the shit outta ya! This works better than you can imagine (even though it sounds wack as shit) so make sure you do this.

2.

Now we have our totem, we need to know when to use it. Total babe, from the film, needed to use his totem to check if he was dreaming, so that's when he used it. But doubt, fear, anxiety and worry often come outta nowhere and wash over us and we don't notice they fucked our shit up until after they subside. Same with anger. That's why people apologise after they have lashed out as opposed to before. "Sorry to do this, just letting you know that at about midday tomorrow I am gonna get some serious sand in my vagina and start acting like a moody D-bag, just warning you now so you are prepared!" said no one ever.

As funny as this sounds, it is similar to the approach we need to take to be aware of our doubt. Now I don't want you worrying about the future and getting yourself into that state, but I want you to be clever about this and just before you start writing your daily goals before bed for the following day (and this needs to be before you write them, not after), I want you to have a quick think, and I mean quick (set a 60-second timer on your phone if you need to and don't go over), about all the things the following day that might cause you a bad useless emotion, in this case, doubt.

You don't need to write these down, just make a mental note, and while you think of the thing, look at your new engraved bling, and picture yourself the next day smiling through the doubt, powering through it, smashing right through it like a male porn star does a watermelon. Again, don't do this for more than 60 seconds, and then immediately write your awesome goals so you don't go to sleep thinking about negatives.

---

This will work so much better than you think, in fact, it totally works. It's a very basic association, and you are associating something bad (your useless states), with something awesome (your new invest-in-yourself engraved totem)! The double cool thing is that after a few days you won't even need to do this exercise as your totem will have taken over! And then you can repeat the process for your other rubbish states.

Just to explain, fear, which we are coming to in a few chapters, is not a useless state. Useless states are states that either render you useless or prevent you from making the right decisions and are usually based on absolutely nothing. These include doubt, worry, anxiety, dread, boredom, disgust, panic, cruelty, jealousy, hate, frustration and disappointment.

There's probably a few more but I think I got most of them. If you suffer from any of these, ever, they are taking away from your absolutely amazing and life-affirming states like interest, enthusiasm, curiosity, amusement, excitement, gratitude, joy, elation, triumph, humility, charity, sympathy, and ultimately love!

Use your totem to remind you that you are you, and you have the ability and power to be your best you, and chances are, you haven't experienced full 100% amazing you yet! Now, just like a shitty rom-com with Huge Grunt in it, Let's go deep on emotions...

---

## Summary

- Ex 1.0

Be awesome!

  - Write down 5 things you are absolutely awesome at!
  - Do not be afraid to be honest here, if you're killer at it, acknowledge it

- Ex 1.1

Find a totem

- Choose something you like that fits like jewellery or that you can keep on your person and order it now
- Use your totem as an anchor to remind yourself of where to go when you end up in a particular negative state
- Pre-empt tomorrow's possible stresses by taking a moment to acknowledge them the night before

- Don't be afraid to sell yourself – it's not bragging if it's true
- Selling doesn't always mean there has to be a monetary exchange, you can sell a service for a favour, or sell someone on your ideals
- You need to know what you are awesome at to know what to double down on and what needs work.

# Chapter 27

# Emotions

Paul Ekman identified 6 basic emotions (anger, disgust, fear, happiness, sadness, and surprise). There are a bunch more, but let's work with these...

You can basically trace the source of any situation with these 6 core emotions.

Whether it's your partner asking you to take out the bins, your car passing its MOT, your boss not giving you time off, your boss giving you time off in return for a reach-around, your kid not going to bed as easy as usual, or your career not being where you want it to be, you will encounter one of these 6 core emotions. Each has a plethora of sub-emotions, all of which can be umbrellaed under just 2 emotions: love or fear, which we will come to later on.

So why am I bringing this up? Because the average human will all too often make decisions based not on fact or experience, but instead on the emotion they are feeling at the time. The kicker here is that the emotion they are experiencing will most likely be based on their own or someone else's past experience or ill-informed forward-thinking.

Let's say you wake up to an official-looking letter hanging out of your letterbox.

You open it and it says you owe the council £4.5k in back payments for council tax. Now let's say just before you opened that letter you stubbed your toe and overheard on the radio that the government is cutting funds for teaching, and you're a teacher. The £4.5k repayment letter is now 10x worse after stubbing your toe (anger, frustration, pain), and the government cuts to your career (anger, frustration, worry, anxiety).

Now let's say that the same letter comes through the post, but as you are opening it, your mum rings you up and tells you that the malignant tumour the doctor thought they found was actually just a cyst and there's now nothing to worry about (happiness, elation, relief). The letter from the council now doesn't seem as pressing, right?!

Now let's say that the phone call from your mum was instead to say that they had just won the lottery jackpot and £3.1 mil was being wired to your account as you speak to her because you're the favourite child. Now the letter from the council seems less pressing, but for an entirely different reason. Just as a quick mini test: if you thought to yourself that the council bill mattered less after your mum winning the lottery as opposed to her health being well then you need to rethink your priorities (I would have put an emoji here).

The thing to note is that your reaction to the letter changes depending on your emotions, and more than that, your emotions will differ depending on a bunch of other variables.

Now let's use a more real-world example. Your partner, or housemate, or parent is in a bad mood because of something that happened to them at work. Something that has nothing to do with you, but because you live with that person you are gonna have to hear about it when they get home. Let's say that up until this point you were having a killer day, you closed a massive deal at work, or taught your kid how to ride a bike, or something equally awesome.

Now let's say that you need your partner to do a really annoying job that only they can do, something like phone up your internet service provider because your broadband has stopped working but the account is in your partner/parents/housemate's name and only they can make the call. No matter how much you don't want to ask them, you gotta! How up for making that call is the other person? Would they be more up for making the call if they had had a similarly awesome day at work as you did?

The fact is, the job of calling your internet service provider is what it is: annoyingly automated and mind-numbingly long, but ultimately the problem will get fixed and it's not gon' kill ya! But the other party's emotions come into play and affect you.

You can almost definitely think of a similar situation that would have happened to you in the last week. Maybe you're the one that acted like a dick because of the situation? In business, if you are trying to sell a product or service and close a deal, you will very often come across extremely emotive prospects. Your ability to close will be stronger or weaker depending on your ability to stay calm and use strategy and logic instead of emotion.

So let's plan ahead. This works like a dream every time and you will be absolutely blown away with the results. The only time it won't work is if you get emotional. Trust. This works with anyone but I suggest you try it on your partner, or a close friend or family member to see how much of a golden ticket it is.

And as a forethought, if you start getting emotional (angry, pissed off, livid, ornery, disgusted, whatever) then use your totem to remind you whassup! Remember you have to make a mental note that the situation could get feisty before you enter it to make sure you don't react badly when the inevitable happens, so make sure you log that and remember it when going into any situation that could turn into a nause.

I'll use my wife to make the example, but you can do this with anyone. Wife is pissed off because she feels fat. My initial reaction could be to say things like "you're not fat" or "you look amazing, don't be so silly". Neither of these work for two reasons:

1) It doesn't matter if you're fat or not, if you feel fat, you feel fat.

2) Your partner is not looking for your sympathy, they are looking for a way to not feel fat.

So much so that unless you can miraculously change their brain chemistry or the way mirrors work, or chop off their bingo wings leaving no marks or scars, sympathy will not help. More so, by trying to sympathise you may get another response based out of another negative emotion: "You don't know how it feels! Blah, blah, blah!!!"

When my wife has these days, I would try everything I could think of to talk her out of the way she felt, but the bit I was missing is that she feels like that, and me saying "don't feel like that" won't help at all! It's like someone telling you to calm down when you're vexed, it just pisses you off more.

In this case, and I would imagine most of you can relate, she would tell me she looks fat, I'd tell her to stop being stupid, she'd tell me I didn't understand, I'd start getting annoyed or upset that she wasn't listening to me, and then we would have an argument.

My wife knew it wasn't my fault, and I knew it wasn't hers, but we would play push and pull and never meet each other in the middle. Reason being that by this point we were both making decisions based on emotion and not logic. You will have had an experience before when someone told you to calm down when you were doing your lid about something. Does it help? Does it fuck!

So, here's the hack... and it's a goodun'! It takes discipline but as you are noticing, a little work makes your life much easier, so I implore you to try this out and prove it to yourself, then you can start using it as and when you need. I'll use the "I feel fat" example...

Here's how the conversation should go:

---

Wife: I look fat, I hate my body, nobody understands!

Me: Fucking right you feel fat (match emotion). You're surrounded by media shit that makes you feel that way and I don't understand how you put up with it, I'd be livid if I felt like you do now, this must be horrible for you!

Wife: Arghhhhh, stop trying to give me advice.

*I look at my totem*

You're pissing me off! (notice she is not pissed off with me, she is pissed off with how she feels. And more so, this is where most of us get emotional and react based off of our emotions).

Me: Bless you, baby, I don't wanna piss you off, I am here to help (this will feel like you are going against your fundamentals. If someone shouts at you, you wanna shout back, or if someone blames you, you wanna blame back or get defensive, or get angry, or point the finger). How can I help you out? You want me to go get some cake and try and catch you up?

Wife: *Reluctantly smiles*

Me: *Hugs wife* Baby, I'm here when you need me, I'll go and make you a cuppa, or get you a glass of wine if you'd prefer, and when you want to vent some more just come and start ranting at me, I love you and I've got your back, and just so you know, I don't understand how you feel, and if I could take your pain I would! This must be rubbish for you! *Kisses forehead and walks away*

---

Now apply this to pretty much any conversation that gets heated. Two things to note, and one of them is a biggy!!

1. By controlling yourself you are controlling the situation. You never have to wait for a situation to control itself or settle itself down (cuz then it might not), take action and fix it yourself.

2. People can never, ever come back at you when you either totally own up or agree. I will say that again and I suggest you write it down as many times as you need to so it never leaves your mind! People can never, ever, ever come back at you when you either totally own up or agree.

Let's talk about that for a second. I absolutely hand on heart swear down guarantee that if you agree with someone, no matter what mood or emotion they are running off, they will eventually lose steam and give in. When they realise they are arguing with themselves they will only have so much energy. For this to work you MUST stay in control and not drop the ball, which is harder than you think, but it is 100% worth it.

You can work the same sort of scenario with your parents, friends, whoever. If you are driving and someone cuts you up, do you really need to start shouting and bibbing your horn and flipping them the bird, like you've just caught them in bed with your spouse? Is it really worth your time or effort, and does it make the situation any better? No, it just prolongs it.

With negative situations, you want to dispose of them as quickly as possible and redirect to positive. Weirdly enough, more often than not, the spectrum of negative and positive are so close that a really bad situation can quite easily become amazing, and vice versa.

You close the deal, have a couple of drinks to celebrate, then drive home and crash because you're drunk and then lose your job, then you go to prison, fall in love with your prison warden, work super hard on making your body and mind strong while you are stuck in your cell, exit prison a better version of yourself, marry the warden, have kids and live happily ever after. Or something like that! I really urge you to try to redirect your rubbish emotions to get to the best possible outcome quick smart.

This works in literally any situation. Many people talk about manipulating, but I think that's ethically wrong. You don't need to manipulate anyone. You just need to be in control of your own emotions. I bet that nearly every detrimental situation you've ever been in has a direct correlation to your mindset. But why are our emotions so strong, and why do they affect us so much?

I used to have a drug addiction. In fact, I've had a lot of addictions, all of which left me out of control. I have had sex addictions, smoking addictions, drinking addictions, drug addictions, eating addictions, TV addictions (television, not transvestite). I could go on. Addiction = no control. I've had junkie friends that said if they could only do heroin once every few months then it would be totally amazing. Fact is I've never met a heroin addict that could control their addiction.

Well, it's not an addiction if you can control it.

I remember realising I had a drug addiction when I was going to sleep thinking about cocaine, waking up thinking about cocaine, and spending the time in between night and morning tossing and turning. It also didn't matter how much I had. I used to smash the whole bag and then get more. I was out of control. Quitting an addiction means you are most definitely going to encounter emotions. In fact, a mixture of different emotions: familiarity, love, hate, fear etc.

For now, all you need to know is that if you can learn to control your emotions then you can learn to control you. Booze is probably the easiest way I can exemplify this as most of you will be able to relate to drinking yourself into oblivion and making bad decisions. We've all done it. Don't be shy.

Emotions are just like fire: you stop putting wood on and the fire goes out and then dies. Feed the fire, and not only will it stay alight, but if you feed it too much it will grow and grow, and in no time be uncontrollable. You don't want an uncontrollable fire! You want a fire that fits its purpose. If you're camping you want a fire to keep you warm and cook marshmallows on, it only needs to be a certain size to live out its purpose. Feed it too much and you won't be thinking, "Mmmm I love cooking marshmallows." You'll be thinking, "Shiiiiiiit where's the water...? There goes my tent."

You need to control your fire! It's hard sometimes, damn straight, but life is hard, so just learn to be in control and kick your ass when you are about to go out of control. Use your totem. The world wants you to be out of control because when you are out of control you spend more, you react, and you make bad decisions, and bad decisions for you will always be good decisions for someone else.

Look at it like this, if I was selling you a pen, and you already had a great pen that you love, why the shit would you wanna buy mine? But what if I was selling you a new heart, and you had just had news from the doctor that if you didn't get a new heart you would die in a week, and there wasn't anyone else selling hearts? No matter how much of a dick I am, or how much mark-up I throw on top of the RRP, you are gonna buy my product, even if it means selling your house.

Immediately one deal is so much more valuable than the other. This is true of everything; people will buy if they need the product. Arguments only happen when there isn't anything more important to absorb the energy. Like I mentioned earlier, we only have so much energy, don't waste it on emotions that will take you two steps backwards.

On the other hand, some emotions are worth more than their weight in cocaine, I mean gold. Sorry, had a blip! The average emotion will work in exactly the same way as a fire; feed it and it grows, stop feeding it and it dies. When your partner starts going bonkers at you, don't react, don't feed the emotion, don't add to their emotion with your emotion, just kill it, kill it dead. Do not fuel the fire. Instead, use your energy to spark up one of their good emotions.

There was an amazing advert on UK TV a few years ago, I can't remember what the ad was for, but it went something like this... There was a mum walking around a supermarket with her young kid, the kid must have been about 5. The kid starts having a tantrum, kicking and screaming in the canned goods aisle. Now before I tell you what happened in the rest of the ad, just take a moment to think about how you would react to that.

For those of you that have kids, think about the emotions you would experience if your little rotter started wailing like a banshee next to the soup in your local supermarket. What would you do?! Well from my experience it's rare to go shopping without hearing a mum or dad lose their shit and start shouting at their toddler. Idiot move. The kid doesn't know better, and shouting will just teach them it is acceptable to act like a dick in the future.

Own this, guys, you know if I'm talking to you. So, either way, in the ad, the mum matches the kid. She lies down in the middle of the aisle and starts kicking and screaming. The kid is dumbfounded! He looks embarrassed and stops his BS just to bring the situation back to normal. Now I know this is an ad but it was so on point. If you match the emotion without getting emotional, you can control the situation. Do you want to wing your life or be in control? Funny thing is, the more control you have, the better you can wing a situation.

I want to take the time here to talk about NLP in a bit more detail, just in case you think I am delving into that territory. I am not. Matching someone to call them out on their crazy is one thing, manipulating people into buying things they don't want is another.

As with anything, you get amazing practisers of NLP, but you also get absolute shits! I am neither. There are always positives to be taken from anything but the matching I am talking about goes no further than what we have discussed. I do not sit back when someone sits back to try and get them to buy the pen they don't need. But that's just me, you need to make up your own mind... But be ethical.

---

## Exercise 1.0

What do you get emotional about? It might be you are chilled AF most of the time but behind the wheel of a car, you are a treacherous D-bag. It might be that you are a really nice person but when it's that time of the month you lose your shit and turn into a dragon. It might be that you don't like it when you hear a phone go off at the cinema, but you'll scream at the TV in a bar when the football is on and other people are trying to eat. Grab your journal...

At the very top of the page write 'MY EMOTION DIAGRAM'.

I want you to draw a picture of yourself in the top half of the page, nothing that takes too long, a stick person (fucking politically correct, Lee 1) with obvious features will do, but it needs to have a huge smile! Next, I want you to do the same in the bottom half of the page, and you guessed it, this one has a massive frown!

Around the positive one at the top of the page, I want you to note situations where you shine and always win. Could be you're a legend when it comes to dealing with upset kids, or you are great in heated family arguments or something like that. Don't be embarrassed to write attributes about yourself that you know are true.

Surrounding the bottom negative asshat version of you I want you to do the same with things you lose your shit with. Now it is imperative that these are things that when you think about them, they do not actually matter. Obviously, you don't have to write down 'I get angry or upset when I hear about people getting murdered' or something equally harrowing. I mean things like: calling your insurance broker if you end up screaming at the phone every time 'that' automated voice says, "Thank you for waiting, our team of experts are waiting to serve you, you are now 27th in the queue."

After completing this, I want you to strike through each negative and sign your initials next to each strike. Don't scribble them out, I want you to still be able to read them through the strikes. Then I want you to put a big cross right through the negative you picture!

---

Exercise complete. Say goodbye to the old you. You can do this as often as you like, and in case you are thinking, 'Oh God, he's getting me to draw a stickman (stick person) and blah, blah, blah,' then no worries at all, carry on being out of control and shouting at other drivers or having arguments with your partner or friends or whatever. No drama from me.

That's enough on emotions for now, next we need to do some practice to get you holding yourself right and coming across in the best possible light. Onwaaaards...

---

## Summary

- Ex 1.0

Your emotion diagram

- – Draw a happy version of yourself in stick person form at the top of your page

- Draw a sad version of yourself in stick person form at the bottom of your page
- Next to the happy you, write out all your positives
- Next to the sad you write all your negatives
- Strike through all negatives and sign your name next to each one

- You need to be in control of your emotions
- You need to feed the positive emotions and starve the negative ones
- You can choose which emotion to feel as long as you are aware.

# Chapter 28

# Eliminate All

# Negatives

Let's say you invite me over to your house because you think I'm pretty neato. You are expecting me at about 06:45 before you have to leave for work and peek out the window just before only to see me getting out of my car and walking round to the boot. I open the boot and pull out a big, black bin bag. You wonder what I have in the bag but think nothing of it. You walk to meet me at your front door and get there just as I knock, knock, knock. You open the door and welcome me.

We exchange pleasantries and you suggest we go into the living room. Just as you are about to ask me what is in the big, black bin bag I say, "I hope you don't mind me bringing my bag in with me?"

I put the big, black bin bag on the floor and begin to open it.

I pull out some latex gloves from my pocket and put them on while you watch in amazement.

I reach my hand into the bag and before you know it I am emptying the contents of my big black bin bag all over your house, and the bag is full of actual shit. I'm smearing shit on your walls, throwing shit at your ceiling, rubbing shit into your gorgeous cushions that you picked up on 'special offer' from Ikea, all the while rubbing my dirty shoes all over your equally gorgeous turquoise Havana rug.

What would you do? I am hoping you would kick me the fuck out like Uncle Phil (rest his soul) does to Jazz on FPOBA.

So you throw me out of your house and peer through the letterbox to check I am leaving, but instead, you see me ripping the roof off of your Audi convertible and emptying the remaining dook from my big, black bin bag all over the interior of your freshly valeted TT. You run to the kitchen, grab the biggest knife you can find, shoot back to the front door, throw it open screaming obscenities at me, and chase me off. Phew. Done.

Wrong!

You clean up the house the best you can and get ready for work. You take an Uber and figure you'll get the car sorted after a day in the office. You get to work, I've been there already.

In fact, your friends' houses, your parents' house, your local coffee shop, everywhere you go, I've been there already and covered it in shit! When you finally catch up with me, what would you say?! I can imagine a bunch of four-letter words, and you may even get violent. And rightly so! I just F'd your S right up! I put my crap everywhere, all over your life, and now YOU gotta clean it up, cuz I'm fucked if I'm doing it, I hate shit! Pissed off much? Livid? Angry?! Upset?!

Question: What's the difference between this scenario and watching TV or listening to the radio, or reading the newspapers?

Answer: You can see the shit I've left.

It's obvious. It stinks and looks bad and you just wanna get rid of it! I know that as you are reading this you are already thinking, "But I need my TV to relax at the end of a hard day," or, "But I love the Big Show on Radio 2," or, "But the Guardian is highbrow and educational."

Sorry to break it to you, but these mother Fs have got you exactly where they want you and are dumping their shit all over your brain 24/7, 365 and most of the time you won't even notice. And for those of you that do notice, how come you haven't prevented it?! Stopped watching, stopped listening, stopped reacting!?

Well, the answer is the same for you as it is for me, as it is for everyone! It's soooo hard. It doesn't take more than a few minutes to research the issues related to negativity, stress and misinformation. I firmly believe that negativity is more of a killer than pretty much anything else. And even worse, it is soooo contagious.

I am sure you can think of something you have moaned about in the last 24 hours, you may even be able to think of something negative you have said in the last hour. Why?! Where's it come from? The media mostly. It's all just scare tactics and fear to keep us vibrating at a slow, dull, greyness that keeps us part of the script: school, college, uni, job, family, mortgage, pension, die.

The whole thing is a set-up if you ask me! Have you ever heard of or met someone super successful that adopted the above already much-trodden path? Something to think about.

So back to negativity...

How do negative people make you feel?

Let's get proactive... What things in your life are negative for no reason?! How do you react to something going wrong? Can you relate to getting a parking ticket and it ruining your day? Can you relate to some idiot driver sitting up your backside, and even after he overtakes, you spend the next few minutes, or hours, moaning about it to your friend, partner, family, or stranger?!

Ever had a blemish on your skin that ruined your day? Do you complain?

Grumble? Moan? Does your partner or friends or family moan or whinge?

It absolutely takes energy to do this, and even more importantly it takes time. And what do we know about time? It is the most important thing in our lives. Negativity is a complete and utter waste of your life. It's a killer. If your life is spent in prison, of any sort, is it a life or just an existence? Do you find yourself telling other people to stop moaning and being naggy but don't even notice when you are doing it yourself?

C'mon guys, we gotta be real.

So, here's one of my favourite exercises, and it's one of my favourites because it took me the longest time to complete it. I am pretty sure I have never failed at an exercise as much as this one! It took me weeks, and I mean weeks to not fail. The first week or so I failed every time within the first hour. I would love to hear how you get on with this, hit me on my social and let me know how many days it took you to do this and what happened when you finally completed it.

---

## Exercise 1.0

So, the concept is simple, well it seems simple, but you gotta remember you are fighting a lifetime of people leaving their shit in your house, so it won't be instantaneous. The deal is, you can't say one negative thing to anyone, for a whole day – 24 hours, baby! I imagine a bunch of you are thinking, "Sure, whatever, I got this." Good luck, my brothers and sisters.

Two things that this exercise does:

1) it makes you aware of your own negativity. You can then remedy and begin to eradicate.

2) it makes you realise how much BS you are hearing daily, aka how much shit people are leaving in your front room!

I can't stress this enough, you cannot be surrounded with any negativity if you are to successfully make your first big transition. And if you do have to put up overhearing someone regurgitating some absolute dross they heard on the news, or whether Idiot A is gonna suck off Idiot B on celebrity island farm Chelsea Essex fuck fest 9000, at the very least you need to be able to switch off and stay focused on your mission without letting the shit infiltrate your brain.

So how do we do it? First port of call is you! As a great man once said, *I'm looking at the man in the mirror, I'm asking him to make that change/change his ways*. As soon as you can complete the previous exercise for at least half of a day you will start to make obvious and noticeable positive changes. The rest will snowball.

Next thing to do is let everyone you are close to know that you will not be indulging in negativity, especially in your own home, office, or place of work. You need to be prepared for people to laugh or make jokes, I could write a load about why you shouldn't listen to them, but I'll put it like this: fuck 'em! Stay strong and stand by your beliefs! Remember the cynic!? One of the most wonderful things about making a transition is that people notice, and they follow.

You know what I mean: you know that feeling when someone says, "Dude, I made loads of cash doing matched betting," or some other obvious-when-you-know online marketing campaign is big at the time, and instead of saying, "Nah man, I got my own plans," your brain goes into 'quit on everything and do that as it's easy money' mode.

And with absolutely no training, experience, or clue what it is you are jumping in to, you get super excited and drop your long game, if you had one (which you probably did not if you were considering a 'get money easy scheme'). The only people that make bank off of money-scams are the people scamming! There is such a thing as get rich quick but there is definitely no such thing as getting rich easy!

Anyways, when you start being positive 95%+ of the time, not only will you set the scene, but people will follow.

You join the gym and quit before getting results, nothing happens. You join the gym and get results, people become interested, and in a lot of cases follow suit.

How'dya think smoking became what it is?! Someone smoked and people followed.

We want to be in the 1%, not the 99% so we need to be in control and lead.

To stay in a state of positivity we have to make sure we maintain no matter what.

There are so many distractions and traps life will set to try and make you lose your cool. You have to reality check morning, noon and night, especially if you are new to being positive. No off days, this is not a diet, this is your new life.

Sometimes you'll drop the ball, and that doesn't matter. What matters is whether you can pick the ball back up quickly, or catch it before it hits the floor.

Like I said at the start of this book, I am no better than anyone else, and I won't tell you that by doing XYZ you will have the exact same results or experience as I have had, that would be dumb. What I know though is that all of the exercises I am offering here are simple as hell but will set you on the right path with nothing other than commitment.

There is no golden ticket or corner-cut you can do to get where you wanna go, it has always been the same. Commit, and keep going! Do it and get it done! Reprogramming our mindset is the same as changing a tyre on a bike or car: you either do it and get it done or you don't. If to change your tyre you had to run barefoot, backwards, through a field of bamboo, with your pants down, while in a thunderstorm and you are wearing a hat with a conductor on it, you probably wouldn't do it, right?

But the things I am suggesting are nowhere near that hard. It doesn't have to be hard to make a transition. It has to be consistent, committed and measurable. Remember the snowflake that turns into a snowball that turns into an avalanche. That's what it's gotta be!

If you are diagnosed with cancer, what do you want to do? You wanna kill that evil shit! You gonna tiptoe around it or go full force?! The last thing you want is to have it grow. Kill it, kill it dead with fire! Negativity affects more people in the UK and US than cancer does because it affects everyone, and even worse, it doesn't have to.

If you get cancer then you can't just flip the switch on that. You can with negativity.

Pharmaceutical sales are at an all-time high, medicated kids and adults alike are either upping their dose or trying to wean themselves off of drugs they should have never been prescribed. We are in such a dull bubble of normalcy that it feels weird to start breaking through.

You know that feeling when someone walks into a room and either it lights the place up, almost like they are glowing and radiating more than everyone else, or the opposite when someone walks into a room and it's like they've brought a black cloud in with them. Which one do you want to be?!

The following are amazing flexes for you to get so used to that they become natural.

1. Smile always. Sounds simple, but it's hard. You know when someone you love really pisses you off, but they do it with a big grin and sparkly eyes and it makes you go all soppy and ultimately give them the benefit of the doubt. That's the power of a smile, my friends! A great way to start, and to give you that positive glow when you walk into a room, is to always remind yourself to smile when you enter into a new situation, a new room, or conversation, or wherever, whether it's at home, in a shop or bar, or at work. It gives people an immediate positive view of you, and portrays you as warm, welcoming, inviting, happy, and all those other amazing traits that boast an absolute legend! Plus, and possibly more importantly, forcing a smile actually makes you happy (check it out on Ask Jeeves). Be aware of your smile and how you look and hold yourself. People will make an immediate judgement of you within milliseconds, and although it's not impossible to change that judgement later on, it is waaay more work than getting it right from the outset.

2. Make eye contact. Similar to 'smile always'! You will remember me talking about the eye contact game? How are you getting on with that by the way? Obviously, you don't want to look like you have bodies under your patio, but regularly maintained eye contact is essential to make good strong connections with people, and once you get it right it is gold dust.

3. Stay composed no matter what. This is so important!!! Never, ever, ever, ever, ever react based on emotions. If you think I am going over ground I've already covered, damn straight!!! It's fookin' important! If you can stay calm and collected in a situation where everyone else is trippin' then you win. That simple. If I'm having an operation where the surgeon is poking around near one of my organs with a scalpel, I'm gonna want them to be chilled, calm, cool and collected. It's like the kid that doesn't get their way,

they kick and scream and tantrum, and does it help?! Does it fuck! Don't be the out-of-control child, be the in-control adult.

4. Be a role model. Yup, be a role model. Do things so well and so right that people want to copy you. Be so nice and so cool to people that it's hard for others to find fault with you. Be your best you and it will radiate off you like something that radiates a lot, maybe a radiator.

5. Change your voice tone if you need to. This is definitely one you will be unaware of, because:

    a) Most people hate the sound of their own voice anyway so they just figure it's not great.

    b) It's one of those things like having BO or bad breath where people are too polite to let you know.

So you need to check for yourself by asking a friend that won't BS you, and you need to make sure you don't react with emotion from their answer. Ask your bestie what parts of your voice are annoying, or boring, or not ideal and then work on them. This will get you far. I have a really good friend that mumbles a lot and no matter how many times you say, "Sorry, what?!" he still doesn't speak clearly!

Thing is he is hyper-intelligent and always has great things to say, but often it's impossible to listen because his voice is mumbly AF! You don't have to be like an OTT daytime TV presenter, but if you can look someone in the eye, smile wonderfully and speak with clarity, intonation, and colour, then you are on your way to winning pretty much anyone over!

Delve deep right away. In any situation, go deep as quick as you can (hehe). I mean deep with conversation and understanding. If you are going to bother having a conversation with someone then make sure it is worth your time, and theirs! If it's not, as much as you are used to small talk, cut it out! I don't mean to ask them how they are and then ask if they are circumcised or how heavy the flow is on their period! I mean to make the conversation worthwhile. Ask them about them, ask them interesting questions they won't hear most of the time and show genuine interest in what they are saying. And don't just ask then switch off. You will always learn something when someone is talking passionately if you choose to listen, and they will always open up and talk passionately to you if given the opportunity!

Eliminate your negatives!!!

Notice when you are being negative and train yourself to acknowledge it and replace it with a win. It is your duty to not only make your life amazing but to make other people's lives amazing too!

$60 + 60 = ?$

---

## Summary

- Ex 1.0

The no negativity game

- − Don't say anything negative for a whole 24 hours
- − If you fail, start again
- Negativity is a disease
- Being the most positive person in the room pays dividends, every time.

# Chapter 29

# One Twenty

One hundred and twenty minutes AKA 2 hours AKA a shit ton of milliseconds. What can you do in 120 minutes?

Let's break your life down. Nowadays the average human lives over the age of retirement. In the UK the retirement age is 65-67 years old. So let's ignore the fact you should never retire, cuz you can't retire from your life, and work with the average life expectancy. At the time of writing this, the average life expectancy in the UK is about 80 years old. So let's say that we are all gonna live to 80 years old.

But what is 80? Well, 80 sounds like 80 until you break it down – 80 years is the same as 960 months, or 4,160 weeks, or 29,200 days, or 700,800 hours, or 42,048,000 minutes.

This will mean different things to each of you, but the one that got me was the hours... We only got 700,800 hours in our lifetime! And that's if we live 'til 80. Daaaayuum. And the first few years of life we can't remember (for me the years between 14-20 I can't really remember either, well they were hazy, to say the least), and I'm guessing the last few years are gonna be shady at best. This isn't a lot! Even worse, how many of them have we made count, like really count!?

There is an awesome TED talk on procrastination where Tim Urban drops some bombs on how to best manage your time, it's totally worth a watch. At the end of the talk, he shows a picture of the life span of a 90-year-old in months depicted as empty blank boxes, one box for each month. The amount of boxes is worryingly few and completely eye-opening.

If you search '90 year life span in months' you can see for yourself. I actually set this as my tablet background for a while to keep me on track. Fact is, for most of us, we are nearing or already over halfway through the part of our lifespan where we can really make a difference. Don't get me wrong, you can always make a difference, but I'm guessing it's easier when your hips aren't replacements and you are actually aware if you've pooped yourself or not.

Let's go through the same process as before but with a day. The average day is made up of 24 hours, as you know.

You gotta know what you are doing in your day, you can't just wing it, it doesn't work. So let's break it down... 24 hours in a day. The quack says you should sleep 8 per night, so let's roll with that: 24 - 8 = 16. The average workday is 8 hours: 16 - 8 = 8. Let's say you eat 3 meals a day, and take an hour per meal to prepare, eat, and clear up afterwards: 8 - 3 = 5. Let's say you have a family, or partner, or dog, let's give them a couple of hours too: 5 - 2 = 3. Now let's take one more hour just for damage limitation or unknowns: 3 - 1 = 2.

Baby, you still got 2 hours a day to do you. Go to the gym, join a club, learn a new skill, write a book, build something, start a business... whatever you desire! Also, bear in mind I have been very conservative with these times. If you are healthy and fit you can totally live well on 6 hours of sleep per night, and most people don't spend 3 hours a day preparing and eating food.

Let's talk about those 2 'you' hours! 2 hours a day may not seem like much to you, or maybe your bad brain is saying things like, "Yeah but that's my Candy Crush, Netflix, porn, or pub time," and you need that to unwind after a day at the job you hate... If this is you then GET A BETTER JOB!

So, those 2 hours, let's make them work for us and don't forget your burst practice cuz it is a multiplier. An average week for most people is 5 days, Monday through Friday. If you're this far into this programme then you aren't most people. I don't have days off but just in case you're not there yet let's roll with 6 days per week and 1 day of rest. 6 x 2 = 12 hours.

If you go to the gym 6 times a week, for an hour at a time, you will have done did 6 hours of keeping fit per week, which is 624 hours per year. That is more than enough to get you in the best shape of your life! If you do anything, and commit, and don't give up, you will be competent at that thing within a month, and a master within a year. People never believe me when I say this, but the people that have already lived like this or are halfway through a cycle know it works.

Don't be a hater! Just to put a point on it, I am writing this book in 'my' 2 hours per day, along with a whole bunch of other stuff including setting up and running 2 new companies, learning how to bake, flipping stuff online and a whole heap of other things, all the while working full time, being a rad dad and husband, keeping my health up, sleeping, eating, and I still have time to play online scrabble, meet friends, and play Xbox every now and then. More so, I still have time to do sweet FA sometimes and be spur of the moment too!

Just FYI, that 2 hours per day, over a year, is 730 hours if you include Sundays. Now let's make you feel bad. And you need to be honest here, remember, we don't lie to ourselves anymore. Do we? Did you just lie?! Did you?! Are you still lying?! Are you?! I could go on but I'll stop... Will I?! Oh God, I just lied! ARGHHHH.

## Exercise 1.0

Grab your journal and find an empty page. Write 'Honest Me' at the top and sign your name next to it. Answer the following with a score between 0 and 10 (0 being none at all and everything's cool, 10 being you're completely concerned about it and something needs to change):

1. An average day, how many hours are you spending watching B S on Netflix/TV/YT or similar?

   This constitutes anything non-educational or non-inspiring. If you want to watch reality TV (which is never real btw) then you can do it in your 2 hours, although I highly recommend you don't. Making time to watch inspirational and educational material is integral to your transition and will always make you feel better after than watching some rubbish about Cynthia's new vajazzle or if that washed up cameo 'actor' that only ever appeared on a few episodes of EastEnders is going to eat a witchetty grub or not.

2. An average day, how often are you twiddling your fingers without knowing what to do?

   This means scrolling through social media without any reason to be, going for cigarette breaks, basically doing anything aimlessly or without purpose? If you're honest with yourself here the truth will shock and appal you!

3. An average day, how often do you realise you don't have the things you need?

   You know if I'm talking to you: you go to cook dinner and you're out of an ingredient you need and you have to go to the shop to get it. Or you spend loads of time each day thinking about what you are going to eat. Or you leave for work and realise you're out of fuel. Or you don't have fresh clothes for the morning and end up leaving the house without having your shit clean, dry, or ironed (which in turn makes you feel less confident and has a critical repercussion on the rest of your day).

4. An average day, how much time are you spending going backwards?

   This constitutes as anything you are doing that is dragging you down, making you less positive, preventing your transition. Things like moaning, nagging, whining, and basically being a little bitch.

5. And finally, on an average day, how aware are you of all of the above?

---

Fact is, most of us don't make mistakes when we are aware. How many times have you walked through a door someone held open for you, or been given the right of way when driving and you didn't realise that you forgot to say thank you until it was too late? Why? Because you just weren't being conscious in those moments, for whatever reason, usually stress or worry will be the deciding factor here.

Now put the shoe on the other foot; how do you feel when someone doesn't notice something you have done?! Especially if it took effort and you didn't have to do it, like holding a door open for someone. There are a bunch of reasons for this, some obvious and some much less obvious as to why we operate at this almost unconscious level. You may believe it is because of stress, exhaustion, worry, the news, the media, or that the queen is a lizard and we are being hypnotised by the Illuminati, whatever, it doesn't matter. Fact is, when we are not awake, present, or in control, we make stupid mistakes.

These mistakes can more often than not cost us days, months, years, our health, our relationships, our job prospects, and ultimately our life.

Every time I relapsed with my addictions it was because I was not thinking. It was like I was on autopilot, just going through the motions. It wasn't that I thought, "Hmmm is this a good idea?!" It wasn't until after I had made the stupid mistake that I realised it was a stupid mistake! And then it's too late. This is not an excuse. Quite the opposite. Here is a small list of things that most of us have the potential to do on a daily basis that waste time, effort, energy, and ultimately life.

Watching TV, small talk, pressing snooze, giving up halfway through a plan (no matter how small the plan is), arguing, smoking, doing drugs, drinking too much, lying, cheating, getting mad, moaning, negging etc.

I won't go on! You know why I won't go on?! Because you already know what you are doing is a waste of your life! You know! Throughout this programme, your consciousness will have shifted whether you like it or not. Some of the most basic of hacks and exercises I have given you so far will have enabled you to reflect in a way you previously didn't. This is why I use baby-steps for everything! The foundation is easy to implement but the aftermath or repercussion is monumental! And all of these little baby steps, these tiny little bits of Lego, can create anything!

If I held up a can of cola and asked you how much it is worth, you may say £1.50 or something like that. But you are assuming what is inside the can is actually cola, and not a rolled-up piece of paper saying "read this if you are a poopy pants", or diamonds. The can covers up its insides, as we do. I believe there are 4 types of people in the world, don't worry, I'm not gonna go NLP on your ass, this one is my own device! Out of the 4 types of people, I think only 2 exist. Lemme explain:

Type A - People that are completely evil.

Type B - People that are completely love.

Type C - People that are mostly evil and sometimes love.

Type D - people that are mostly love and sometimes evil.

**Type A** completely evil: these are your classic evil mother Fs! And if I asked most of you to think about people that are completely evil you would immediately go to Hitler, paedophiles, human traffickers, Simon Cowell etc.

**Type B** Completely love: Straight up amazing with not a bad bone in their body. I reckon you would think of Mother Teresa, your local special needs school care worker, your dear old nan, the dog from 'UP!'

Problem is I don't actually believe for one moment that Hitler, paedophiles and human traffickers are 100% evil. Don't get me wrong, they are in the bracket of absolute worst people in the world, but surely they can't be absolutely evil? Well, maybe Simon Cowell! As for Mother Theresa, I bet she was a bitch sometimes! And apart from the dog from 'UP!' who is just a complete don, I don't think anyone is completely 100% pure amazing love! Well maybe not in this lifetime, I'm yet to see or experience it, and I don't know anyone else who has either.

**Type C and D** are what's really going on: the 'sometimes love but mostly evil', and the 'sometimes evil but mostly love': we slip between these types on the regular. I'm not gonna dwell on this as the point of this chapter is to get you using your time, but this basic understanding is super poignant.

The majority of your time is being wasted by your auto-pilot. Some days you're on form, knocking 'em out the park, pumped up and making the best decisions. These days are the ones that get us places, get us moving, progress us forward! They are integral, and they ensue immediately after we control ourselves. I can't even count the number of times I have said out loud to people, "I'm quitting cigarettes," or, "I'm gonna change my diet and join the gym," or, "I'm gonna write a book"!!!

You ever had that? Got absolutely gassed on a plan, on something that's gonna change your life for the better, and then when you wake up the next morning you just go through your usual motions, and then by the time you realise it, you have already sold yourself out of doing the thing you were completely sold on the previous night?! Yup! Welcome to being a human!

Look, a lot of control is based around time and structure. I know it sounds lame but is your dream house, curing cancer or building hospitals in countries that need them lame? Is your career as an actor, artist, writer, musician, F1 driver, Olympian, is that all lame?! Having your perfect body, is that lame?!

Fuck the haters, man, you gotta get to it! All of these things, and whatever other awesome career or life-affirming game changer you are thinking of all needs structure, control, and time. There are no ifs or buts to this. You can try and tell yourself otherwise, but it's just not the case, and your next 120 minutes are ticking away...

So we need to start being in complete control of our time, or as close as humanly possible. It is running away from us as we speak and we need to tame it the best we can. Time is running out for all of us, do not be an idiot and waste it.

Start little if you want, in some ways it helps to move you in the right direction, and it also enforces the realisation that what you are doing works. However, don't leave it too long before moving on to upheaving and rebuilding your whole day otherwise it is easy to slip back into bad habits.

---

## Exercise 1.1

Grab your journal! Now, by this point, you should have a nice amount of pages written out in your journal! If you have been doing your daily goals morning and night for just 1 week you will have 14 pages, plus all the extra bits I've asked you to write down and exercise.

I want you to take this opportunity to have a little flick through what you've done so far.

---

That's progress in your journal right there! You did this! You chose to do it! I actually had nothing to do with it, even if you think I did! You chose to spend money on your future by picking up this book, you choose to spend time reading it, and you spent time writing down some really tough things just to make your life better!

You are already fucking awesome! See!? It was there all along, and YOU did it! And now the bit you have all been waiting for: how to reprogram your brain.

---

## Summary

- Ex 1.0

Honest me questions

- Answer all the 'honest me' questions, honestly
- Ex 1.1

Revisit

- Take a few minutes to flick through your journal and see the progress first-hand
- Subdividing time allows you to see how much time you've got and how much time you're wasting
- Utilising just 2 hours a day ends up in a monumental amount of time across a year
- 80 years is the same as 960 months, or 4,160 weeks, or 29,200 days, or 700,800 hours, or 42,048,000 minutes.

# Chapter 30

# pNF

Little p, capital N, capital F.

Ever heard that expression: "it's the journey, not the destination"? Well, I have found that it is all about the destination. The destination makes your journey better, every time. I am not saying the journey isn't important, but until something is focused on finished, it is more a rambling through the jungle lost than it is a journey. And to note, you should be enjoying the journey, I'm not saying don't enjoy the journey, I'm saying you need to accomplish shit to progress.

If your destination is stacking shelves in your local supermarket, do you think your journey will be better or worse than if your destination is being an astronaut for NASA?! A journey needs a destination, and the value of the destination is dependent on the calibre of the journey. Yeah, I said calibre. And what?!

Think about how frustrating it is when you are searching for somewhere that serves food cuz you're hungry AF but you can't find anywhere cuz it's Sunday, or late, or you're in the ass-end of nowhere. What happens? You end up hungry, disappointed and pissed off! You need the destination. Same difference if played in reverse: you want pizza but you won't leave the couch, you ain't gettin' pizza!

A lot of the information we are given, as you have hopefully realised by now, is for want of a better expression utter ass-crap. We are told to take our time and enjoy life, we are told to relax and take two weeks off a year, we're told to chill out! Motherfucker, you can't enjoy life to its fullest if you are constantly lost in the jungle with no purpose!

That's just existing. Lemme say that one more time: with no purpose, you are just existing. You're not living, you're just going through the motions on autopilot. It won't help anything! Plus, if you take your time and take it as it comes, then when are you gonna actually start living? When you're too old to get a hardon or remember your own kids' names. That's too late.

Unfortunately, a lot of this misinformation is based in the past, in our subconscious. As I outlined earlier, your transition cannot be based in the past. Your transition also gives zero fucks about your past. This should be great news for a lot of you, no more playing the victim and blaming your past, no more blaming things that have already happened and can't be changed to sculpt what hasn't happened yet!

So let me explain my version of past, Present and Future, or as I want you to call it: past NOW FUTURE. I'll explain the now in a bit, but first let's finally kill the past. Don't worry, I'm not gonna ask you to ignore your past, quite the opposite, but we do need to know how to use it to our advantage, and we need to know how much of our energy and time we should put into it.

To begin we need to look at this mathematically. It's easy maths, don't stress. Think of your past, now and future as a pizza. For the average human, about 80%-90% of your pizza is gonna be past pizza: old, out of date, not current, stale, and useless for the majority of things, cuz its already been eaten! Our subconscious brain lives in the past and it uses our previous experiences to assume our future experiences.

This leaves a worryingly low amount of brainpower to focus on your future.

Even more worryingly, this leaves us with minimal brainpower to actually be living in the now. Most people tend to dwell on their past and worry about their future: "I won't or can't do this or that because I had a bad experience before," or, "But what if that goes wrong?" respectively.

When you put it down on paper the whole thing is mad!

Why would you want to spend the one part of your time on earth that is current and controllable (your now), by using it to worry about things that haven't happened yet and may never happen (your possible future)?! Your possible future can be negative or positive, but its possibilities are based on what you do with your now.

It's totes cray-cray! I see this every day. These factors are bred directly from fear. We will go through this in detail in the next chapter but all you need to know right now is that there are only two main emotions, love and fear, and every other emotion or feeling is a derivative of one of these two key emotions.

You can all think of a time that you dwelled on the past or worried about the future. If you are like most people you probably do this multiple times per day. Again, this is existence, it is not living, and it definitely will prevent you from being able to transition. The thing they don't tell you at school is that your future is completely dependent on the actions you make in your now. In this chapter, I will completely explain the best ways to use your past, now and future, and the detrimental repercussions that can occur if you misuse them.

# Past

Your past is very important, of course it is, it allows you to make decisions that make your life easier: put your tongue in a blender when you're a kid because there was still cake mix on it = never put tongue in the blender again.

Sometimes our past experiences, actually scratch that, pretty much always our past experiences completely shit up our future decisions. So to make this easier to understand I will put these into categories of positive and negative.

Things that your past can help with:

**Pain**: remembering what hurts, what is dangerous, what to avoid and/or what will hurt others.

**Positive experiences**: feeling confident because of something you have done or been a part of. This could be remembering how you felt when you passed your driving test, or when you went on your first date, or had sex the first time and it was good, or the feeling you got when you had your first kid or bought your first house.

**The negative version** of this is not moving forward because you are living off of past success, and guess what, yup, past success is in the past and will not help your future. Ever done that thing where you keep bringing up stuff that you did ages ago? Like it still warrants praise!? It's not that it doesn't mean anything, but using your now to keep bringing up your past is a waste of your energy and potential, and FYI nobody cares.

**Remembering**: people's names, likes, dislikes etc these are all really handy traits of your memory, but they are so obvious we don't need to speak about them. The remaining worthwhile things to talk about on the positive side are, well, not really too much. I am sure you can think of a couple more things but I can almost guarantee that they will be basic human traits, like remembering people's names or similar.

Now let's talk about how bad your past can be. The main thing to consider is the fear that your past can bring, which in turn prevents you from making important decisions in your now that will make your future better. Every worry you have ever had is based on your past! Every single one! Think about it! And even worse, your fears may be built from other people's fears, built from their pasts!

---

## Future & Now

I won't go into good and bad luck again because you know that already, so let's just focus on the luck you can change.

Your future and now is WAY more important than your past, and in true spectrum form, they change priorities from time to time depending on different factors. Your future holds all of your wildest and most awesome dreams, so why do people have wild and awesome dreams and end up in a job they hate or learn to love until they retire?

This is why I ask people to commit to the daily goal practice. It is a way of marrying the two most important parts of this puzzle: your future, and your now. I know a lot of self-help gurus will be getting sand in their vaginas upon hearing my take on this, but guess what, zero shits given!

The reason I believe they are of equal importance is because of duality. You need your future to gas up your now, and you need your now to actually build your future! It's that simple!

Just writing your goals down in your journal ain't gonna do shit because it's just writing. The reason it is so important to write your future goals down is that it gets you amped and forces you to push your now harder than you would have without thinking about your future, dig?

The two can't exist without each other, and if you let one slip then the other slips too. You stop thinking or caring about your future and your now turns to shit, and vice versa, you stop pushing your now and future won't get any better. Forget your past, just focus on your now and your future, in equal measures. Bounce between them and consistently reality check yourself.

Let's baby step: I want you to come up with something you want to do in your future, your immediate future, ideally in the next few minutes or hours. I want this thing to be something that you do all the time and would not usually think too much about. Something like doing the grocery shopping or going to get fuel for your car or going to the gym or something. Let's use grocery shopping as an example.

Let's say you've run out of milk and you know you are gonna want a coffee tomorrow morning, so without thinking too much (or seeing it as anything more than an annoying chore) you don your flip-flops and scooch on down the street to your local Co-Op. You get to the shop, pick up your coconut almond milk, cuz that's how you roll, go to the teller, pay, scooch back home, and Robert's your father's brother. You had a future thought (need milk for coffee) and took an action (thong-up and scooch).

The problem here though, is that apart from the milk, which cost you money, and the scooch to the shop, that cost you time, all you ended up with is tomorrow's milk. I mean, that's cool, cuz you needed the milk for your coffee, but that's pretty much it.

Now let's play out that same experience but with a little amped up foresight.

You want your milk for your coffee tomorrow morning, but this time you see it as an opportunity. You dot your good hand as a reward for spotting a potential opportunity and then spend a few seconds scheming up a way you can take advantage of the situation. It's time to slip your feet into your favourite plimsolls. Now I know this sounds funny, but just by wanting your future to be better (in this case the immediate future, just to get milk from the shop) it will force you to be aware there are opportunities to be had, and it gets your brain working to figure out what those opportunities could be.

I'm definitely going to write another book on this, but just trust me now, everything is a business and you are always working on commission, even if you don't think you are. With that in mind, everyone is a potential prospect for whatever business you are running, and the shopkeeper is no different. So, we are going to sell the shopkeeper something. This may be as simple a 'sale' as getting information (knowledge is potential power, remember), or something slightly less simple as signing them up for your new online course. You heel-toe quicksmart to the shop, pick up your milk, and head to the counter. Now I should mention, certain situations in life are waaaaay easier to 'sell' than others. Shopkeepers and checkout folk are one of the easiest. Why?

Because:
1. They HAVE to talk to you, whether they want to or not (sly, I know)
2. You have X amount of 'dead time' while at the till that can often just be an awkward silence
3. If you are one of the only people that asks an interesting question or says anything other than, "Yes please," in reply to, "Would you like a bag with that?" then not only will you make their time at work go quicker (which they will love you for) but also you will brighten up their day, and you will immediately become memorable and interesting to them

So, back to our example. You get to the till, and instead of the usual slightly awkward 'dead time', or nausey small talk you would make, you take the opportunity with one of the following (feel free to concoct your own relative to your own needs). I will use some obvious ones I have used/use to give you an idea.

Just in case you are unsure of standard small talk you may have with a checkout person: how long have you got left on your shift? The weather is XYZ! Etc., etc.

All of the following can start with: "Hi, my name is ___, don't think we have spoken before, how's your day going?" To be fair, that on its own will usually spark a much more valuable (for both parties) conversation than usual.

Questions:

1. What do you do outside of work?
2. What is your favourite thing about your job?
3. Do you have plans for the future?
4. What hobbies do you have?
5. Do you have kids?

Etc., etc., etc.

Statements:

1. I run a company doing ___, you must meet loads of interesting people working here, is there anyone you would recommend me talking to?
2. I'm doing ___ this weekend and looking for new places to try out, any recommendations would be amazing!

3. I am thinking of doing ____ next year, what are your thoughts on that?

Etc., etc., etc.

I KNOW loads of you are thinking WTF? But try it! I get so much business from conversations like this with people most other people would never think to pitch to. There are a few reasons for this:

- Even if the person you are talking to doesn't have an interest in whatever it is you are talking about, you can nearly always guarantee they will either know someone, or know someone that knows someone. I recently got a bit of work because I had chatted to the receptionist at the dentist about music and she had a brother who was married to an events planner. I asked for her details and asked if it was okay to contact her and she was more than willing to help (people always want to help if they can). I messaged the events planner on LinkedIn and supplied her a band for a huge event she was running and now we are her preferred supplier. This is one of so many examples.

- It makes you memorable. If you give someone an experience different from the norm, they will almost always remember you. And being remembered gives benefits. Next time you go to pick up milk for your coffee, lovely Jenny behind the till will remember you and say something like: "Oh you're that lovely person from the other day that mentioned you did ____, so weird, I bumped into my friend/tutor/doctor/mum/whatever today and they needed ____ – I'll drop them a message now if you would like, what's your number/website/contact etc?"

- After hardly any time whatsoever, you will be on first-name terms and that in itself will make the whole experience that much better for both parties. In turn, the likelihood of you staying in their minds, and them mentioning you to other customers long after you have left is staggering.

Point being with all of this is that bouncing in between your Now and your Future is paramount to be able to force yourself to start not only encouraging opportunities but more importantly to create opportunities.

If you do this with every person you meet, or at least as many as you can, you will start getting a name around the village, then around the town, then who knows!

If you live in the Future you will miss opportunities in your Now that are necessary to build the Future you want. Similarly, living solely in your Now prevents you from taking into account the roadmap you need to get to where you are going! I suggest you spend enough time with your goals that you can taste them, smell them, and breath them, but not so much time with them that you end up daydreaming your life away.

Create the opportunity, quickly analyse it, and if it makes sense, or at least feels like it does, then jump at it, even if it is a risk and outside your comfort zone. Risk is paramount, and most people won't take the necessary risks needed to succeed. We've all been told to hold back and play it safe, but that won't get you anywhere! But why won't we risk? Fear! Or a derivative of. Let's talk about it.

## Summary

- Live in the past and you are not living
- Worry about the future and your now is screwed
- Live solely in the now and you will get nothing done
- Bounce between your now and your future and you will win hard!

# Chapter 31

# Love And Fear

Did you know that every single emotion, word, action or feeling can be traced back to either love or fear? From love comes contentment, happiness, success, peace, and all the other lush, wonderful emotions. From fear comes anger, hate, guilt, shame, anxiety and all the horrible, nasty emotions.

From my experience, and from listening to and observing others and studying psychology, most people tend to run with amounts of each of these, and I am yet to meet someone that is just completely one. I don't think it is possible, or worthwhile. Like the existence of duality, and the spectrums that everything works on, we tend to bounce between the two constantly.

You may be a really happy, positive person, but you're scared of dying. You may be super confident with your career but you are scared to ask someone on a date. You may be content with your bank balance but you constantly worry about screwing up your tax returns. Even though I am yet to meet a 100% love or 100% fear person, I can tell you I have never met a genuinely happy and successful person that doesn't live through love way, way, way more than fear! It is impossible to be happy and successful without living mostly in love.

Like I explained before, you should strive for success in all parts of your life, as a student, a parent, a son or daughter, a family member, career-wise, health-wise, confidence-wise. Every part of your life needs to be successful. Would you swap your perfect relationship for unlimited money? If you answered yes then it would only be a matter of time before you would answer the same question with the opposite answer. Rich and lonely or happy and broke? Neither of these things are ideal. You need it all, most of the time! Of course sometimes terrible, horrendous, and sad life events are inevitable, but the rest of the time you need it all.

Remember there is not an absolute amount of happiness or success in the world.

Just because someone starts a successful business, does not mean that you can't. There isn't a chart that exists where it is logged, or a certain amount of 'happy chips' or 'sad tokens'. This is just in your mind. Just because someone else writes the script for a blockbuster movie, doesn't mean you can't.

It is this disbelief in what is actually possible that stops most of us starting, and guess what... this kinda shit comes straight outta fear. Fear of failing, fear you won't be good enough, fear people will laugh, or whatever. Living in fear prevents you from living in love. Living in love helps to keep you from living in fear. Which one sounds better?!

It's the same with light and dark. Imagine being in a completely pitch-black room, no light. No windows or anything. You can't see shit. Imagine this as fear. What could possibly remedy this? One tiny little match will obliterate the complete darkness. A candle will do even more. And a floodlight, or 10 floodlights, will completely alleviate the problem. Now reverse that example: you are outside in the sun, it's gorgeous and everywhere is bright and buzzing. No matter how much darkness, if there is still some light, no amount of darkness can make it pitch black.

The only way for something to be completely pitch black is for there to be no light, as in absolutely no light whatsoever. But the tiniest amount of light will do something. If you think of your scale as light and dark, or love and fear, then bearing all of this in mind you only need the tiniest amount of love, or light, to start to make an impact that the dark cannot compete against.

The feeling of not being good enough, being scared, worried, anxious, all of these things just need that first little beam of light to begin the transition. Now if you can amplify that light, that tiny little bit of light, and make it lighter, then the darkness just keeps getting lighter.

We are coming to the end of this programme, and the reason I have left this chapter until the end is because when I explain what I'm about to, most people they think I'm crazy, and I wanted you to be ready so you don't just take it with a pinch of salt, but instead start living your life by it.

So, my simple rule about fear...

Fear always.

What do I mean?! I mean fear is about to be one of your best friends, and you are going to learn to hang out with him/her a lot more.

Let's use a hack. And as with the majority of my hacks, this one has to be experienced. We have to be aware of the amount of love and fear we have in our life currently to know where we need to amplify the love.

---

## Exercise 1.0

For the next 24 hours, I want you to make a note for every time you have an obvious fear or derivative of fear, prevent you from doing something. Stick a cross on your 'bad' hand every time this happens, and make a note in your journal of what the fear was. Remember, derivatives can be any of the following: actual fear, worry, anxiety, doubt, jealousy, vindictiveness, anger etc. Basically, anything that ain't love, baby!

_____

When I do this exercise with others, if they are being honest with themselves, they are living in fear for a large part of the day and in turn a large part of their life. They need more light.

"I want to be a singer but I think people will laugh at me," or, "It will be too much work," or, "I don't have time." Fear talks us out of what we should be doing. "What if XYZ?" or, "I can't call them on a Sunday," or, "I'll do it tomorrow when I've got the courage up." Fear ruins our progress. "He must have a small dick to drive that car," or, "She's got really fat," or, "I hope they fail." Fear makes us assholes.

So fear, we should be afraid of it, right, and ignore it and focus on the light?

Well, sorta. Well, actually not entirely.

Fear, in fact, tells us exactly what we should be doing! It's a torch into the jungle. It shows you exactly where you need to go. It gives you a green light. If fear is preventing you from becoming a singer, it means you should fight it and start the journey. If fear is stopping you making the call or asking the girl out, DO IT! It's giving you a clue. If fear is making you act like a self-entitled holier than thou douche bag then it's holding its hand out to let you know something needs fixing!

Use fear as a first step marker. Trust me on this one: everything you desire is a few steps after something big and scary. You can't complete a video game without killing the evil boss! Kill the evil boss!!! Cuz as soon as you do you will have levelled the fuck up! You will be stronger, wiser, and happier.

When you feel fear, run at it.

---

## Summary

- Ex 1.0

Notice your fears

- – For the next 24 hours make a note of all of your fears
- – Make sure you include derivatives of fear including anxiety, doubt, hate, anger, worry etc.

- Fear is a green light, do not run from it, run at it
- Fear is only scary until you've conquered it, then it's just the norm
- Everything you desire will be scary at first
  - – Scary = unchartered territory. Charter the shit outta it!

# Chapter 32

# Rinse and Repeat

To implement anything I have taught you, and to successfully complete your first big transition, you must commit. I have brought this up a lot, maybe you're sick of it, but there is no way around it, you MUST commit. Your daily goal practice is not daily if it's not daily. All the exercises and hacks I have explained are completely dependent on your ability to control yourself and commit to them. Using 'the scale' or any of the other hacks to keep you aware, as far away from autopilot as possible, confident and motivated is the key here!

This is not a diet! This is a life change. You will transition again when you learn more, but you have to go into this believing that your daily efforts will pay dividends in the long run. They will, I absolutely 100% guarantee it. This shit works! And you know why it works…? You! You have the power to fake it or make it. The old fake and make. Stuff doesn't happen to you, it happens because of you. Eat enough burgers and you'll get fat, send enough emails and you'll get a response, ya dig?!

Giving up is harder work than committing, it just feels like it is the other way round initially until you start to reap the benefits, and more often than not, with the really big stuff, the benefits won't happen overnight.

You are totally capable of being more amazing, wise, powerful, fast and successful than you originally imagined, and the best gift in the world is that it's up to you.

We aren't brought up being told this, our schools don't tell us that we can make things possible, instead, they tell us to be realistic. This notion is even stronger when affirmed by parents, family and friends that were sold the same bullshit, and so the cycle continues. But you can break the cycle, you can create a new feedback loop. You just need to know you can, then you need to run with it.

Commit now and control your future, don't let it control you. The reason most people flake is that the initial change of scenery is more than they are willing to commit to. It feels alien and uncomfortable because it's not what they are used to, just like hating olives when you were a kid and loving them now, the good shit takes work.

Noncommittal, wussy thinking and lack of action has crippled humanity and prevented so many of us from moving forward. For all of you that moan about the 1% being lucky or born into it, stop it! A large percentile of those in the 1% are there because they worked harder than you! While you were chillin' it they were killing it! The old chill and kill. Granted, some of the 1% are completely born into it and are privileged and entitled cock munchers, but the others though, they worked, committed, and pushed, ran at fear and ignored the haters.

Legends.

One of the most beneficial ways to commit and push is to rinse and repeat. When someone achieves a goal, it is always because they have mastered it, and you can only master something by doing it, over and over and over, and over. Can you think of any successful athlete, actor or actress, musician, artist, poet, writer, producer, director, businessperson, milkman, postman, baker, builder whatever, can you think of any successful person that just picked it up, or had beginner's luck, or didn't put any work in but still reaped the rewards?!?! Who are you kidding?!?!

They all worked like crazy bastards, and it only seems crazy to us because we are told that average is okay, normal is good, standard is safe, mediocre is alright. Utter wank! The burst practice I taught you, that only works if you rinse and repeat, every day until it's done, and then you need to move on and repeat with the next thing you want to accomplish. You don't have to be any good at anything to get started, but you will get better if you commit. Remember, doing something really bad is 100% better than doing nothing at all!

No more excuses! You've come this far so you have proven you can commit, in this case to reading some idiot trying to drop knowledge bombs all up in your shit. Rinse and repeat is the process that will make you superhuman. Do it, do it again, do it again, do it again. Every day, until it's done, and then move on. That's it. It is soooo simple.

By this point, you should have had enough time to implement some of your new positive brain loops, and upon the successful completion of one, you now know that you can reprogram as and when. So I want you to reprogram a new loop. This loop needs to be anchored for whenever you finish a task. The reason I want you to do this after you finish a task is to start to reprogram your brain to understand that the task needs to be completed again.

We usually commend ourselves at the end of daily tasks, but cracking open the champagne for each job done is a farce. It allows the brain to relax. Think back to a time you accomplished something huge, it felt better than accomplishing something small right?! Of course it did! We want more of those big wins, and they come off of loads of regular little wins.

So, from now on whenever you complete a task, tell yourself, "I will complete this task again, but next time I will complete it better because I learned XYZ this time." Try not to be too loosey-goosey with this, you want to dominate your brain, not compete with it. Tell it when you are going to do stuff, and then get that stuff done. When you complete your next day to-do list, or daily goals last thing before bed and first thing in the morning, it continually reinforces the notion of why you are doing what you are doing.

When I break down all of my personal accomplishments it has always been because of me, and it was always due to the amount of regular and consistent effort I put in. When I first started playing drums and guitar and singing, I practised every single day, without fail. I did shit and I got shit done. The same thing happened with my wife; I wanted her, I committed way before we were in an official relationship: I did wife, I got wife done. Same with my business, my kid, my health, this book. All the things you desire are just a matter of work away. Notice I didn't say time. There's a reason. Time, it seems, we can't control, but we can control the work we put in, the effort, the passion, the heart. All of those things we can control within the time we have.

Let's do an exercise to prove the power of rinse and repeat.

## Exercise 1.0

I want you to learn how to do something over the next week by practising every day. The skill I want you to learn is how to make an owl noise using just your hands and mouth. If you can already do this I want you to learn something similar, like wolf-whistling, or making that water droplet sound by flicking your cheek. Something like that. The owl is perfect because most people struggle with it, but when you get it, it feels great, you know, cuz you can sound like an owl.

Why am I asking you to do this?! Well, it is a skill that will take you about a week, but to do it in a week, you will need to practice it every day, ideally a few times a day. You will have to go online to research how to do it, and the feeling of accomplishment the first time you can do it is actually surprisingly life-affirming. In turn, this will prove to you that you can do anything, you just gotta commit, then rinse and repeat. Remember after each practice session to drop your anchor and order yourself to repeat the process.

---

Now I totally understand a bunch of you will be thinking, "This guy is telling me to use my time wisely and work hard, and now I have to waste my time trying to sound like an owl." Well, I feel you, but the true fact of the matter is that you are doing way more here than learning how to impersonate a nocturnal flying swoopy mush with a panoramic vision opportunity. You are planting a seed, a very strong seed, a seed that will grow tall and powerful and enable you to repeat this process with anything.

Some things take longer, granted, but the premise is the same. The reason I have asked you to do something that seems un-useful is because there is no pressure to do it, you have to choose to do it. If I said I want you to learn to sell more products, or go to the gym, or learn to do jazz tap, then the fear comes out and your brain will try and talk you out of it.

With this exercise, which I am gonna call the hoot hoot 3.0, you really have no need to do it other than me asking you to and you accepting the challenge.

For those of you that are already smashing life a new one, and are feeling beyond this, no problem, let's replace the hoot hoot 3.0 with something scary, something that you have shit riding on. You'll know what it is without thinking too hard, you always know, remember?! I'd love to hear what you are choosing to do, and I'd love to hear how long it took you to get your owl down, post videos of your owls on my social so I can see what you got/have a cheap laugh!

Anyways, back to rinse and repeat. Another hack that totally works, and actually this is great for every single part of your transition but you can start by using it for the rinse and repeat, is to get someone else involved, the more the merrier, huh?! You must have heard the old adage 'strength in numbers'? The reason gym classes make you work harder than doing a circuit in your living room is because of the comradery and accountability.

Having a gym buddy, or group, pushes you to maintain your commitment, pushes you to work harder, for longer, more often, and it completely increases motivation. One study I saw said that 95% of people that start a weight-loss programme with a buddy successfully completed the programme, whereas an average of 50% of people that start a weight loss programme on their own quit.

So we can use this for our own benefit, with whatever it is we are doing. Let's say you struggle to get your coursework at college done, or you don't cold call as many prospects as you should to get your business cooking, or you don't go running regularly enough, or you don't eat well because you don't like cooking, or whatever... Get a buddy, or ideally 3 or 4 or more people to make the same commitment and work with them. Start a study group to get your coursework done, or cold call at the same time as the rest of your team, or get a jogging friend or even better join a running club, or cook with your partner or children or friends.

You must have had it before where you made plans with someone, then at the last minute wanted to bail but felt you couldn't because you didn't want to let them down, so you went, and then ended up enjoying it. NB: It's funny that we struggle to let others down, but we let ourselves down all the time...

---

# Exercise 1.1

Let's take action on this immediately. Think of something you want to do, something that's been bubbling away in your mind since you started this programme, and call up a friend or family member, and get them to commit to starting it with you. If you want to go into business, or start a hobby, or learn a new skill, then this is the time to start. Call them now! Right now! Do not deliberate on this.

---

This is a great way to practice the art of persuasion too, you can convince and sell the idea to your friend or family member. Double win!

Take control and make it happen.

And now, to our final chapter...

---

# Summary

- Ex 1.0
Owl hands
    - Learn how to make an owl sound with your hands
    - You need to figure this out
- Ex 1.1
Start something
    - Whatever it is, start something now!
    - Call a friend and tell them you are starting whatever it is
- Everything takes commitment and time
- When you know what you want, work out the route and then rinse and repeat.

# Chapter 33

# WLV / DsGsD 2.0

So, last chapter, motherfuckers. How are you feeling? What have you learned? One of the biggest issues I have with self-help kinda stuff is that it assumes that there is only one way to fix your shit. I don't agree with this, and I want you to make this programme your own. Take the bits that are really working for you and leave the rest. You will find on second, third or fourth read that you will pick up super helpful things you may have missed the first time, and your opinions will change with your transition, so definitely start the journey again with your new information and rinse and repeat.

I titled this chapter (and purposefully left it till last) WLV, which stands for a whiny little victim. I didn't wanna bring this up earlier in the book because it took me a long ass time to get to the point where I realised I was being a little bitch, and you have to be at a certain stage in your transition to have someone call you a little bitch and accept it without reacting negatively. I am not calling any of you whiny little victims, but I am pretty sure most of you will appreciate that up until recently you could probably label yourself with this exceptionally clever abbreviation (again, use of an emoji here would be great).

Okay, thanks for reading, bye!

Joking, you have me for another few minutes.

Joking, bye!

Sorry, I will stop now.

Look, like we've talked about, bad luck is gonna happen, you can sorta prepare for it, but by doing so you may spend a lot of time prepping for something that never actually happens. Instead, I suggest you learn to react well and stop being a WLV. Learn to understand that fear, worry, anxiety and whatever else are inevitable and you will have to deal with them sometimes, but they always usually pre-empt something awesome.

Course if you start a new job or something you are gonna be anxious, but that's part of it! It's part of the inevitable cycle of stuff. The cycle that needs to be completed for cool shit to happen.

If nobody had ever pushed through the anxiety or fear or worry then literally NOTHING awesome would have ever got done!

Most people nowadays get anxious about leaving their houses or taking their driving test or going to the dentist, it's fucking crazy! This is life! It is your life and you know you don't wanna be regretting all the small thinking you did and time you wasted when you're on your deathbed. This programme was written to give you the opportunity to be happier, more confident and far enough outside of your comfort zone that you can make some super beneficial changes that help you on your journey through this fucking bonkers life.

This is my first ever venture into writing, and I know there are loads of mistakes and errors, and probably bits where I thought I'd made a good point but to loads of you, it didn't make sense or contradicted something else I said previously that is inevitably gonna bite me in the ass by some troll on some site somewhere. But you know what, like really know what...?

I don't care. I mean it, I couldn't give two shits, because for every mistake I've made I will gain insight, and for every little thing that happens to me as a by-product of this book I will react to it, and I will continue to learn and get shit wrong and then learn, and then make my life better.

You can't ever be right, you can just be a little less wrong, and that's what I will do, continuously, 'til my body drops and doesn't get up again. I will make mistakes and learn and force myself far enough outside of my comfort zone to the bit that feels weird and awkward the first time round but leads to all the dope shit!

I have never been happier. I know I have to write that, but in previous years, before I levelled up a few times, I would have written it and knew I didn't mean it or couldn't back it up. I mean it now. I am happy, I am healthy, I am strong, and I just want to keep going. I'm hungry now, and it's amazing what a bit of hunger will push you to get done.

I want the same for all of you, for everyone! I want you to all come away from this knowing that you have a lot of work to do, and I want you to start doing it. I know when I write my next book I will be laughing at all the stupid mistakes I made in this one: the length of the process that could have easily been shortened and streamlined; the amount of money and time wasted on fruitless attempts to do XYZ; the fact I've only just learned how to use semicolons. And then I'll laugh at my second book when I write my third. And that's it, I will level up until I die!

I often joked with friends while writing this book that it could have just had one page that read like this:

## Chapter 1

Stop being a little bitch and start getting your shit together.

## The end.

But I knew it wouldn't sell and people would be pissed off if they did buy it, but it really is that simple. You know when you are being lame, you know when you should and when you shouldn't, you know what's right and wrong, and you know what you want, and you know when to use semicolons and when to just use commas. Go fucking get it, whatever it is, and stop wasting time.

DsGsD!

I'm not gonna end on the standard, "You got this! You can do it," because you know right now whether you can or not! Instead, I just want you to know that if you don't try then you will never know.

I heard someone on the radio when I was driving into town last weekend on one of our local stations. She was a comedian and was on the show talking about her upcoming tour. It was a really good interview. She explained that she ran comedy nights for years before she had the bottle to get up and try out her own material. The bit that stuck out was when the presenter asked: "So how come it took you so long to give it a go yourself?"

She explained that her dad had died a couple years back and it was enough for her to think, "Fuck it, life's too short." She said that she always knew she wanted to be a comedian but was so sure that she wouldn't make it that it wasn't even an option to figure out, more just a daydream at work or a chat that came out when she was drunk with friends. I think about this stuff all the time, and as the previous chapters will have explained, life IS too short.

It is too short to worry, too short to be anxious, too short for fear, too short for lying to yourself, and too short to waste. Do not waste it anymore, no matter what happens and how bad it seems at the time.

I know it sounds lame AF but if my message changes just one life for the better then that's the beginning of the kind of dent I'm looking for, then I will push until I have helped loads of people realise they can be themselves, and then I'll keep pushing. Be you, like actually you, and own it!

Fuck the haters, fuck the naysayers, fuck the anxiety, fuck the fear – DO SHIT, GET SHIT DONE!!!!!

If you only take one thing from this programme then let it be this: Wet Nose = Cool Body. Moist noses are also one of the ways that canines can regulate body temperature and cool down. "Dogs don't have normal sweat glands, like people," says Dr King, "so they secrete sweat from the pads of their feet and their noses."

Thank you so much for your time,

all the best.

Lee xoxo

:) :p :O ;P ;\ etc., etc., etc.

# END

# ABOUT THE AUTHOR

Lee (or Lee-Lee as his step-kid calls him) is a business owner, musician, university lecturer, and public speaker based in Brighton, UK. As a drummer he is also endorsed by global brands Vater, Remo and Liberty Drums, and runs the Instagram channel @drum_hacker

Printed in Great Britain
by Amazon

43528879R00220